Gender equity in the early years

Gender equity in the early years

Naima Browne

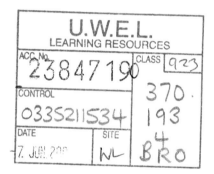

Open University Press

Open University Press
McGraw-Hill Education
McGraw-Hill House
Shoppenhangers Road
Maidenhead
Berkshire
England
SL6 2QL

email: enquiries@openup.co.uk
world wide web: www.openup.co.uk

First published 2004

A catalogue record of this book is available from the British Library

ISBN 0 335 21152 6 (pb)   0 335 21153 4 (hb)

Library of Congress Cataloging-in-Publication Data
CIP data has been applied for

Typeset by RefineCatch Limited, Bungay, Suffolk
Printed in the UK by Bell and Bain Ltd, Glasgow

For Rehana, with love

Contents

Acknowledgements   viii

Introduction   1

1   Where are we now?   5

2   Seductive science   22

3   The appeal of 'new' pedagogies   41

**4   Girls' and boys' understanding, playing and talking about
     gender**   60

5   Mummies and superheroes   78

6   Reflections on what we do   94

7   'Recuperative masculinity' strategies and superhero play   112

8   Are more men needed?   132

Afterword   156

Bibliography   159
Index   173

Acknowledgements

First, I should like to thank all the early years educators and the children who so willingly and enthusiastically talked to me and answered my questions.

Thanks also go to Rosalyn George, with whom I discussed many of my ideas, who kindly read several draft chapters and whose comments were always so valuable.

Last, but definitely not least, thanks to my family for their support. Thanks to my mother who was always willing to read and discuss the work in progress. Special thanks to Phil for his ongoing support and encouragement. Finally, thanks to Rehana, who helped in so my many ways, not least by being certain that the book would get written.

Introduction

There are significant and ongoing changes currently taking place within early childhood provision in the UK and it is therefore critical to reflect on how gender equity within the early years phase is likely to be promoted by central government initiatives and the developments being introduced by early years educators. This book aims to place the concerns and interests of those working in the early years field in the UK within a theoretical framework in order to enable educators, and others, to reflect on the impact of 'new' insights, initiatives and approaches to development, learning and teaching in the early years.

Before writing the book I had expected that early years educators would be concerned about issues such as the impact of the introduction of the foundation stage and of the curriculum guidance for this non-statutory provision, the changes from baseline assessment to the development of a foundation stage profile and the inspection pattern of early years settings. From talk with educators it became very clear, however, that the early years field has felt the 'backwash' arising from the increasing concern about boys' 'underachievement'. Many educators have also read the numerous articles in newspapers with headlines such as 'Planet boy, where mum fades from the picture' that urge that we 'accept their [boys'] maleness and teach them to cope with the education system and girls' emotional games' (Turner 2003a). Articles such as this promote the view not only that differences between girls and boys are biologically determined but also that the education system is weighted against boys, as it has been 'reorganised for the benefit of super-ambitious Hermiones with their diligence, neat handwriting and battery of different-coloured pens', with the result that girls' achievements 'eclipse those of boys' (Turner 2003a). Furthermore, educators are aware of some of the insights into child development that are emanating from research into brain structure and development (Kimura 1992; Shaywitz et al. 1995; Gur et al. 1999). These 'insights' support a shift towards biological determinism and the 'insights' therefore need to be re-examined in relation to theories about children's construction of gender and issues of gender equity.

In addition to these 'top down' pressures, early years practitioners in the UK have been looking at models of early years provision in other countries, in particular the pre-school provision in Reggio Emilia in Italy, but little attention has been paid to the extent to which the adoption of elements of the 'Reggio approach' will facilitate gender equity (e.g. Valentine 1999; Dahlberg *et al.* 1999; Abbott and Nutbrown 2001). It was also apparent that many early years educators had become disheartened about their 'equal opportunities' strategies, not least because they felt that the strategies were simply not working.

The fundamental issue that early years educators are grappling with is our understanding of what it means to be 'a girl' or 'a boy', and 'femininity' and 'masculinity', and this is the focus of the book.

A few words about terminology

Gender equity

Throughout this book the term 'gender equity' has been used, rather than 'equal opportunities' because it serves to emphasize the importance of treating children, and others, fairly by considering differences. In contrast, 'equality' is frequently understood to mean treating all children fairly by treating them the same.

Gender is inextricably linked with all aspects of ourselves, including 'race', ethnicity, social class, language background and disability. Furthermore, each child's life experience is unique and children have different 'needs', desires and pressures to conform to certain ways of being (e.g. all girls or all boys). Gender equity approaches, therefore, are not based on the assumption that certain groups of children can be viewed as homogeneous categories (e.g. 'girls' and 'boys') but instead acknowledge and take account of the existence of these differences in order to challenge the existing inequitable status quo. Equal opportunities approaches, however, often fail to acknowledge children's diverse life experiences, and the prejudices and discriminatory practices individuals need to negotiate on a day-to-day basis are rendered invisible. Gender equity emphasizes fairness in both process and outcome.

Educators rather than practitioners

I have chosen to use the word 'educator' rather than 'practitioner' to refer to all adults who work with young children. There are two main reasons for this. First, I believe that all those who are working with very young children are involved in their education. Second, the introduction and widespread use of the term 'practitioner' within the early years field has coincided with the introduction of initiatives intended to regulate and control this phase of education. While not advocating that the early years field should be free from scrutiny and accountability, I believe that it is important that those working within the early years field retain their sense of professionalism and purpose, while simultaneously retaining their ability to work flexibly and responsively. The word 'practitioner' not only conceals the true nature of our work with young children, that of education in its widest sense, but also suggests that work within the early years field is essentially routine and mechanical. Using the word 'educator' emphasizes what those working in the early years actually do.

Organization of the book

The book is organized into eight main chapters that are unified by two main themes that have an impact on the promotion of gender equity. The first unifying theme is the adoption of a critical stance towards the bimodal or binary model of gender underpinning the highly gender-polarized social structures and experiences young children are encountering or to which they are being introduced. The second unifying thread is the ongoing examination of the validity of what is habitually referred to as 'developmentally appropriate practice'.

The book opens with an exploration of how gender equity may be facilitated by critical examination of the various discourses that shape our understanding of 'femininity' and 'masculinity' and of what it means to be a 'good' early years educator. The second chapter analyses some of the scientific research that has looked at biological differences between girls and boys and women and men. Questions are asked about the validity of some of the conclusions drawn and the status of scientific 'truths' about biologically determined developmental and behavioural differences between girls and boys.

In the third chapter the focus shifts to the 'Reggio approach', since at the time of writing there has been a plethora of recently published books endorsing this approach. This chapter explores the principles underpinning the preschool provision in Reggio Emilia and focuses on the extent to which 'the Reggio approach' fosters gender equity. The appropriateness of adopting such an approach in socially, culturally, linguistically and economically diverse communities is discussed.

In Chapters 4 and 5 young children's ideas about what it means to be girls and boys are placed centre stage. How children perceive girls, boys, women and men in terms of 'appropriate' behaviour and interests is examined. Young children's imaginative role play, in particular superhero play, is explored, since it appears to be a powerful medium for young children's exploration of 'femininities' and 'masculinities', of what it means to be 'feminine' and 'masculine', and for coming to understand the gendered nature of society.

In Chapter 6 the focus shifts on to early years educators, their views about young children and their reflections on how their own practice fosters gender equity.

Chapter 7 looks in more depth at 'recuperative masculinity' strategies and considers how moves towards facilitating superhero and weapon play (Paley 1984; Holland 2003) may have a negative impact on gender equity within early years settings.

Chapter 8 highlights how the issue of increased male involvement in the early childhood field has taken root against a backdrop of boys' 'under-achievement' and somewhat simplistic notions of gender identity development, which has led to an emphasis on the value of male staff as role models. The chapter also explores how the gendered nature of the early years field is reflected in the pay, status and promotion of those working within the field.

1 Where are we now?

Early years provision in the UK is currently passing through a period of change and development. A plethora of central government initiatives have had a direct impact on the early years field, including the introduction of the foundation stage (for children in England and Wales from age three to the end of their reception year), the publication of the Curriculum Guidance for the Foundation Stage Curriculum, the replacement of baseline assessment with the foundation stage profile, the introduction of Sure Start, a government programme that aims to work with 'disadvantaged' children, parents and their local communities in order to promote the children's early development to ensure 'they are ready to flourish when they get to school' (www.surestart.gov.uk), and Ofsted's (Office for Standards in Education) involvement in the regulation of daycare and child-minding in England.

Alongside these developments there have been a limited number of initiatives within the field of equal opportunities (e.g. Disability Discrimination Act 1995, Race Relations (Amendment) Act 2000, new Special Educational Needs (SEN) Code of Practice 2002). In recent years, however, boys' underachievement has been both the catalyst and the focal point of central government schemes focusing on equality issues and gender (e.g. the launching of the DfES Gender and Achievement website, the publication of *Raising Boys' Achievement* (DfES 2003b) and the availability of funding from the Best Practice Scholarships Scheme for teachers researching best practice solutions for raising boys' achievement).

There has also been an increase in the number of books and newspaper and magazine articles that argue that differences between women and men and girls and boys have a biological rather than social basis (see Chapter 2).

It has been stated that these policy changes and initiatives have led to a 'silent revolution' in the early years field, which has resulted in a 'complete change in the way early years education is carried out' (QCA 2003). It is worth reflecting on this claim, not to make judgements about its veracity but to consider what the comments have to tell us about how change in the early years field is achieved. The assertion that there has been a 'silent revolution' suggests that at grass roots level there has been relatively little discussion and debate about the various government initiatives and, possibly, what debate there has been has not been widely publicized and disseminated. Those working within the early years field will know that in fact there has been a great deal of debate about the government initiatives but the claim made by the QCA, coupled with the comment that 'Practitioners have simply got on with doing their job' (QCA 2003), not only renders invisible the grass roots discussions but also implies that an educator's 'job' does not include adopting a critical stance to new initiatives. The phrase 'silent revolution' could also hint that there has been a degree of stealth involved in shaping early years provision in ways sought by the policy-makers. This is not to suggest that there has been a conspiracy of silence. Instead, it is an excellent example of the powerful way in which dominant discourses shape our understandings of who we are (in this case as early years educators) and what we feel we should or should not be doing if we want to be 'good' at our jobs.

Discourse theory

The term discourse, which is used throughout this book, can be defined as: 'A body of ideas, concepts and beliefs which become established as knowledge or an accepted worldview. These ideas become a powerful framework for understanding and action in social life' (Bilton *et al.* 1996: 657). The ideas of Michel Foucault, a French philosopher, have been used to explore the interrelationship between discourses, power and knowledge in early years provision (e.g. James *et al.* 1998; Dahlberg *et al.* 1999; McNaughton 2000), and although a detailed exploration of Foucault's ideas lies beyond the scope of this chapter, reflection on some of his ideas helps to provide an alternative way of looking at the issue of gender equity in the early years.

Discourses are powerful in that they produce or create 'reality' by providing words and conceptual frameworks for determining what can be said, written and possibly thought and for making sense of our experiences and the experiences of others. In a sense discourses act as lenses: they determine what you see and what you do not see and therefore can also distort what you see. Within essentialist discourses of gender, for example, stereotypical play preferences of girls and boys would be viewed as a natural expression of biological differences. Educators would feel that such behaviour is natural and therefore would be unlikely to intervene. Indeed, intervention is only likely to occur if children are seen to be to playing in an 'unnatural' manner (e.g. girls physically play-fighting or boys consistently playing with dolls). Wearing post-structuralist feminist lenses when looking at gender-stereotyped play choices, however, would lead one to suggest that the children were not only understanding 'feminine' and 'masculine' as mutually exclusive, oppositional categories but also positioning themselves as stereotypically 'feminine' and 'masculine'. In other words, the children are actively positioning themselves rather than simply being at the mercy of their biology. Educators would, among other things, take steps to help the children to explore their understandings of 'feminine' and 'masculine' as part of a process aimed at supporting them in comprehending who gains and who loses within their current gender framework and working towards helping them to develop less restrictive ways of being 'feminine' and 'masculine' (see Chapters 4, 5 and 6 for more discussion on this point).

Specific discourses dominate within society and the field of early years provision at certain points in time, and these dominating discourses serve to inhibit examination and exploration of alternative discourses by determining what is seen to be 'true' or 'the right thing to do':

> each society has its regime of truth . . . that is the types of discourses which it accepts and makes function as true; the mechanisms and instances which enable one to distinguish true and false statements, the means by which each is sanctioned; the techniques and procedures accorded value in the acquisition of truth; the status of those who are charged with saying what counts as true.
>
> (Foucault 1980: 131, cited in Dahlberg *et al.* 1999: 30)

Returning to the issue of change in early years practice, it is possible to argue that early years educators are not coerced into changing their practices; instead, the dominant discourse presents educators with 'truths' about young children and their needs, and educators then feel they ought to adapt their practices in the light of these 'truths'. These 'truths' are enshrined in policy documents (e.g. the curriculum guidance for the foundation stage), institutional practices (e.g. physical layout and resourcing of settings), criteria for assessment and evaluation of the quality of early years provision (e.g. Ofsted inspection criteria) and assessment and recording of the children's learning (e.g. the foundation stage profile). This book sets out to expose the 'truths' about gender that are contained within discourses circulating within the early years field, not to disprove or prove these 'truths' or 'realities' but to uncover them and enable educators to reflect on how these 'truths' contribute to gender inequities.

Dominant discourses circulating within the early years field also identify who can say what counts as 'true'. In view of this it is important that those entrusted with identifying 'truths' are seen to be involved in developing and introducing new initiatives. The *Curriculum Guidance for the Foundation Stage* (QCA 2001) provides an example of this. It is stated in the foreword that the guidance was developed as a result of: 'drawing on the extensive expertise of a group of early years specialists . . . [including] leading practitioners, academics and representatives from organisations committed to the care, development and education of young children' (QCA 2001: 2). Early years educators were provided with this particular piece of information as it served to validate the guidance and designate it as trustworthy and 'right'. After all, if leading lights in the early years field are not able to identify what constitutes 'good' early years practice then who can? Herein lies a key question and one that early years educators should be asking themselves.

Foucault's ideas on the relationship between knowledge, power and discourse are thought provoking. In essence he argued that dominant discursive regimes (those discourses that have a significant effect on shaping specific practices, in this case early years practice) are powerful because they not only identify what is seen to be 'true' and 'right' in terms of practice but also help to regulate and control our practice, as who would want to do what is generally seen to be 'wrong'? His ideas can be viewed as an invitation to imagine the unimaginable and approach old problems in fresh ways:

> It may not be easy to distance ourselves from social conventions and social representations embedded in metanarratives and discursive practices, as they place boundaries on our knowledge and our critical abilities, but it can be done . . . we must first make visible – unmask – and problematize prevailing (and therefore, usually taken for granted) discourses, and the constructions, practices and boundaries they produce (in Foucault's words 'regimes of knowledge').
>
> (Dahlberg *et al.* 1999: 34)

Considering alternative discourses, rather than uncritically accepting the dominant discourses, could lead to more gender equity within the field of early childhood and it is for this reason that it is worth reflecting on the theories, ideas and principles underpinning current provision and practice in order to identify possible ways forward. This book aims to problematize widely accepted practices relating to gender equity within the early years and in so doing to offer alternative ways of thinking about a key issue in early years provision and practice.

Unmasking discourses

In this book one of the discourses 'unmasked' is the dominant gender discourse that presents gender as a dichotomous category or a binary construct in which girl and boy, female and male, feminine and masculine are understood to be mutually exclusive and in opposition to each other. It is this construction of gender that has led to emotive debates about boys' 'suffering' as a result of strategies introduced to support girls. Talking and writing about gender as a continuum rather than a binary construct is very difficult, as no words exist in the English language to describe this interpretation of gender and society's practices, and norms make it difficult to think outside the box created by the dominant gender discourse. It could be argued that simply using the words 'girls' and 'boys' in discussing gender in the early years is problematic, in that it implies acceptance of the dichotomous nature of gender. In this book, however, I have continued to use the words 'girl' and 'boy' not because I view gender in binary terms but because using a word such as 'children' makes it harder to explore the unequal power relations that exist between and within groups of children. Essentialist constructs of 'girls' and 'boys' are not utilized. Instead, the words 'girl' and 'boy' are used in the knowledge that girls are not a homogeneous group and neither are boys. Ethnicity, culture, 'race', social class, economic status and physical ability are some of the factors that influence how young children experience and understand gender. A nursery headteacher alluded to this when talking about the achievements of girls and boys in her local education authority:

> It's a bit like saying 'All Bengali boys are failing to learn to read', which is nonsense. With some Bengali boys it might be much more to do with poverty than race, actually, that they are failing. But there are also white boys who are failing to learn to read and there are white boys who are flying just as there are Bengali boys.
>
> (Nursery headteacher, female 2002)

Subsequent chapters offer alternative ways of thinking about gender.

Two further discourses need to be examined in a little more depth in this chapter as they have implications for gender equity within the early years. The first is that of the importance of maternal care and the second is that of developmentally appropriate practice.

Mother care

During the second half of the twentieth century the attachment theories of Bowlby (1951) had a strong impact on early years settings, not least in the way in which the concept of attachment to the mother was used by policy-makers to drag their feet on developing comprehensive nursery provision in the UK (Browne 1986). Despite the work of child psychiatrists such as Rutter (1981), which led to a re-evaluation of Bowlby's original ideas, some of Bowlby's ideas continue to influence early years provision and practice at the start of the twenty-first century, most obviously in terms of the gender-based patterns of staffing in early years settings (see Chapter 5 for further discussion). A less obvious, but equally important, consequence of the importance placed on mother–child attachment is evident in most educators' views about ideal staffing ratios, with high adult:child ratios being valued (Ball 1994; Penn 1997; Dahlberg *et al.* 1999).

If we are to move beyond our current position it is important not only to reflect on the validity of 'truths' in early years provision but also to reflect critically on who benefits and who loses from early years practice and provision that is informed by these 'truths'.

In the UK and the USA there is a strong adherence to what Singer (1993) has termed 'attachment pedagogy'. This pedagogy is based on the belief that continuous and constant maternal care is necessary to ensure secure development, and secure emotional attachment is a prerequisite for learning. Where such maternal care is not possible (e.g. the mother goes to work), the next best thing is care in early childhood settings that is modelled on the mother–child relationship. Adherence to these views was evident in a nursery teacher's comments: 'Well, I'm a great fan of all that stuff about children needing to be emotionally secure and feel comfortable within their setting and with the adults, so as to actually fulfil their potential and also that the adults are exceedingly important' (nursery teacher, female 2002). The view that maternal care is best has led to an imbalance in terms of the proportions of women and men employed within the early childhood because early childhood care is seen as the responsibility of women both in the home and in early years settings. The consequences of this pattern of staffing for gender equity are explored in more depth in Chapter 8.

Dominant discourses within the field of psychology position mothers in different ways depending upon their patterns of interaction with their young children. Those mothers who spend a lot of time with their children, preferably one-to-one, playing and talking with them and preparing them to fit in with the educational system, are seen as 'good', while those who do not relate to their children in these ways are classified as 'bad' or 'needing support', and the care they provide is seen to be deficient, with the children being labelled as 'deprived'. The 'truths' about what constitutes 'good' mothering are culturally based. That which epitomizes 'good' mothering in diverse cultural and socio-economic groups has, however, not been acknowledged, as the voices of these diverse groups have been silenced by the dominant discourse. As explained earlier, discourses not only have a powerful effect on people's view of what counts as 'normal' but also have the power to change people's outlook, sometimes without them being aware of it. Ann Dally provided a vivid illustration of how dominant discourses can be seen to operate:

> Recently two women consulted me because they were unable to live in peace with their pre-school children and as a result felt depressed, inadequate and hopeless . . . Both were being criticised by their own

mothers or mothers-in-law who insisted, 'If you can't look after your own children, you shouldn't have had them' . . . these critical older women had raised their own families with considerable assistance from others. One had always had a nanny and the other had been much helped by neighbours in a working-class street with her own mother just around the corner. The differences in circumstances were immeasurable, *yet both generations of mothers had so accepted the current theories of what a mother ought to do that none of them spotted the discrepancies.*

(Dally 1982: 10–11; emphasis added)

Research would suggest that disregarding alternative ways of 'mothering' has not been of benefit to children and their parents, not least in term of mothers' mental health (Burman 2001). Despite this, the mother–child dyad continues to be presented as ideal for young children's development, which has implications for who is seen to be responsible for providing or organizing for the care of very young children. Replicating the mother–child relationship recognized by the dominant discourses in early years settings requires high adult:child ratios. Staffing ratios are frequently viewed as a measure of the quality of the setting. Burman has argued, however, that the cosy image of the mother and child dyad is a fabrication that gained currency in Western societies after the Second World War, as mothers as full-time carers were never and are still not widespread (Burman 2001).

It is also possible to argue that the focus on the mother–child dyad has led to individualistic approaches to both teaching and learning in the early years:

in English nurseries by comparison with the collective nurseries of Italy and Spain there was little sense of a committed group of staff sharing and working towards common objectives. This fragmented and individualistic approach was mirrored with the children . . . There was little sense of the children as a group able to help or influence each other.

(Penn 1997: 52)

In UK early years settings, then, the emphasis on the importance of learning in a one-to-one relationship with an adult has led to a lack of value being placed on children learning from their peers. It is interesting to note here that in Japanese kindergartens teachers prefer high child:adult ratios and feel that one adult to 30 four- and five-year-olds is a desirable staffing ratio (Tobin *et al.* 1989, cited in Munton *et al.* 2002). The staff accept that this staffing ratio leads to a certain degree of chaos within the kindergarten but argue that the high child:adult ratio prevents kindergarten teachers from being too motherly in their approach, which is important because kindergartens are seen to provide young children with the opportunity to make the transition from a sheltered home life to the 'tumult of the real world' (Tobin *et al.* 1987: 539, cited in Munton *et al.* 2002: 27).

Examination of beliefs and practices in a wide range of cultures highlights the culturally specific nature of patterns of child care, which in turn are based on culturally located discourses about children and their learning and development. Most children's life experiences do not mirror that of the child presented in psychology textbooks. Many children are being cared for by a variety of adults in a range of settings. Many children in early years settings will interact more with their peers than with the adults. Even when at home it is possible that there are sisters and brothers to play with and to compete with for adult attention. When one considers what happens in real life rather than in textbooks it would seem that the exclusive mother–child dyad is the exception rather than the norm, although the dominant discourse would have us believe the opposite. The key point is that young children are interacting with a wide circle of other people and participating in a wide range of discourses, some of which may conflict with the powerful dominant discourses. The result is that young children are likely to encounter different understandings about what it means to be a 'girl' or a 'boy'. Children are not presented with unambiguous messages about gender that they can swallow whole; instead they are active participants in creating their personal ideas about gender and are involved in a process of making decisions and judgements about the various versions of 'femininity' and 'masculinity' incorporated within different discourses. Individual children's concepts of gender are likely to be influenced by both adults and other children, and this needs to be considered when reflecting on the appropriateness of gender equity strategies utilized by early years educators. The role of both adults and children in the early years setting should be acknowledged, considering how children come to understand what it means to be a 'girl' or a 'boy'. This issue is explored in more depth in Chapters 4 and 5.

Staffing ratios in various early years settings not only reflect diverse societies' dominant views about the role of early childhood settings and the role of women in child care but also provide an insight into how children are constructed in diverse societies. The following section explores how culturally specific accounts of child development have implications for gender equity within early years settings.

The 'child' and science

Different discourses have had a powerful impact in the field of early years practice and provision. For more than 200 years, in many Western societies, science has been highly valued for its apparent objectivity and exactitude. It could be argued that this reverence for science is one reason why the recent scientific 'findings' discussed in Chapter 2 have been taken so seriously and have begun to be used as 'proof' that gender differences have a biological basis (e.g. Gurian 2001; Biddulph 2003). Not many educators that I spoke to had the confidence to reflect critically on the motives behind scientific research. One nursery teacher, however, asked very pertinent questions about scientific research:

> Nursery teacher: I don't know, I think because it is brain research it is taken terribly seriously and actually it's the same as any old research and we should be quite wary of it and wonder who is doing it and why they're doing it . . .
> Interviewer: So why do you think they might be doing it?
> Nursery teacher: I don't know . . . maybe because I think the men are, at the moment, are feeling really threatened in society because of the way that women actually are taking a much greater role.
> (Interview with nursery teacher, female 2002)

Developmental psychology has achieved the status of a science in people's minds because the methods by which research is carried out are judged to be rigorous and 'scientific' and the findings therefore are seen as objective 'truths'.

The 'normal' child and developmental psychology

It was not until the mid to late nineteenth century that childhood as a discrete stage was deemed worthy of study, but the field of developmental psychology has had a substantial impact on early years provision and practice in the UK and is currently a dominant discourse within the early years field. The phrase 'developmentally appropriate' is frequently used by educators and policy-makers and is shorthand for a complex set of understandings, beliefs and assumptions about young children and their learning based on the research of developmental psychologists. Few early years educators feel confident about challenging what is currently the dominant discourse on children's learning. Developmental psychology rests on the assumption that children develop naturally, and the role of society and culture is largely ignored. The work of Piaget has been hugely influential in the early years field, not least in terms of presenting the child as a 'lone scientist' learning and developing naturally and progressing through a series of clearly identifiable, universal stages on the road to adulthood. The developmental stages and markers currently used in the early years field have arisen from the distillation of a plethora of research studies too numerous to mention. In distilling the research findings what has been lost is knowledge about the individual children being researched, including their cultural context and their gender. The result is that the child in developmental psychology, the child against whom children in our settings and families are measured, is not a real child but is, in a sense, an amalgam of all the children researched. The 'natural', 'normal' child of developmental psychology is male, white and middle class, and, as stated earlier, learns by operating as a mini-scientist. This fabricated child not only signifies the 'norm' but is also seen to be the 'natural' child, as factors such as culture and gender have been rendered invisible by the distillation process. No child matches this 'norm' but some children's development will more closely match the 'norm' than will others'. Those children who do not match the norm are seen as different, exceptional, usually a problem, 'noise in the system' that requires attention in order bring the child's development into the range regarded as 'normal'. The normalizing effect of the dominant discourses circulating within the early years field leads to comments such as: 'the research in terms of language development says it [boys' language development] is different, slower. That's not true of all children, we've got a child here who would talk the hind legs of a donkey without any trouble at all' (headteacher, nursery school, female). A nursery teacher, talking about the differences between girls' and boys' patterns of play, mentioned a girl who was unusual: 'We had one girl last term, or the term before. And she spent the whole of her time outside and she's the only girl I've met so far like that. She'd play with the boys all the time and be just dashing around, climbing' (nursery teacher, female, 2002).

These sort of comments draw attention to the children who are judged not to fit the norm but in doing so reinforce the normalizing effect of the dominant discourses. More recently the ideas of Vygotsky and Bruner have been incorporated into the dominant discourse on early years learning and teaching, but I would argue that the notion of the naturally developing child is still a very powerful concept for early years practitioners:

> I'm Piagetian, because I think a lot of what he said turns out to be true. Half Piagetian and half Vygotskian because scaffolding by adults is exceedingly important, you should have really interesting things to see and feel and do and be scaffolded by supportive adults who see you as an individual who *can* achieve . . . I think that children are empiricists – wherever they are and wherever they go they would be exploring the world with their senses.
>
> (Nursery teacher, female)

The *Curriculum Guidance for the Foundation Stage* (QCA 2001) perpetuates this notion of the 'normally developing' child, and the document is littered with phrases that reflect the dominant discourse. The early learning goals, for example, are seen to be 'achievable for most children who have followed a relevant curriculum' (QCA 2001: 3). The 'stepping stones' that identify markers of progress towards the early learning goals are presented in four age-related bands, and while the document states that 'They [the stepping stones] are not age related', it then goes on to state:

> although it is likely that three-year-old children will be better described by earlier stepping stones, shown in the yellow band, progressing through those in the blue band, with later stepping stones in the green band normally describing older children in the foundation stage.
>
> (QCA 2001: 5)

Comments such as these and others, such as 'stepping stones shown in the green band will usually reflect the attainment of five-year-old children' (QCA 2001: 27), belie later comments that the stepping stones are not presented in a hierarchical order (QCA 2001: 27).

The notion that children's learning and development can be quantified, measured and tested is related to the concept of childhood as a 'stage' in human development. The desirable end state of this human development is seen to be adulthood. This may seem obvious and 'natural' but, as Archard (1993) noted, the concept of adulthood as a state predominates in Western societies, while in many other societies adulthood is seen as a process, 'a continual becoming, a never-completed maturing' (Archard 1993: 36). In societies where adulthood and childhood are seen as stages and states rather than processes, adulthood is defined by:

> the possession of properties which clearly and distinctly separate it from childhood. In the normal course of events the *acquisition of these properties follows an invariant developmental process*. Maturity is both a desired end state and a description of physical age; chronological and qualitative progress coincide.
>
> (Archard 1993: 36)

Archard's analysis of different perceptions of childhood and adulthood make it crystal clear that conceptions of childhood are socially constructed and, furthermore, calls into question the validity of the notion of universal developmental stages through which all 'normal' children pass.

The notion of the 'naturally developing' child has implications for gender equity. First, it masks the ways in which gender (and culture and social class) has an impact on the nature of children's life experiences and the ways in which these life experiences are interpreted. A consequence of this is that not only what children learn but also certain life experiences and learning are viewed as irrelevant or unimportant.

Second, the failure to take account of the ways in which diverse experiences and discourses contribute towards children's learning and development can lend support to the view that differences between girls and boys are 'natural'. Emphasizing the 'naturalness' of children's development has also led to educators monitoring and measuring individual children's development to ensure that they do not stray too far from the 'norm', but few questions are asked about the validity of this norm.

The continued emphasis on the naturally developing child and on stages and norms of development fits well with Kohlberg's (1966) theory of gender identity formation, in which children are said to go through a number of predictable stages in a certain order before developing gender constancy (i.e. they know that superficial factors such as hair length or even play preference do not alter one's gender). Gender constancy, according to Kohlberg (1966), was not usually achieved until the child was approximately 6 or 7 years old. Since the 1960s Kohlberg's theory has been criticized (Macoby 1998), yet his ideas still have currency within the early years field and influence practice.

The focus on sets of measurable outcomes suggests that 'children' are homogeneous and those who meet the milestones are fine (i.e. normal), while those that do not are outside the norm, and this leads to anxieties about groups of children and individual children who, because of their diverse life experiences, which are influenced by the interaction of race, gender and social class, are not conforming to the white, male, middle-class norm of development. Research by Farver and Shin (1997) into children's communicative strategies found that Korean-American children's pretend play themes focused on familiar everyday activities, while Anglo-American children's pretend play themes were based on more fantastic and dangerous themes. The researchers pointed out that while these findings could indicate that Anglo-American children's play was 'a more mature form of pretence' (Farver and Shin 1997: 552) it was important to bear in mind research findings that have shown that the form and content of children's play is influenced by the cultural values and abilities of children's play partners, be they same-age peers, siblings or parents. Furthermore, and very importantly, the differences in play themes may be a reflection of differing social goals during play. Korean-American children's play themes, which have minimal social conflict and are easily shared with others due to their familiarity, may reflect the emphasis on 'harmonious interpersonal relationships' that characterizes Korean culture (Farver and Shin 1997: 553). This stands in contrast to the dominant culture of Anglo-American children which values independence and self-reliance that is then reflected in the play themes through which they pursue their own interests and concerns, even if this involves a degree of conflict. Without this acknowledgement of the impact of culture on children's experiences and learning paths it is probable that the Anglo-American children would be regarded as 'advanced' or certainly on track in terms of their communicative strategies, while the Korean-American children might be described as needing extra support and possibly as disadvantaged. I would argue that failure to take into account the gender discourses to which a child has access may similarly lead to certain girls and boys being described negatively in terms of their development, as these gendered discourses lead to children developing a range of understandings of what it means to be a 'girl' or a 'boy', which, in turn, may result in diverse developmental pathways.

An adherence to developmentally appropriate practice also serves to limit the role of adults and children's peers. The adults may be consigned to providing a stimulating, rich environment that individual children can explore and in so doing develop to their full potential. Such an approach removes children from their social and cultural location and underplays the role of adults and other children in helping children to make sense of their experiences. The focus is squarely on meeting the needs of individual children:

> most of the time I try not to think about equality of opportunity. I just try to think of 60 different individuals with 60 different curriculums. Because we're small, small is beautiful, we have the luxury of doing that and the whole staff, we sit down once each half term and talk about all the children.
>
> (Headteacher, nursery school, female)

This can lead educators to feeling ambivalent about intervening in children's play and learning. On the one hand, many educators understand 'good' early years practice to be that which requires a very light adult touch and minimum interference, since children should be encouraged and enabled to learn through self-directed, self-chosen activity. On the other hand, many educators have taken on board the ideas of Vygotsky and Bruner and now view adult intervention as necessary in terms of 'scaffolding' children's learning, although this intervention does not necessarily extend to intervening in play choices or to helping children to develop a conscious awareness of their understanding of gender. Many early years educators, therefore, continue to feel uncomfortable about intervening to help young children to understand gender issues, although they are increasingly conscious that non-intervention can lead to sexism within the setting. Furthermore, children's 'free choice' in terms of play is not really free, as they will make their choices on the basis of what is available and, equally importantly, will be influenced by the discourses to which they have access. This is discussed in more depth in Chapters 3, 4 and 5 but it is important to note here that non-intervention on the adult's part could result in children not experiencing and exploring other ways of being.

The continuing influence of developmental psychology leads early years educators to focus on aspects of development such as cognitive development, while isolating children from their social, cultural and political context, with the result that gender equity is seen to be an 'extra', something political and something that is not integral to 'good' early years practice.

Such an individualistic approach tends to blur the fact that children are part of wider society and their communities and, furthermore, that children learn from each other and not just from adults. This has implications for gender equity work because, as later chapters show, children participate in and share discourses that provide clear messages about gender; it is not only the adult that children learn from. This is an important point to bear in mind when considering how effective adult 'scaffolding' is likely to be in helping children to develop and refine their understanding of gender. Duveen (1993) has drawn on Vygotskyian theory to help to explain how children develop their gender identities. He has argued that: 'the social marking of people (themselves and others), of material culture and of space provides the scaffolding, which enables children to sustain an organised gender identity' (Duveen 1993: 2).

Whether or not we can be said to have 'an organised gender identity' is open to debate (see Chapter 4) but what is important here is the idea that children's learning about gender proceeds on the 'social level, and later, on the individual level' (Vygotsky 1978: 58, cited in Duveen 1993: 2). Duveen queries the extent to which development can be viewed in terms of the passage of ideas from the interpersonal or interindividual level to the intrapersonal or intraindividual level because in his research he found that the same set of social practices (in this case gender marking in an early years classroom) resulted in differentiated gender identities. In other words, children who were in the same class with the same teacher appeared to develop different understandings about gender. He argued:

> What is missing from Vygotsky's account is an appreciation of the significance of social identities as the structures mediating between the interpsychological and the intrapsychological. His formula describes a world in which every individual acquires the same understanding from a set of social practices. Yet where differences emerge between individuals in relation to the same system of collective meanings this formula is inadequate.
>
> (Duveen 1993: 3)

Duveen's analysis is relevant to early years educators because it suggests that we need to talk with the children to find out about their understandings of gender and to discover the range of discourses to which they have access before considering how to develop children's understanding of gender further, rather than simply imposing a set of practices and strategies in the belief that all children will learn the same thing. Once again, the child needs to be placed within his or her social and cultural context.

This focus on the individual, which underpins developmentally appropriate practice, extends to the educators, in that individual educators shape the provision using what they know about individual children. Concentration on the individual is in part a reflection of dominant discourses in wider society. In Japanese kindergartens, for example, large classes are seen to be an effective strategy for promoting the Japanese values of 'groupism and selflessness' (Tobin *et al.* 1987: 543, cited in Munton *et al.* 2002: 27). In the UK such groupism may be a helpful goal for early years educators keen to work on issues of social justice. McNaughton (2000) has discussed how a move from individualism to critical collectivism in the early years field would support the development of gender equity. In essence she has argued that early years educators need to become more willing to discuss and critique decisions that influence how they relate to children and what they do with children, to explore the 'gendered power implications of daily teaching decisions and knowledges' and to experiment with and reflect with others on strategies for gender reform (McNaughton 2000: 181). Educators keen to bring about change in their setting need not only to try to involve others (e.g. colleagues, parents and children) in the process but also to be willing to engage in a process of critical reflection. Without such a process it will be hard to shift patterns of practice based on long-established 'truths' about young children's learning and development and the role of the adult. A good illustration of this inertia is provided by a nursery teacher who, after having been to a conference with two other colleagues from the setting (the headteacher and the deputy headteacher), was keen to introduce playing with guns into the nursery. She talked about how she went about this and the outcome:

> Nursery teacher: The three of us agreed that it would be a good idea to let the boys play with guns and we felt a bit guilty because all these years of saying 'No you can't play with guns'. So we went back to the nursery and, really, without democratic process we said we are going to do this, we're going to let the boys play with guns.
> Interviewer: Without a democratic process means you didn't ask the other adults?
> Nursery teacher: We just told them really. We gave them an explanation about why it was good idea but we didn't really collect any evidence for ourselves and bring it back to people and say 'Do you see what we mean?' and 'Do you think we should carry on with this?' We just did it regardless of what they thought and I know that many of them were against it because they hadn't attended the conference and didn't understand it . . . It was only when I decided to do [some research] that I actually asked people's opinions. As it happens they all agreed that it would be a bad idea to ban gun play – that was the outcome of it. The other outcome was that there was only two of us ever involved in it, the others just watched it.
> (Interview with nursery advisor, female)

Although her colleagues apparently 'all agreed', only she and one other colleague were actively involved in developing the play with guns, which would suggest that the rest of the staff team opposed the strategy but possibly felt unable to voice their views because the senior management was clearly in favour of the strategy. Furthermore, it was clear from talking to the staff involved that there had been no discussion of how the initiative benefited or disadvantaged the girls and boys who were not interested in gun play. This issue is discussed in more depth in Chapters 6 and 7 but it highlights the need for educators to consider girls and boys simultaneously, rather than focusing on girls and boys in isolation from each other.

Educators need to be willing to be self-critical and work with colleagues to develop a critical collective, but they also need to be conscious of the way in which dominant discourses operate to regulate their belief systems and practice. Foucault's notion of dominant discursive regimes operating as regulatory mechanisms is useful here, as it helps educators to reflect on how taken-for-granted 'truths' about children's learning are not necessarily 'right' in any definitive sense but are simply one way of defining what is 'normal' and 'right'. Such an understanding is crucial if educators are to adopt a critical stance to the plethora of government initiatives, some of which are endorsed by people accorded the status of experts, and to challenge customary practices in order to adopt a transformative approach to gender issues in the early years.

The *Curriculum Guidance for the Foundation Stage* (QCA 2001), for example, makes relatively little reference to equality issues, as educators attest:

> Interviewer: Can I ask you a little bit about the curriculum guidance for the foundation stage? Do you think there is enough in there about equal opportunities?
> Teacher: I don't think there's anything, is there?
>
> (Nursery teacher, female)

In the early years the dominant discourse of developmentalism has served to relegate issues of gender equity to the sidelines, along with issues such as social class and 'race'. Inspection of settings takes account of equity issues but only as far as to determine the extent to which children are measuring up to pre-existing norms and expectations. As central government has tightened its control over early years practice and provision in the UK there has been an increase in targets to be achieved, 'guidance' documents for educators and inspection of settings. One nursery head was clear about the reasons for this increased surveillance:

> Well I think that is a sort of control freakery gone mad actually! Because actually people were slightly nervous of nursery teachers. Actually I still think people are quite nervous of nursery teachers

because they are much more anarchic than anybody else. So I think it was a way of trying to regularize them and control them and, um, it won't work!

(Nursery headteacher, female)

If early years educators are to retain their 'anarchic' tendencies they need to continue to be critical and reflective and ensure that they maintain an open mind when considering how children learn about gender. Furthermore, they need to be conscious of the power dimensions of decisions they make about gender issues and to consider how diverse groups are likely to be differentially affected by gender equity strategies that do not take account of the gendered nature of power relations between girls and boys, an issue that is explored in more depth in Chapters 6 and 7 in relation to superhero play.

Where to from here?

This chapter has highlighted how early years educators need to be critical and reflective and to be aware of how certain discourses are privileged and the effect this has on silencing or giving voice to specific groups of children and adults. In addition, moving away from an individualistic approach within early years practice may facilitate gender equity, not least by acknowledging that the pattern of children's development is not 'natural' and universal, and that various discourses influence what we see, focus on and value. Relocating children within their social and political milieu also facilitates consideration of the effects of different discourses on children's developing understanding of gender issues. The following chapter, which explores how gender differences have been explained within the field of science, provides an opportunity to reflect on how a specific discourse, science, has been used to define 'knowledge' about gender differences.

2 Seductive science

One would think there must be something neurological because people have tried very hard to, you know, change things with their girls, to make sure they are playing with trains . . . and it's just not on. I used to believe it was possible to have all that sort of equal opportunities and make sure that that everybody did the same. Now we much more openly talk about how we are going to engage the boys.

(Headteacher, female)

Research into the development of the brain prior to and during early childhood has secured a place on the early years agenda. The research has particular relevance to those concerned with gender equity within early childhood because, as the comments above suggest, practitioners' teaching approaches are influenced by their understanding of how young children develop and how girls' and boys' development may differ.

The idea that there are clear differences between the brains of males and females is far from new. In the nineteenth century, it was argued that it was wrong to expect girls to cope with the same education as boys, as their mental capacities differed: 'The first thing of importance is to be content to be inferior to men – inferior in mental power in the same proportion that you [women] are inferior in bodily strength' (Mrs William Ellis 1843, quoted in Kamm 1965: 167). Recently there has been a resurgence of interest in the notion that biology can explain many of the observable differences between girls' and boys' behaviour. This chapter outlines some of the many scientific research findings and resulting theories connected with the development of observable gender differences in young children, and explores the validity of the research findings and conclusions drawn.

Are girls' and boys' brains different?

Size and physical structure

In the nineteenth century, research showed that human brains were proportionally larger than those of their fellow primates. The simplistic connection between brain size and intellectual ability was made:

> the large proportion which the size of man's brain bears to his body, compared to the same proportion in the gorilla or orang, is closely connected with his higher mental powers . . . that there exists in man some close relation between the size of the brain and the development of the intellectual faculties is supported by the comparison of the skulls of savage and civilised races, of ancient and modern people, and by the analogy of the whole vertebrate series.
>
> (Darwin 1871: 54)

It was a small step from here to claiming that women, whose brains were found to be smaller than men's, were also therefore intellectually inferior to men.

Paul Broca, who founded the Anthropological Society in 1859, was one of the earliest researchers to use brain size as 'proof' of women's intellectual inferiority:

> the brain is larger in mature adults than in the elderly, in men than in women, in eminent men than in men of mediocre talent, in superior races than in inferior races . . . other things equal, there is a remarkable relationship between the development of intelligence and the volume of the brain.
>
> (Quoted in Gould 1981: 83)

During the second half of the twentieth century thinking changed and there was increasing scepticism about the validity of attempting to explain differences between girls and boys on the basis of brain structure. This increased scepticism owed much to the growing understanding about the ways in which biological explanations for 'race' and IQ were flawed.

It is only relatively recently that the issue has been re-examined by professionals concerned with the care and education of young children, and although most people would probably not equate brain size with intellectual ability the idea is still promulgated by some authors. Michael Gurian (2002), for example, writes that the neocortex, the thin outer grey layer of the brain's cortex, is 'associated with human thought and higher intelligence' and notes that male brains have greater mass than female brains. He claims that 'difference in brain size affects the amount of brain material' and concludes that 'basic kinds of intelligence [are] likely [to] be influenced by these differences' (Gurian 2002: 23). In fact there is little evidence to support this claim. The research evidence suggests that although male brains are larger than female brains this difference does not hold true when one compares the brain size with body weight; in other words, proportionally, men's brains are not larger than those of women. Furthermore, although Gurian seems to be suggesting that the greater mass of male brains is due to more 'brain material', it is important to be aware of the diversity of form and function of what Gurian blithely refers to as 'brain material'.

The brain is composed of grey matter and white matter. The grey is composed mainly of the heads of nerve cells (neurones), while the white matter is composed of nerve fibres and other material (e.g. myelin sheathing) that facilitates communication between the areas of grey matter and between the grey matter and the rest of the body. Research would tend to suggest that the density of neurones (nerve cells) is lower in males than in females (Falk 1997). So females have a higher density of neurones (grey matter) but males have more white matter (brain tissue that enables communication between groups of cells in different parts of the brain). What does all this tell us about female and male brains? Merely, perhaps, that the brain is too complicated to allow for simple comparisons and facile conclusions.

It is certainly true that debates about the similarities and differences between female and male brains have moved beyond consideration of overall size, and the theories about brain function and gender are becoming more complex. One idea that has captured people's imagination is that female and male brains are structured or 'hard wired' in different ways, which results in somewhat different capabilities and patterns of behaviour.

Left brained, right brained?

There has been a wealth of research into the functions of different areas of the brain. Due to research in the mid and late nineteenth century the generally accepted view has been that in most humans the left hemisphere is the centre for language and speech (Finger 2000). The right hemisphere is more concerned with analysis of space and shape, emotional and visual memory and interpretation of tone of voice and prosody (inflections). With advances in technology it has been possible to study living, healthy brains instead of drawing conclusions from diseased or impaired brains. Some of the studies have pointed to brain laterality, in other words the tendency for some functions of the brain and thought processes to be concentrated in one or other of the hemispheres (Meyers-Levy 1994).

Research by Myers and Sperry in the 1950s paved the way for the development of a gender-based view of brain structure and activity that is still in circulation today. Myers and Sperry's (1953) research led to the view that a bridging structure, the corpus callosum, which is composed of a bundle of nerve fibres, serves to transfer information between the two hemispheres of the brain. Then, de Lacoste-Utamsing and Holloway (1982) reported that analyses of female and male brains during autopsies had shown a clear sex difference in terms of the size and shape of the corpus callosum. In women the corpus callosum was found to be larger than in men. A wealth of research studies has tended to support the theory that in women there is better communication between the left and right hemispheres of the brain than is the case for men, and while women tend to be left-hemisphere dominant and therefore more adept with language, men are right-hemisphere dominant and better at visual–spatial tasks (e.g. Kimura 1969; Coltheart *et al.* 1975; Corsi-Cabrera *et al.* 1989; Meyers-Levy 1994). Findings about the differences in size of the corpus callosum added weight to the notion that female brains are less lateralized than male brains (McGlone 1980) and led to writers asserting that girls have more 'cross-talk' between the hemispheres of the brain than do boys (Gurian 2001: 27). This idea has permeated the field of education and led to the view that the lower levels of inter-hemispheric communication in boys result in greater specificity in brain function which on the one hand can enhance their visio-spatial skills and on the other hand serve to hamper the development of boys' language. Gender-based differences in brain structure and activity have been used to explain why many boys seem to find learning to read and write more difficult than do girls, and to explain why boys seem to be better than girls at maths and science.

Educators and parents also wonder whether this physical difference in brain structure can explain the widely held view that girls and women find it easier to talk about their emotions as language is located in the left hemisphere and emotions in the right. Currently, the theory of gender-based brain lateralization and gender is well established in the public mind, although the validity of this view is open to question.

If a major difference between female and male brain activity is the degree to which it tends to be hemisphere-specific or inter-hemispheric it ought not to be surprising that one of the most oft quoted differences between female and male brains concerns the 'bridge' between the left and right hemispheres of the brain. A point to bear in mind, however, is that the findings linking brain lateralization and the size of the corpus callosum are controversial. To begin with, the research by de Lacoste-Utamsing and Holloway consisted of autopsies on only nine male brains and five female brains, which is a very small sample from which to draw conclusions. Furthermore, the women who had died were old or ageing, whereas the nine men were young and had been killed in accidents. Later research studies attempted to replicate de Lacoste-Utamsing and Holloway's findings but the results were inconclusive (Jancke and Steinmetz 1998). One set of research findings found that the difference between males and females was smaller than the difference between left and right handed people. Another study examined the corpus callosum of 122 age-matched healthy adults and 24 aged-matched children between the ages of two and 16 using non-invasive magnetic image resonance (MRI) techniques. This study found differences in the shape of the corpus callosum in adults but no significant sex-related differences in the shape of the corpus callosum in children (Allen *et al.* 1991). Another study, six years later, found no sex differences in the size of the corpus callosum in children aged 4 to 19 years (Giedd *et al.* 1996).

The diverse and frequently contradictory research findings could be attributed to the type and size of the sample, the methods of measurement and a failure to take account of factors such as age and 'handedness'. At this point in time there seems to be little consensus about the corpus callosum, although interesting research by Jancke and Steinmetz (1998) investigated the size of the corpus callosum relative to the overall size of the brain, and found that women with large brains had a relatively small corpus callosum, while men with small brains had a relatively larger corpus callosum, which led them to suggest that brain size, not gender, is the determining factor when considering the size of the corpus callosum.

It is perhaps not surprising that there is uncertainty surrounding the corpus callosum when one considers some recent scientific research findings. With the advent of non-invasive methods of studying the brain, research studies have found that between 70 and 95 per cent of the research subjects had a left-hemisphere language dominance. On the basis of these research findings it would seem that up to nearly a third of people do not have left-hemisphere language specialization. For these 30 per cent it could be that the language functions are spread more evenly across both hemispheres, in which case the language functions may be located more in the right hemisphere so that these people would have right-hemisphere language dominance (Knecht *et al.* 2000) or alternatively their brains might lack lateralized specialization. In 1998, Jaeger and her colleagues were researching whether the brains of women and men showed similar patterns of functional organization for language or whether men's brains were more strongly lateralized. The researchers found that women used both left and right hemispheres for both simpler and more complex language tasks. Men, however, used both hemispheres for the simpler language tasks but their left hemisphere was more active than their right hemisphere when dealing with complex language tasks (Jaeger *et al.* 1998). This piece of research certainly calls into question the theory that language is left-lateralized for everyone. Research by Hyde and Linn has challenged the theory that girls and women are more verbally skilled than boys and men (Hyde and Linn 1986), while further research by Hyde has suggested that gender-based discrepancies in mathematical ability may be negligible in young children, although small gender-based differences may appear in older children (Hyde *et al.* 1990). These findings should lead us to tread cautiously when making claims about hemispheric dominance and gender-based differences in the functioning of the two hemispheres of the brain.

Jaeger (quoted by Donovan 1998) has commented that the deeply rooted belief that language function is situated within the left hemisphere was based largely on the study of men's brains, and she makes the point that:

> Unfortunately we've had the mistaken impression that what we've learned from male subjects can be applied to women as well. In fact, virtually all our ideas about the brain from the fields of neurology, psychology and linguistics are modelled after studies of the male brains, as are all ideas on cognitive function in our textbooks. They will need to be re-evaluated [and] new cognitive models designed.
>
> (Donovan 1998)

The existence of conflicting research findings also has obvious implications for arguments relating to educational provision, not least in that they make the situation less clear. We cannot confidently claim that certain types of teaching and learning approaches will suit girls or boys on the grounds of their brain laterality and hemispheric dominance.

Different rates of maturation

Differences in brain structure have not been the only factor said to affect girls' and boys' behaviour and attainment in the early years. Research findings suggest that girls' brains mature more rapidly than do those of boys. There are a number of distinct differences between the appearance of children's and adults' brains and Caviness and his associates used MRI scans to measure the maturity of children's brains (Caviness *et al.* 1996). The more closely a child's brain matched that of an adult the more 'mature' it was said to be. Caviness *et al.* found that, using this measure of maturation, the brains of 11-year-old girls were as 'mature' as the brains of 17-year-old boys. Findings such as this are hard to believe, and few of us would claim that an 11-year-old girl is as mature as a 17-year-old boy, so perhaps the development of structures within the brain is not a very good measure of 'maturity'. It could be that the actual functioning of the brain is a better measure. Adults' and children's brains differ in terms of the electrophysiological activity that occurs and this activity can be measured using electro-encephalograms (EEGs). Anonkhin *et al.* (2000) examined the EEGs of youngsters and found that those of 11-year-old girls were similar to those of 17-year-old boys. Perhaps this is proof that boys' brains mature at a slower rate than girls' and if so this has consequences for educators and parents.

On the basis of this scientific evidence it is possible to assert that girls in Year 6 and 7 are as mature as boys in Years 11 and 12. Our everyday experience should tell us that this is not the case. A closer look at some of the maturational differences between girls' and boys' brains may help to clarify the picture.

Language and brain development

It has now become common knowledge that girls' language skills develop sooner than boys', with the result that by the time children start nursery there is already a clear difference between girls' and boys' linguistic abilities.

> So I'm very clear that there is a difference between girls and boys language development, and all the research in terms of language development says it [boys' language development] is different, slower. That's not true of all children . . . We are not talking about *all* boys but if you are looking at a normal sample you would expect more boys to be referred to speech and language therapy than girls.
>
> (Headteacher with speech therapy background)

How true is this claim, however, and if there are differences are they biological, as we are increasingly led to believe, or are these differences linked with socialization patterns?

According to Gurian, not only do girls speak their first words earlier and develop a better vocabulary than boys, but also by the age of three 99 per cent of girls' speech is comprehensible, while it is not until boys are aged four and a half that 99 per cent of their speech becomes intelligible (Gurian 2001: 35). Since Gurian does not refer to specific research findings to support his assertion it is not possible to comment on the validity of the research he refers to. Macoby (1998) has cited the work of Shucard *et al.* (1987), which found that 6-month-old girls had more activity in the left hemisphere than the right when listening to verbal stimuli, while for boys of the same age the pattern was reversed. Working from the premise that the left hemisphere is the centre for language, Macoby concluded that 'there are hints of a neural substrate that enables girls to progress faster (or at least differently) with respect to language' (Macoby 1998: 107).

Before we jump to conclusions, however, it is important to bear in mind that language is not only 'processed' in the left hemisphere, as outlined earlier in this chapter: language may also be processed by the right hemisphere, and for many people, girls and boys, both left and right hemispheres are involved. Second, even by the age of 6 months, babies have experience of socialization processes, so it is possible that any differences between girls and boys that are emerging at this age are as much a function of socialization forces as expressions of innate biological differences. Third, insufficient research has been carried out to be able to state with any certainty that differences in language development are due to brain structure and function. This does not mean that observable differences between girls and boys may not exist in terms of their different rates of language development; it simply means that we ought to be wary of explaining these differences purely through references to disparities in the brain development of girls and boys.

Self-regulation and brain development

Another area of development in which there appears to be a gender-based difference is related to self-regulation or self-control. 'That's the only thing with boys, their boredom threshold is quite low and of course once they are bored they don't want to do anything anyway except be disruptive' (Head of private nursery school). Gurian simply states that 'boys get bored more easily than girls . . . Girls are better at self-managing boredom' and then goes on to state that once boys become bored they will 'act out' and disrupt the class (Gurian 1991: 46), but is there a biological root to this apparent difference? According to an article in the *Times Educational Supplement* (*TES*), some differences between girls and boys can be attributed to nature rather than nurture: 'Boys tend to be action-orientated, impatient, imaginative, inclined to take risks . . . their learning and motivational skills are different [from girls']' (Duffy 2002: 16). The article fails to provide research evidence to support this assertion.

There is, in fact, a great deal of research that would confirm the experience of the headteacher quoted above. Macoby draws on a range of research findings (Rothbart *et al.* 1994; Eisenberg 1996; Kochanska 1996) to argue that boys may show lower levels of self-regulatory behaviour than do girls of the same age because of differences in the rate of maturation of the relevant brain structures (Macoby 1998: 107–11). If we look at brain structure alone it would be possible to adopt the view that differences between girls' and boys' self-regulatory behaviour are 'natural', but alternative explanations are possible. Macoby (1998) raises the possibility that the apparent delay in boys' self-regulatory systems may be linked with girls' greater linguistic skills. In other words, what may be a relatively small difference between girls and boys in terms of brain structure may be exaggerated by the fact that girls' greater facility with language plays a key role in helping them to regulate their own behaviour. It is also possible, of course, that parenting patterns are such that while parents allow their small boys more leeway with regard to their behaviour, small girls are encouraged to conform and control themselves at a younger age than boys. A comment by a headteacher certainly suggests that in early years settings boys may not be expected to exercise self-control, as the adults tailor provision to suit the boys: 'We tend to catch the boys at certain times because we can tell if they would rather run around. There is no way you are going to get them to come and write their name' (Headteacher, private nursery).

Processing emotions

Research by Schneider *et al.* (2000) and Killgore *et al.* (2001) has suggested that there may be brain-based differences in the way that boys and girls process emotion. According to Kilgore *et al.*, in very young children emotions are initially processed within a sub-cortical area of the brain known as the amygdala, and there is little or no connection between this area of the brain and the areas of the brain linked with language. From around the age of seven, girls' brains are said to develop in such a way that emotion is processed in the cerebral cortex, and this means that there are numerous connections between the area of the brain concerned with emotion and the areas of the brain concerned with language. One result of this is that older girls and women are able to talk about how they feel. For boys and men the picture seems somewhat bleak, as they continue to process emotion in the sub-cortical area of the brain and this apparently makes it very hard for boys and men to articulate what they are feeling.

The lesson we need to learn from current brain-based research is that we need to treat the results of scientific findings with caution. There may well be differences between the structure and functioning of girls' and boys' brains but a great deal more research needs to be done before we jump to conclusions about the consistency of these differences, the cause of these differences and their implications.

The effects of hormones

> The boys were into Batman and rushing around . . . having swords and guns and wanting to hit at things and this is going to sound really sexist but there's all that business about boys producing more adrenaline.
> (Nursery teacher, female)

> Girls seem to have a more caring side to them, which seems to come naturally, possibly hormones or genes.
> (18-year-old student teacher, female)

In addition to research exploring structural and functional differences of the brain there is considerable interest in the role hormones play in shaping the structure of the brain and influencing, girls' and boys' development and behaviour.

Hormones are chemicals in the body that act in two main ways in the brain. First, hormones may have an organizational influence, in that they may play a key role in determining the structure of the developing brain. Second, hormones may have an activational influence, in that they may 'trigger' expressions of patterns of behaviour. Recent research findings have suggested that certain hormones may have an organizational effect prenatally on the developing human brain.

Oestrogen and testosterone are commonly referred to as the 'sex hormones', and these have a powerful impact on the development and functioning of the human body. Oestrogen, the female sex hormone, is produced by the ovaries, is responsible for sexual maturation and the reproductive cycle and is necessary for the growth and healthy maintenance of bones. Testosterone, the male sex hormone, not only stimulates the development of secondary sex characteristics but also is important for the development of muscle and bone. The testes and the adrenal glands situated on top of the kidneys produce testosterone. It would, however, be a mistake to think that males do not require oestrogen and females do not produce testosterone. Low concentrations of testosterone are produced in females by the adrenal glands and ovaries and although males do not produce oestrogen as such, it is created in boys and men by the conversion of testosterone.

Gurian is clear about the activational influence of testosterone and oestrogen, in that he claims that he does not 'want to stereotype but can't avoid what is before us . . . testosterone is a sex and aggressive hormone' (Gurian 2002: 90), while 'estrogen [*sic*] is an "intimacy" hormone' (Gurian 2002: 89). The message is clear: expect boys to be aggressive and girls to be more focused on maintaining relationships. However, prior to around the age of around 8 both girls and boys produce similar and small amounts of the sex hormones, so arguably any differences in girls' and boys' behaviour cannot be linked with these hormones. Given this somewhat complex picture, is it sensible to talk about the effects of testosterone on little boys and oestrogen on little girls?

For a long time it was believed that the so-called sex hormones had no impact on brain development, but now some scientists and sociobiologists would argue that it is pertinent to talk about the effects of testosterone and oestrogen on very young children, as some research studies have suggested that these sex hormones have an effect on the development of the brain. Some would go as far as to suggest that the brain is hard wired and 'gendered' before birth.

Hormones and early brain development

What gives us a male or a female brain, then, is not a matter of our genes; for we have seen how a genetic male may have a female mind, and vice versa. It is a matter of the hormones that our developing bodies make, or which surround us in the womb. What matters is the

degree to which our embryonic brains are exposed to male hormone. The less they get, the more the natural feminine mind-set will survive.
(Moir and Jessel 1991: 36)

In the early 1970s research into girls with a condition known as congenital adrenal hyperplasia or CAH suggested a strong link between brain development and hormonal environment prior to birth. Girls suffering from CAH produce large quantities of male hormones prior to and after birth, and the most obvious manifestation of this condition is the masculinization of genitalia. If the condition is untreated, the girls develop a masculine appearance. Research comparing the behaviour of girls with CAH with their unaffected sisters found that girls with CAH have better spatial awareness, are more likely to be aggressive and to choose to play with 'boys' toys' (e.g. vehicles, guns), engage in more rough and tumble play and, despite the fact that they have normal levels of oestrogen, show less interest in babies than do unaffected girls (Money and Ehrhardt 1972; Berenbaum 1990). This research is often cited to 'prove' that 'sex' hormones shape the development of the human brain.

While the brain is developing in the womb, hormones control the way the neural networks are laid out. Later on, at puberty, those hormones revisit the brain to switch on the network they earlier created. Men who are known to have been exposed to a below average amount of male hormone in the womb, are also found to have a female pattern in the distribution of their skill functions in the brain.
(Moir and Jessel 1991: 43)

It is important to remember that there are a number of problems with the studies on girls with CAH. First, the sample size is small. Second, the girls must be psychologically affected by the fact that, until they have corrective plastic surgery, anatomically they may look more like boys than girls. In addition, comparing siblings does not remove the socialization factor, as children within a family do not all have exactly the same social experiences. It is feasible that parental attitudes towards girls with CAH and their unaffected sisters may be very different, which in turn may lead to very dissimilar experiences of upbringing

Research into the development of autism seems to suggest that testosterone levels *in utero* may play a major role in determining whether a child develops autism or Asperger's syndrome. Scientists at Cambridge Autism Research Centre have found that young children who were exposed to higher than normal levels of testosterone while in the womb have smaller vocabularies than do those children who had normal or lower than normal levels of testosterone. The scientists have also claimed to have discovered that higher levels of testosterone *in utero* tend to result in poorer social and communication skills. The Cambridge team argue that testosterone is known to stimulate the development of the right hemisphere and suggest that this growth may take place at the expense of the left hemisphere. Although potentially interesting, this research needs to be considered in the light of previous research findings, which suggest that in up to 30 per cent of people the left hemisphere may not be the centre for language (McKie and Gold 2002).

Analysis of the side-effects of certain drugs given to pregnant mothers has added weight to the argument that the foetal hormonal environment may affect the personality of children. Mothers who are diabetic and more likely to have miscarriages have been treated with diethylstilbestrol (a 'female' hormone). Researchers have claimed that boys born to these mothers are less assertive than 'normal' (Bland 2001), although the research did not take into account the possible effects of differences in mothers' behaviour towards their sons and the effect that this might have on a child's emotional and social development. Other research has suggested that girls exposed to diethylstilbestrol while in the womb had better developed spatial skills than the 'average' girl (Meyer-Bahlburg *et al.* 1998). So we are left with the question: does diethylstilbestrol have a 'feminizing' or 'masculinizing' effect or are the action and interaction of hormones prenatally too complex to be explained by current scientific research findings?

Support for the argument for the prenatal 'gendering' of brains does not always come from the study of children or mothers with specific medical conditions and behaviour. A number of studies appear to support the theory that the physical structure of the brain is noticeably changed by prenatal hormonal action. It has been claimed, for example, that an ultrasound scan at around 26 weeks shows that the corpus callosum in female brains is noticeably thicker than that in male brains (Achiron *et al.* 2001). However, as discussed earlier in this chapter, other research studies question the extent to which the corpus callosum differs in males and females.

If hormones affect children before they are born what happens in the case of opposite-sex twins? Miller (1994) claimed that evidence from studies of twins supported the view that prenatal hormones can be transferred between babies while in the womb and that the result of this hormone transfer, although not always evident in boys, resulted in girls become more 'masculine' (as measured by spatial development and motor coordination). Miller's argument was that this hormone transfer affected brain development: 'testosterone affects the females greatly but . . . either little female hormones are produced by the ovary prenatally, or the male is little affected by any female hormones that may reach him' (Miller 1994: 524). It is interesting to note that Miller's hypothesis runs counter to the research findings regarding diethylstilbestrol, briefly discussed above.

Research by Rodgers *et al.* (1998) focused on opposite-sex twins and their toy preferences because they believed that choice of toy and play style were among the most consistent differences in girls' and boys' behaviour. On the basis of previous research findings into prenatal hormone transfer it was expected that girls with a twin brother would be more likely to play with 'male' toys (e.g. vehicles, balls, bricks) but no such tendency was observed. Rodgers *et al.* argued that their findings did not support the hormone transfer theory, although they did acknowledge that more research needs to be carried out into the levels of hormones achieved through hormone transfer. It could be that hormone transfer does occur but the level does not reach a critical level and therefore has no effect on brain development. Alternatively, high levels of hormones may be transferred, but if this were the case the work of Rodgers *et al.* would suggest that even high levels have no effect on brain development. Gender-typed toy play has been attributed to socialization factors (e.g. Macoby and Jacklin 1974) and it must be said that the average age of the children in the Rodgers *et al.* study was 8 and therefore it is not possible to exclude the effects of socialization.

Hines *et al.* (2002) researched possible links between the level of testosterone in pregnant mothers' blood and 3-year-olds' sex-typed toy and game preferences as reported by the parents. The study was fairly sizeable, in that it involved 679 children and their mothers. Hines *et al.* (2002) stated that in the case of the girls a clear, positive, linear relationship was apparent between prenatal testosterone and postnatal gender behaviour but no such relationship was apparent for the boys in the study. So higher levels of maternal testosterone during pregnancy seem to increase the tendency for daughters to engage in 'masculine' type play, while sons seem to be unaffected by their mothers' testosterone levels during pregnancy. Two possible explanations were put forward by Hines *et al.* to explain these somewhat puzzling findings. First, because boys' prenatal levels of testosterone are much higher than girls' prenatal levels, the variation in the mothers' testosterone levels will have proportionally less effect on boys than on girls. Interestingly, the second possible explanation is rooted in socialization rather than biology. Hines *et al.* drew on research by Fagot (1978), Perry and Bussey (1979) and Langlois and Downs (1980) to support the argument that since girls are less strongly discouraged than boys from engaging in cross-gender behaviour, girls with a hormone-related predisposition towards 'masculine' behaviour are more likely to be able to engage in such behaviour, while boys with a hormone-related predisposition towards 'feminine' behaviour will be strongly discouraged from exhibiting such behaviour. It is significant that a study looking at the effect of mothers' testosterone levels on children's gender-role behaviour required the researchers to draw on theories relating to both nature and nurture in an attempt to make sense of the findings. More research clearly needs to be done on very young children in order to exclude or minimize the effects of the socialization.

It is apparent from recent research that the effect of hormones on brain development is complex and intricate. It is not merely the case that more testosterone makes a 'male brain' and less testosterone a 'female brain', although this is the traditional view on sexual differentiation (Gurian 2001: 41). Fausto-Sterling, a biologist who has critically examined many scientific research studies related to gender, is confident that 'the claim that clear-cut evidence exists to show that fetal hormones make boys more active, aggressive or athletic than girls is little more than fancy, although harmless it is not' (Fausto-Sterling 1992: 131).

While it seems possible that at some point during early to mid pregnancy hormones may play a role in the development of sexual dimorphism of the brain, we do not yet know for certain which hormones are involved and, just as importantly, the scope and significance of any resultant differences in the structure and operation of the brains of females and males. The brain is, after all, a very complex organ and the wealth of conflicting research findings would tend to suggest that, while differences may exist between female and male brains, these differences may not be very significant, as the human brain appears to possess the potential to perform the same task in numerous ways.

Hormones in early childhood: The T factor

> But boys' testosterone levels rise at the age of 4 don't they? So that's why they like fighting.
>
> (Nursery teacher, male)

If the impact of hormones on early brain development is still not completely understood, what could be said about the effect of hormones circulating in the bloodstream during early childhood?

Steven Biddulph (2003: 36) has made the bold claim that boys and girls have the same levels of testosterone levels up to the age of 4, but at the age of 4, for reasons no one knows, boys' testosterone levels double. By the age of 5 the testosterone levels have halved (i.e. are the same as the girls) – 'just in time for school'. His claim is unsubstantiated but this 'truth' has now entered public consciousness to the extent that teachers have referred to it when trying to explain gender differences among 4- and 5-year-old children, and increasing levels of aggression and physical activity among 4-year-old boys are explained in terms of this testosterone surge. Articles in the media perpetuate the myth:

> As soon as the first jolt of testosterone kicked in at about the age of four, my boys became, well boys. They wanted to fight each other or their father; they loved to climb, hit, kick, swing and roar around.

They were not responding, as I had previously believed, to some sinister social conditioning. They were obeying their nature.

(Turner 2003b: 4)

It has not been possible to find any research evidence to support the claim that boys experience a testosterone surge at the age of 4, although there is plenty of evidence for high levels of testosterone among infant boys in the first three to 21 hours after birth (Terasawa and Fernandez 2001). In baby boys levels of testosterone are also elevated during the first two to four months, but by around the age of 6 months testosterone levels fall to prepubertal childhood levels and remain low until around the age of 9 or 10 (Winter *et al.* 1975; Quigley 2002). These high levels of testosterone are due to high levels of luteinizing hormone (LH) and accompanied by high levels of follicle-stimulating hormone (FSH), which is needed to ensure healthy development of the specialized male reproductive cells. This very early testosterone surge is never mentioned by those who argue that differences between young girls' and boys' behaviour is partly hormonally induced, probably because the high level of circulating testosterone in infant boys does not appear to be associated with increased levels of aggression or activity.

Although testosterone levels do not markedly differ in children until around the age of 10, it is worth considering the effect of this hormone, not least because it is widely believed to cause aggression in boys. A study of 28 pre-school children, both girls and boys, aged 4 and 5 years old has revealed some interesting patterns in testosterone levels (Sanchez-Martin *et al.* 2000). When children were playing amicably testosterone levels were low, but being on the receiving end of aggression raised the testosterone levels of both girls and boys. However, when the testosterone levels of the girls and boys are looked at separately it would appear that there was a positive correlation in boys between testosterone and serious aggression in social situations but not for playful fighting. This pattern was not observable in the girls in the sample. The researchers were led to conclude that 'Testosterone can be a useful biological marker for aggression (and behavioural patterns reflecting different levels of sociability) in children (especially boys).' They also postulated that girls and boys express their conflict behaviour in different ways. This last idea would suggest that there could be a socialization element at work, which would account for the children's different responses to aggression. It also raises a number of questions, including whether the testosterone levels of the aggressor are higher than those of the 'victim'; in other words, does testosterone cause aggression or is it produced in response to aggression? Is it possible for the body to 'switch off' testosterone production and, if so, is the mechanism different in girls and boys? Are the levels of testosterone produced in girls and boys very similar when on the receiving end of aggression and, if so, how, if at all, are boys' and girls' responses different? A small-scale study of very aggressive boys aged 4 to 10 years found that their testosterone levels were no higher than those of a control group of unaggressive boys (Constantino *et al.* 1993). This would suggest that we need to be cautious about linking aggression in young boys with high levels of testosterone. Research with adults has shown that testosterone may indeed cause aggressive behaviour but, as noted above, testosterone may also be produced in response to aggression (Mazur and Booth 1998), and we need to be wary of applying research findings based on men to young children in the early years. Testosterone may be implicated in aggression by adult males but this does not necessarily hold true for little boys. Furthermore, it is important to keep 'male' and 'testosterone' separate. They are not synonymous, and for educators in the early years it would appear that thinking about the possible action of testosterone is not very helpful when attempting to understand and support the young children in our care.

Why might there be differences between girls' and boys' brains?

According to evolutionary biologists, gender differences exist because of our role more than 10,000 years ago as hunter-gatherers. Males were the hunters who roved far and wide to hunt for food and protect the community, while females stayed close to home, caring for children and gathering food in the immediate locality. Men therefore needed to be strong and powerful, to be willing to take physical risks and to have well developed spatial skills. Women, so the story goes, needed to be nurturing and more skilled at interpersonal interactions. It has been argued that differences in the relative sizes of particular structures within the brain are directly related to the different abilities of women and men, as measured by standardized tests (Falk 1997). Furthermore, comparative studies on other mammals have led to the claim that:

> the cognitive specialities of men and women are likely to have evolved for reasons to do with classic 'reproductive fitness' – i.e. superior visiospatial skills may first have developed in polygamous male ancestors of hominids for finding mates (and the way home) whereas enhanced abilities to interpret vocalisations may have been selected in female ancestors in conjunction with mothering.
>
> (Falk 1997: 120)

This may well have been the case more than 10,000 years ago, but it is difficult to believe that changes in human societies have not also been accompanied by changes in human skill patterns and behaviours. One of the cornerstones of the theory of evolution is the concept of adaptation, change over a period of time in order to function most effectively within a given niche. Why, when we start discussing gender-based patterns of behaviour, do we conveniently forget that human societies and lifestyles have changed considerably over the past 10,000 years and that humans must have adapted accordingly?

It is interesting to note that Gurian argues that 'in order for the human species to survive . . . divergence in sex roles was necessary' (Gurian 2001: 39) because until 10,000 years ago humans were hunter-gatherers, but then goes on to state that 'male and female hormones were not as far apart in their constitution a million years ago as they are now. We know this because testosterone is directly related to bulking, or muscle mass, and fossil records show us that male and female bodies used to be closer in size than they are now' (Gurian 2001: 40). These statements appear to conflict and make the argument rather muddled. Are Gurian and others arguing that before the development of agricultural societies male and female humans were more similar than they are now? If so, the argument about the importance of sex role division in hunter-gatherer communities seems weak. If, on the other hand, the argument is that sex role divisions developed and increased more recently (i.e. within the past 10,000 years), surely we can no longer keep explaining our current biology as a reflection of our hunter-gatherer history.

It is worth considering the theory that women are 'natural' carers and men are not because of our evolutionary history. 'A father does not secrete high doses of oxytocin, progesterone or estrogen – biochemicals that hormonally bond offspring to the chemical host. Therefore, men do not have as deep a biological bond with their children as do their mothers' (Gurian 2002: 158) This claim sits very neatly with the view that boys are primed by their biology to be the 'hunter'. Many parents reading this bold statement would not agree with Gurian's view. Fathers can have extremely strong bonds with their children, while some mothers may not feel the same level of bonding. Once again, it seems to me, our biochemistry is used to support a view that may not be valid.

The validity of this view becomes even more suspect in the light of recent research into new fathers' hormonal make-up. In the first of these studies, researchers chose to focus on three hormones – prolactin, cortisol and testosterone – as studies on animals and human mothers had linked these three hormones to bonding and nurturing (Storey *et al.* 2000). Although the study was small-scale – only 34 couples were involved – the findings are thought provoking. To begin with, they found that 33 per cent of the fathers experienced a drop in their testosterone levels during the first three weeks after their baby's birth and it took another three to four weeks for it to return to its normal level. The fathers also experienced a rise in their levels of prolactin in the few weeks prior to the baby's birth. Prolactin, as its name implies, promotes the production of milk in human mothers and the level of prolactin in men never rose to the level required to produce milk, so what is the purpose of this hormone in men? The answer may lie in studies on animals, where it has been found that prolactin promotes parenting of the young. The third hormone, cortisol, rises in women prior to birth and has been found to be linked with high levels of mother–baby bonding. The research found that cortisol levels doubled in fathers in the few weeks leading up to the birth. These findings were confirmed in a second research study (Berg and Wynne-Edwards 2001). This second study also found that the levels of oestrogen began to increase in fathers-to-be from about a month before the birth. The new fathers had raised oestrogen levels for approximately 12 weeks after the birth of the baby. The researchers suggest that the net effect of these hormonal changes is to trigger nurturing behaviour in the new fathers. When they were listening to a crying baby, it was found, the men with the highest levels of prolactin and the lowest levels of testosterone were those who had the strongest urge to comfort the baby. The fact that men may produce 'female' hormones and develop nurturing behaviour suggests that we need to look again at theories that place women as the 'natural' carers.

I would suggest that these research findings not only highlight the complex way in which hormones and behaviour are linked but also demonstrate how 'plastic' the brain is, in that it continues to develop and change in line with life's experiences. In view of this, the evolutionary theory begins to look somewhat simplistic.

Conclusion

This chapter has provided a brief overview of some of the research findings and scientific theories relating to brain development and gender and the effect of hormones on behaviour. Science is a powerful discourse within this society because the dominant culture continues to respect rationality and objectivity, which the field of science supposedly embodies. Scientific findings are presented as 'truths' because they have supposedly resulted from value-free, unprejudiced, rational scientific exploration. However, it is important to bear in mind that science is neither value-free nor objective, in that it serves political, social and economic interests (Longino and Hammond 1995). One has only to reflect on the way in which science research grants are allocated and consider which scientific findings hit the headlines to know that scientific endeavour is deeply enmeshed with the dominant discourses within a society. In view of this we need to go further than this chapter has gone when reflecting on scientific explanations for gender differences. This chapter has used the tools of science itself to highlight problems with many of the research studies. For example, the size or nature of the research sample was questioned and alternative explanations were offered to explain the same findings. This process serves to highlight how scientific 'truths' are little more than interpretations of scientific data, which in themselves may be flawed and lacking in objectivity. As educators we need to be willing to ask more questions about scientific research findings relating to gender and to be far more circumspect about accepting the latest scientific findings as 'true' simply because they are the result of scientific enterprise. Questions that need to be asked include those about the motivation for the research, who carried out the research, why certain findings are publicized and not others and who the subjects of the research are (e.g. age, gender, cultural and socio-economic background). Asking questions such as these enables us to become more conscious of how and why scientific discourses have been used to create 'truths' about gender, which in turn enables us to adopt a more critical stance towards these scientific 'truths'.

3 The appeal of 'new' pedagogies

The 'Reggio approach' to early childhood education is the subject of this chapter, as it is an approach that has captured the imagination of early years practitioners worldwide. However, the extent to which the 'Reggio approach' fosters gender equity is debatable.

In this chapter I outline some of the beliefs, principles and values underpinning the pre-school provision in Reggio Emilia in Italy. The chapter also explores how gender issues are approached in the municipal infant and toddler centres and pre-schools in Reggio Emilia. Questions are raised about the extent to which 'the Reggio approach' is an appropriate approach to adopt by those attempting to ensure that their early childhood provision fosters gender equity in the socially, culturally, linguistically and economically diverse communities served by the various early years settings in the UK.

This chapter draws on observations of infant and toddler centres and pre-schools made during my visit to Reggio Emilia in 2003. While in Italy I also interviewed parents, staff and British and Australian educators, and some of their thoughts and ideas are included in this chapter. In England I interviewed a lecturer and headteacher who had visited Reggio Emilia and also talked to other early years educators in order to gain an understanding of how the 'Reggio approach' was perceived by educators in Britain. Personal reflections on the presentations made to the Reggio Emilia study group by speakers as diverse as parents, pre-school teachers, *pedagogiste* such as Carlina Rinaldi and Paola Cagliari, *atelieristi*, teachers (e.g. Paola Strozzi) and the Commissioner of Education and Culture, Sandra Piccinini, have also been included in this chapter.

The 'Reggio approach'

In the northern Italian town of Reggio Emilia the municipality currently runs 13 infant and toddler centres (*asili nido* or 'safe nests') for children aged from

3 months to 3 years old and 21 pre-schools (*scuole dell'infanzia* or 'schools of infancy') for children aged from 3 to 6 years old. It is these municipal schools that have become world-renowned. Just over 25 per cent of the under-3s in Reggio Emilia attend the municipal infant and toddler centres, with a further 13 per cent of this age group attending infant and toddler centres run by cooperatives, religious orders and a parent association. Approximately 40 per cent of 3- to 6-year-olds attend municipal pre-schools and almost 55 per cent of this age group have places in state and private pre-schools or pre-schools run by religious orders or cooperatives (Municipality of Reggio Emilia 2000).

The first municipal pre-school opened in 1963 but the story of the municipal Reggio Emilia schools starts just after the end of the Second World War, and women played a key role in the development of the municipal pre-schools. In a village just outside the town a school for young children was set up using funds raised from the sale of a German armoured tank and some horses left behind by German troops. The school was run by parents and during the next 17 years several more schools created and run by parents were established. In 1963 the municipality opened the first municipal pre-school, which Malaguzzi described as a 'decisive achievement' because it marked the end of the Catholic church's monopoly on early education: 'They [citizens] wanted schools of a new kind: of better quality, free from charitable tendencies and not merely custodial and not discriminatory in any way.' (Malaguzzi 1998: 52). In 1970 the first municipal infant and toddler centre opened its doors in Reggio Emilia to meet the needs both of young children growing up in nuclear families and of working mothers (Malaguzzi 1998: 61).

Some fundamentals of the 'Reggio approach'

Other writers have provided detailed descriptions and explanations of what constitutes the 'Reggio approach' (e.g. Cadwell 1997; Ceppi and Zini 1998; Edwards *et al.* 1998; Dahlberg *et al.* 1999; Valentine 1999; Abbott and Nutbrown 2001; Giudici *et al.* 2001) so this section serves simply to provide a necessarily brief, general overview of the 'Reggio approach'. The municipal schools of Reggio Emilia of today are underpinned by certain principles, beliefs and values. The first of these beliefs relates to the image of the child. According to Carla Rinaldi, children are: 'rich in resources, strong and competent . . . unique individuals with rights rather than simply needs. They have potential, plasticity, openness, the desire to grow, curiosity, a sense of wonder, and the desire to relate to other people and communicate' (Rinaldi 1998: 114).

In addition, the *pedagogista* Paula Cagliari emphasized that a child should be seen not as an empty vessel waiting to be filled but as an 'active constructor of knowledge, an active builder of interpretative criteria of the world . . . a subject who reinterprets knowledge and strategies for constructing knowledge' (Cagliari 2003a). This process of learning benefits from collaboration with others, so relationships with peers, teachers, parents and culture are very important (Malaguzzi 1998; Vecchi 2001). Children are also seen as communicators and there is an emphasis on enabling and encouraging children to express their ideas and thoughts through a very wide range of forms of symbolic representation. The forms include drawing, painting, words, clay sculpture, collage, building with diverse materials, movement and music.

Teachers

Alongside this view of children who are powerful individuals with rights and protagonists of their own development, is a belief that teachers are partners, nurturers and guides (Edwards 1998: 179). In Reggio schools the teachers stay with their class from the time they start to when they leave (i.e. three years) and this close relationship is seen to offer continuity and security and is an important aspect of the practice. Each pre-school has an *atelierista*, a trained artist who works with the children, and a *pedagogista*. Each *pedagogista* works with the children, teachers and parents in a small number of infant and toddler centres and pre-schools and their role is to support the teachers (e.g. discussing ongoing projects, helping them to develop their professional expertise) and also to help to develop relationships with the parents. The *pedagogiste* are also involved in policy development at municipal level and work alongside colleagues to share and discuss current research.

Teachers in the municipal infant and toddler centres and pre-schools do not simply apply programmes or teach curricula developed by others. Instead, teachers together with the children are 'co-authors of paths of learning' (Cagliari 2003a). Teachers need to be open to the ideas, perceptions and interpretations of children. Underlying the 'Reggio approach' is the view that knowledge is a construction, neither standard nor standardizable, and constructing knowledge is not simply a cognitive process but one that involves the whole individual, involves making connections, some of which are new and unpredictable, and also involves metacognition (Cagliari 2003a). With this view of knowledge it is argued that teaching and learning do not simply involve ingesting facts or copying skills and that learning is not the outcome of direct acts of teaching. Learning and teaching are reciprocal processes (Cagliari 2003a). Teachers are seen to be learners and 'pedagogical researchers' (Gambetti 2001). This is where the concept of *progettazione* comes into play.

Progettazione

There is no direct English translation of the word *progettazione* because it is a complex concept. The term is used to describe the flexible planning that characterizes the 'Reggio approach' and stands in contrast to *programmazione*. The latter term is applied to a method of planning with predefined general educational objectives, programmes of study and stages where teaching and learning are seen to follow a rigid path to a predetermined end. *Progettazione*, on the other hand, describes the process by which teachers design, create, organize and coordinate learning contexts that have a range of possible outcomes and ends. Teachers utilize their knowledge of the children and their past experiences to generate hypotheses of the possible directions in which the project will go (Rinaldi 1998; Cagliari 2003a). Nothing is set in stone and the directions, objectives and ultimate end point of the project or learning journey are open to modifications and changes. Documentation, which entails observation and interpretation, plays a key role in helping adults and children to determine possible future paths of learning.

Documentation

Documentation can include photographs, videos, slides, written notes, sketches, drawings, tape recordings and so on. In the 'Reggio approach', documentation is seen to be an integral part of the learning process and the documentation itself plays a central role in shaping future teaching and learning moments. The documentation process 'not only accompanies the knowledge building process but in a certain sense impregnates it' (Rinaldi 2001a: 86). The documentation is a form of communication that makes the learning processes visible and enables children, teachers and parents to revisit and reflect on what has occurred and make decisions about where to go next (Rinaldi 2001a). Reggio teachers believe that documentation not only values what children can do and have done but also values what children *could* do (Valentine 1999). Carla Rinaldi has pointed out that this form of documentation is very different from the documentation of children's learning that takes place in many other early childhood settings, where evidence of children's learning (e.g. samples of children's work) is collected during the learning process but this is then reflected on at the end of the process and the documentation plays no role in determining the learning path (Rinaldi 2001a).

The curriculum in Reggio schools is not rigidly defined but the children's learning is none the less not without direction. Carla Rinaldi has likened the learning to a journey 'where one finds the way using a compass rather than taking a train with its fixed routes and schedule' (Rinaldi 1998: 119).

Participation

Participation of families is a crucial aspect of the 'Reggio approach'. Staff at the 8 Marzo pre-schools in Reggio Emilia explained what this participation consisted of in practice. The first point that was made was that the relationship between the schools and parents is based on dialogue and exchange: parents' views and insights were welcomed and teachers did not feel that parents came into the school to 'check' on the child's progress or the teachers.

In order to be eligible for a place in a municipal pre-school the parents must be working. This means that they are unable to participate during the day, so meetings, which are open to all the citizens of Reggio Emilia, occur during the evenings. Parents may attend class meetings, during which teachers and parents exchange ideas about projects occurring within the setting and also discuss theoretical principles (e.g. the image of the child in present day society). The staff emphasized that the relationship was not didactic and pointed out that parents could be involved in the decisions surrounding the direction of a project. There may be evenings in the kitchen where the setting's menu and issues relating to nutrition are discussed. There are also work meetings during which parents may be in involved in such activities as cleaning up the courtyard, handling documentation panels and making resources for the children (e.g. a wooden playhouse). Parents also come together with staff and children for parties and celebrations (meeting with staff at 8 Marzo pre-school 2003).

The importance of the environment

Malaguzzi (1998) talked about the importance of creating an 'amiable' environment, one in which children, teachers and parents would feel at ease. The environment reflects Italian culture (e.g. in the use of colour and the importance attached to light) and all the schools have a central *piazza*, which, like the piazzas in Italian towns, is the place for children and adults to meet, stop, interact or simply pass by one another. The environment, designed to facilitate interaction and encounters, is flexible and different spaces can be created or modified to enable the children to pursue their current interests and learning paths. Every school has an *atelier*, a studio that is the focus for visual and expressive education (Malaguzzi 1998), and each age group has a mini-atelier next to its classroom. There are numerous opportunities for multisensory experiences. The environment also includes the outside areas and the town itself.

What is the appeal of the 'Reggio approach'?

When considering issues of gender equity and the 'Reggio approach' it is useful to reflect on how the interest in this approach has grown and the implications of this in terms of developing a context that encourages intellectual critical debate.

During the past decade the pre-schools of Reggio Emilia have been an increasing source of interest and inspiration for practitioners in the United

Kingdom. There exists a plethora of published books and articles detailing the 'Reggio approach'. Some of the books and articles have considered how the 'Reggio approach' can be applied in contexts beyond the northern Italian town of Reggio Emilia. The titles of some of these books in the latter category (e.g. *Bringing Reggio Emilia Home*: Cadwell 1997) have possibly played a role in generating and supporting the view that the 'Reggio approach' is not only a 'good' approach to early years provision but also a better approach than that currently to be seen in early years settings in the UK and the USA.

In recent years early years educators around the world have not only read about the Reggio Emilia pre-schools and infant and toddler centres but have also visited 'The Hundred Languages of Children' exhibition and attended conferences about the 'Reggio approach'. Some educators have also been able to join study tours to Reggio Emilia to try to find out more about the renowned infant and toddler centres and pre-schools in action.

In 1994 a limited company, Reggio Children, was established to facilitate:

> the promotion and dissemination of the theoretical and practical experience developed in the municipal infant-toddler centres and pre-schools (by organising and supervising international exchange initiatives, seminars and training courses on the Reggio experience, publication of books and audio-visual materials, etc.) and support for those inspired by the 'Reggio Approach' who want to create educational institutions that are suitable to children's great potential.
>
> (Municipality of Reggio Emilia 2000: 10)

The company profits are used for the development of the schools in Reggio Emilia and to fund research.

Reggio Children has been very successful in promoting the 'Reggio Approach' in North America, Europe and countries in the Pacific Rim. Between 1994 and 2002 no fewer than 90 study tours were held in Reggio Emilia catering for more than 10,000 visitors from the aforementioned parts of the world. During the same period 'The Hundred Languages of Children' exhibition toured more than 60 cities in North America, Europe and the Pacific Rim.

Educators keen to adopt the 'Reggio approach' have received mixed messages about the appropriateness of such an aim. There is disinclination on the part of Reggio educators to describe the 'Reggio approach' as a model of early years education because the educational work in Reggio schools is dynamic and changing due to reflection and experimentation (Edwards *et al.* 1998). Paula Cagliari, a *pedagogista*, argued that reference to the 'Reggio approach' has two very negative aspects, the first being that 'you are afraid to betray it and that makes you afraid of change'. The second negative aspect is 'the fear that it will not work' (Cagliari 2003b). Carla Rinaldi stated that those involved in the schools in Reggio Emilia do not present a 'recipe' for early years education:

'Education is a process which needs to be constructed . . . which has deep roots within the community. We feel that franchising within education is not possible' (Rinaldi 2003). Despite this claim, however, Reggio Children awarded a certificate of accreditation for two years to the Model Early Learning Center in Washington, DC, and early years practitioners have drawn their own conclusions about the possibility of developing schools using the 'Reggio approach'.

As the interest in the 'Reggio approach' has grown, highly respected researchers and theorists have added their support to the approach. In 1996, for example, Jerome Bruner stated:

> When I came to visit Reggio Emilia . . . I was not prepared for what I found. It was not just that they were better than anything I'd ever seen . . . What struck me about Reggio pre-schools was how they cultivated the imagination and, in the process, how they empowered the children's sense of what is possible.
>
> (Cited in Municipality of Reggio Emilia 2000: 3)

In the UK, interest in the 'Reggio approach' began to take off in the 1990s. This coincided with a period marked by educational reforms and developments (e.g. the introduction of the National Curriculum, testing of children as young as 7 in England, the introduction of the Desirable Learning Outcomes baseline assessment of children as young as 4 in their first term in the reception class). Many early years educators looked askance at what was happening in Key Stages 1 and 2 and were anxious to ensure that the educational experience for children below statutory school age was not changed for the worse by top-down pressures (e.g. Blenkin and Kelly 1994). It is possible to argue that in this climate of anxiety the appeal of the 'Reggio approach' was strong, with its emphasis on the child and focus on the development of a wide range of forms of representation. The 'Reggio approach' was discussed by no fewer than eight well regarded witnesses giving evidence to the Select Committee on Education (DfES 2000a).

The promotion of the 'Reggio approach' and the endorsements given to the approach by well respected practitioners and theorists, coupled with a belief that there exists an ideal approach to early years education, have created an environment in which it is very hard to question the validity of the 'Reggio approach' within the context of the UK. This reluctance to engage in a critique of the 'Reggio approach' has also been maintained by elites within the early childhood scene, a point first made by Johnson (1999) and acknowledged and recognized by Wright (2000). The fact that only a relatively limited number of people have been able to travel to Reggio Emilia has tended to create a dichotomy between 'those who have been' and 'those who have not', with the latter group feeling unable to criticize Reggio practice merely because they have not seen the infant and toddler centres and pre-schools first hand. This dichotomy had been reinforced by the fact that until fairly recently the vast majority of those visiting Reggio from the UK tended to be early years inspectors and advisors, lecturers and headteachers.

Howard Gardner has asserted that it takes at least ten years before one can claim to be an 'expert' on Reggio schools (Gardner 2001: 25) and on this basis most educators in the UK are at the level of novices in terms of understanding and implementing the 'Reggio approach'. As novices, many educators feel less than confident about entering into a critical analysis of the 'Reggio approach'. It seems ironic, therefore, that although one of the tenets of the 'Reggio approach' is that children are encouraged to 'question what we have constructed as adults' (Cagliari 2003a) and are not encouraged to accept 'truths' passively (Rinaldi 2003), the same cannot be said for educators who are attempting to understand the 'Reggio approach'.

Loris Malaguzzi, the founder of the 'Reggio approach', was conscious that many educators prefer not to enter into critical debates about theories and models, preferring instead to adopt the theories and models that are currently dominant:

> and when we tell them about our humble and at the same time extra-ordinary origins, and we try to explain that from those origins we have extracted theoretical principles that still support our work, we notice much interest and not a little incredulity. It is curious (but not unjustified) how resilient is the belief that educational ideas and prac-tices can derive only from *official models* or established theories.
>
> (Malaguzzi 1998: 58; emphasis added)

It is possible to argue that discourses about Reggio that make distinctions between 'experts' and 'novices' and that do not permit critical analysis of underpinning theories are in danger of presenting the Reggio approach as an established entity rather than simply an approach to early childhood educa-tion that is dynamic, fluid and open to change in the light of new insights.

Problems with the 'Reggio approach'

> It's almost like an icon. People think this is perfect nursery education and it's not. It doesn't do the things for children that I want to do, it does *some* of them and it does some of them so superbly that you are just breathless.
>
> (University lecturer, female)

It is important to remember that the 'Reggio approach' emerged and continues to evolve within a particular context. The approach was developed in a prosperous Italian city that, until fairly recently, had a fairly stable population with very little immigration from other countries. In such a context it is likely that the culture of the town was fairly homogeneous. The citizens had a shared inheritance in terms of the effects of the Second World War and the years of fascism and had a common history of active citizenship (the very first preschool with which Malaguzzi became involved was that set up by parents at the end of the Second World War). The people of Reggio Emilia contributed to and lived through the struggles in the 1960s and 1970s that had resulted in the Catholic Church losing its monopoly on early childhood education. Reggio Emilia also has a tradition of valuing communal activity rather than individual enterprise. The city can be said to have had a substantial stock of what is called social capital (i.e. cooperation, mutual support, trust, norms of reciprocity and networks of civic involvement) and in communities such as this voluntary cooperation or participation is easier (Putnam 1993). Reflecting on the sociopolitical history of the city makes it clear why fundamental principles of the 'Reggio approach' not only exist but also, until recently, have been appropriate within the given context. Citizens of Reggio Emilia, however, are conscious of changes in the city:

> Until recently the cultural mix wasn't an issue. It was a very wealthy area, farmers have made lots of money, they got very wealthy farming pigs. Now there are immigrants, some are illegal immigrants who bring problems ... 20 people living in a room, begging, illegal employment, unemployment. The people of Reggio do not want the city to change.
>
> (Parent of child in Reggio pre-school 2003)

Although immigration from the south of Italy has been occurring for decades, during the 1980s and 1990s the city witnessed an increase in immigration from other countries. Reggio educators are also acutely conscious of how the city is changing from one with 'a consolidated tradition to one with new and uncertain futures' (Piccinini 2003). Reggio educators talk about the challenge this presents but have not clearly articulated the nature of this challenge (Rinaldi 2003).

A major issue that the 'Reggio approach' is silent about is the notion that an individual's identity develops as a result of the interaction of gender, class and 'race' (Zinn and Dell 1996). This is one issue that will need to be grappled with if the 'Reggio approach' can be said to facilitate gender equity. In view of this, one must question the extent to which the current 'Reggio approach' is transportable to other contexts, especially to socially, culturally, linguistically and economically diverse communities within the UK.

The interface of theory and practice

When considering the extent to which the 'Reggio approach' deals with issues of gender it is necessary to bear in mind the possibility that practice may not match the theory. Malaguzzi was aware of this and warned that: 'It's important for pedagogy not to be the prisoner of too much certainty, but instead to be aware of both the relativity of its powers and the difficulties of translating its ideals into practice' (Malaguzzi 1998: 58). Critical analysis of both the theories underpinning the 'Reggio approach' and the day-to-day practice in the infant and toddler centres and pre-schools certainly suggests that in some instances a disjunction exists between the theory and the practice. It is also possible to argue, however, that the pedagogical theory itself does not adequately deal with gender issues and the concept of gender equity.

The superficial aspects of the 'Reggio approach' are the consequence of a series of choices made by those involved in developing the approach. The choices shaping the 'Reggio approach', like all educational approaches, have been guided by a set of values: 'school, for us, is a place where, first and foremost, values are transmitted, discussed and constructed. *The term education is therefore closely correlated with the concept of values*' (Rinaldi 2001b: 38; original emphasis). But values themselves do not exist in a vacuum, independent of the cultural, historical and political context: 'Values, therefore, are relative and are correlated with the culture to which they belong, they determine the culture and are determined by it' (Rinaldi 2001b: 39). When considering issues of gender equity in relation to the 'Reggio approach' it is therefore necessary not only to examine the values underpinning the approach but also to consider the cultural context within which the values are defined.

Carla Rinaldi (2001a) has listed some of the values underpinning the educational work in municipal infant and toddler centres and pre-schools in Reggio Emilia. The first is what she defines as the 'value of subjectivity', and relates to the construction of 'self' (which encompasses personality, individuality and identity). This value recognizes that who we are is socially constructed and self-constructed (i.e. we are active players in our self-construction but who we are is also mediated and influenced by the cultural context).

The second value is that of difference, which, Rinaldi has argued, is connected with valuing the uniqueness of each individual. Difference in this context is seen to encompass 'gender, race, culture and religion' (Rinaldi 2001b: 40). Rinaldi lists four further values – of participation, of democracy, of learning and of play, fun, emotions and feelings – but it is the first two values that are particularly pertinent to issues of gender equity.

Value of subjectivity

In relation to constructions of self, Rinaldi highlights the important role played by 'interactional qualities' and goes on to argue that the implications of this are taken seriously by the pedagogical methods used within the infant and toddler centres and pre-schools (Rinaldi 2001b: 40), which include observation, documentation and small group work. While it is certainly true that the 'Reggio approach' emphasizes the importance of interaction, collaborative working, discussion and sharing ideas and competences, less attention seems to be paid to what children may be learning about gender relations and gender roles during these interactions. No mention is made of the teacher's role in helping children to talk with adults and with each other about how they see themselves and their gender. It is possible that such conversations do occur but when I visited a pre-school in Reggio Emilia an observation of a teacher working with a group of 3-year-olds suggested that this was not the case. The group was composed of four girls and one boy and they were working on the idea of sending messages as a means of communication with other children in the school. The two girls who were sitting next to the teacher were involved in a great deal of discussion with her and with each other. One of the other girls appeared to 'tune in and tune out', while the fourth girl spent most of her time quietly watching the only boy in the group. The boy was sitting furthest away from the teacher and spent the whole time rocking on his chair, twisting around in his seat to play with items on the shelf behind him and shuffling back in his chair in order to push the unit behind him. At no point did the teacher engage him in the conversation or attempt to include him in the group, although she did address a few comments to the girls who were not actively participating. The teacher also made eye contact with all the girls but not the boy.

What messages could the children take from these interactions? Girls are expected to talk and discuss? Girls are expected to listen to other children when they are talking? Boys are not expected to join in if they are not interested? Boys are allowed to be fidgety? Girls are more interested in communicating with others than are boys? Girls are more interested than are boys in writing and drawing? Children develop gender identity not by simply 'absorbing' messages about gender (see Chapter 1) but by reflecting on how the teacher and other children respond to them, and others within the group provide the children with some possibilities about what it means to be a girl or a boy. The teacher appeared to be unaware that the children's patterns of involvement and behaviour could be interpreted as part of the process by which the children were developing their gender identity.

The literature on children's group interactions in other Reggio pre-schools suggests that this observation is not atypical of the social dynamics within the Reggio pre-schools and infant and toddler centres. For example, a group of

5- and 6-year-olds, made up of two girls and two boys, were working with an inexperienced *atelierista* on building a bridge, and the documentation revealed that the boys, Luca and Ferrucio, constantly played a central role in leading the discussion and the development of ideas (Rubizzi 2001). One of the girls, Caterina, was sometimes attentive, while the other girl, Martina, was described as seeming 'absent'. At one point Caterina exclaimed 'I have an idea!' but no one asked her what her idea was (Rubizzi 2001: 106–7). Interactions such as these, where the girls' silences are ignored by the adult or where the girls' attempts to participate actively are overlooked, while the boys are allowed to direct the activity, provide children with clear messages not only about what is acceptable behaviour for girls and boys when working together but also about whose views and ideas are seen to be most valued. A highly experienced *atelierista* with 30 years' experience of working in the Reggio infant and toddler centres and another teacher commented on the documentation and suggested that the *atelierista* should have asked Caterina to share her ideas, and should have tried to find out why the girls were not fully engaged and then helped them to become more involved (Rubizzi 2001: 115). It was noted that this is not an easy task in view of the fact that children 'have their own preferred approaches and personalities, it is unfair to constantly hold back someone with an approach like Luca's. What is more, with his intelligent impetuousness he often contributes to giving direction to the work and carrying it forward' (Rubizzi 2001: 114).

This response does little to deal with the gender issues that were an integral part of the interaction and reveals a great deal about the adults' concerns. One interpretation of what occurred during the group work could be that the children were developing an understanding of themselves through 'traditional' masculine and feminine discourses. It has been argued that children's play and interactions reproduce the power relations inherent in dominant understandings of what it means to be female or male (McNaughton 2000). If the children are understanding themselves through the 'traditional' feminine discourse they will feel that it is normal for girls to be quiet and well behaved, to listen to others and to be unassertive. The boys, on the other hand, understanding themselves through 'traditional' male or 'macho' discourses, would feel that it is perfectly normal for boys to assert themselves, 'hold the floor' during discussions and exercise power through making decisions about what was to be done. The teachers' comments suggest that they understand the children through 'traditional' gender discourses. The focus of the teachers is moving the project along, and the issue of unequal power relations appears to have been unobserved or ignored.

Observations of children's free play in the municipal pre-schools would suggest that the children understood their gendering in terms of 'traditional' discourses. In one example a 3-year-old girl was rocking a doll in a toy buggy while nearby two boys ran around shouting. One of the boys, running fast, deliberately and repeatedly rammed an empty buggy into the girl's buggy. The girl tried to ignore him but then both boys started piling up the girl's push-chair with scarves and hats. She patiently removed the scarves and hats but when they put the scarves back into the buggy she pushed the boys away and moved away. The boys followed her and continued to disrupt her play. No adult intervened.

In another instance, the children were playing outside. The adult was playing skipping with the girls and a group of boys were running around pretending to shoot others. Every now and then the boys would run up to girls, push their hands in the girls' faces and run off. The girls responded by pulling their heads away from the boys' hands and closing their eyes, and then carried on playing skipping as if nothing had happened. Again, the adult did not intervene.

An early years practitioner who visited Reggio Emilia some years ago recalled a similar instance:

> When I was there the children were outdoors and one of the schools had a hill, an artificial hill with a pulley which the children could ride down, and there was one little boy who completely took command of that and was not simply just hogging it but knocking people over as he went by, and that was completely ignored, it was sidelined, that was *not* something they [the adults] were going to deal with it. He was a boy being a boy was the message I took from it and I think the children did as well because some girls did complain about it, but they were just told 'Oh, he does that, he'll be better in a while.' Now whether that, I mean there may be a way of interpreting that which is about that this child has got a need so therefore we'll let him do it, but the fact that it's a gender issue as well means that maybe it probably ought to be looked at more closely.
>
> (Lecturer, female)

The children in these three examples seem to understanding themselves through 'traditional' discourses of masculinity and femininity. For the boys, understanding themselves through 'macho' discourses meant that they felt it was 'normal' to be rough and aggressive and to exercise power through physical methods. For the girls, understanding themselves through 'feminine' discourse meant that they felt it was normal to be quiet and patient and to try to avoid conflict. Despite the rhetoric about Reggio pedagogical methods attaching importance to the role played by 'interactional qualities' in helping children to develop their self-identity (Rinaldi 2001a: 40), it would appear that the adults in pre-schools are not concerned about helping the children to think critically about the dominant discourses that are shaping their understanding of gender.

In the Diana pre-school, the oldest children write a book, *Advisories*, for the new 3-year-olds, introducing them to the pre-school and the staff. The book is written from a child's viewpoint and uses the children's ideas and language. Paula Strozzi talked about a group of eight children, five boys and three girls, who were deciding what needed to be written about a teacher. One of the girls said 'She [the teacher] has a really beautiful body' and another added 'She's about as tall as my mum'. The girls also commented that 'Maybe she puts on shiny make-up' and described her as 'elegant'. The boys made a range of comments, including: 'She's not very tall', 'Her bosoms are wide and beautiful', 'She has a private thingy, ha, ha!' and 'She never takes a bath so she stinks! Ha ha!'

When asked about the boys' comments Paula Strozzi suggested that the boys were merely playing with irony and sarcasm. She also justified the teacher allowing the boys to talk in such a way by arguing that 'it is important to allow children to express themselves, it's important that children are not censored by adults and that children find appropriate words to describe something' (Strozzi 2003). An alternative understanding of this event could be that the 5-year-old girls were entrenched in their 'traditional' feminine discourse, in that they were talking about a teacher's physical appearance in terms of her sexual attractiveness (e.g. her body, elegance and make-up). The 5-year-old boys' description of the teacher revealed that they were equally strongly entrenched in their 'traditional' masculine discourse, which includes a strong element of overt masculine sexuality that renders girls and women as powerless sex objects. This incident closely parallels one described by Walkerdine *et al.* (1989: 66), in which two small boys use sexually explicit language when defying their nursery teacher and in so doing seize power by positioning their teacher as a 'powerless object of sexist discourse' (Walkerdine *et al.* 1989: 66). The boys in the Reggio Emilia pre-school and the boys described by Walkerdine *et al.* (1989) were both exploring issues of power and this was made possible by the multiple ways in which they, as boys and children, and the teacher as adult and female are variously positioned within different discourses. The teachers have authority and power as adults and teachers but, as Walkerdine *et al.* (1989) have argued, the boys are able to oppress their female teacher by drawing on a patriarchal discourse. The teacher's response to the boys in Reggio Emilia would suggest that she felt that it was acceptable and 'natural' for boys to express their sexuality in this way. The teacher is faced with a dilemma. Does she acquiesce with this shift in the power relations between herself and the boys on the grounds that to be positioned as a 'good' teacher within the dominant pedagogical discourse she must emphasize the importance of children developing 'naturally' and at their own rate? Paula Strozzi's comment about the importance of children being able 'to express themselves' and not to be censored by adults would suggest that the boys' behaviour was interpreted as part of natural and normal development, and therefore 'good' teachers would know not to intervene. No reference was made to the power dimensions of the exchange, which is not surprising, since the Reggio Emilia approach is strongly influenced by developmental psychology, which, as discussed in Chapter 2, results in gender equity issues being sidelined. While it is possible to concur with the view that the adult should not act as a 'censor' in this situation, it is important that the adults should encourage dialogue and enable the children to think about alternative gender discourses, other ways of being 'a girl' or 'a boy'. Adults also need to consider how the 'Reggio approach' needs to change in order to become a transformative practice in terms of gender equity through the challenging of 'traditional' gender discourses.

Paula Strozzi, talking about investigations with children, commented that: 'The point is that we are entering a world of views, and it is very important for us to say that there is not only one truth, because the truth can always be falsified. It is important to be able to explore a world full of surprises' (cited in Nimmo 1994: 310). Unfortunately, the 'surprises' do not seem to include diverse understandings or discourses of what it means to be a girl or a boy.

Value of difference

Turning to the value of difference, Rinaldi (2001b) has acknowledged that dealing with differences can be painful and difficult and that there is a temptation to concentrate on 'sameness', but then argues that this is problematic if we are not aiming to 'standardize' and 'normalize' people. She has suggested that educators need to think about the following questions:

- What do we do with differences?
- Are all differences acceptable? If not, which ones are not?
- What concept of equality are we developing?
- Is the aim to make everyone equal or to give everyone opportunities to develop his or her own subjectivity (and thus difference) by interacting with others?

(Rinaldi 2001b: 40–1)

These are certainly very pertinent questions when we are considering issues of gender. The previous section suggests that Reggio *practice* (as opposed to *theory*) does not give everyone opportunities to develop her or his own subjectivity because children do not appear to be given access to a range of discourses through which they can understand themselves as girls and boys. It would seem, therefore, that the concept of equality does not include gender equality because 'traditional' discourses are not contested and gender power relations remain unchallenged.

Reggio educators have done a great deal of work on the differences between girls and boys. There are numerous examples of girls and boys working in single-sex groups (e.g. Rankin 1998; Bartoli *et al.* 2000; Piazza and

Barozzi 2001; Strozzi 2001; Vecchi 2001). Krechevsky, a member of the Harvard-based Project Zero team that carried out collaborative research with Reggio educators, stated:

> Reggio educators purposefully set up single-sex and mixed groups in order to investigate further the approaches to learning exhibited by girls and boys. The research literature also shows that girls typically prefer smaller groups than boys.
>
> (Krechevsky 2001: 250)

Krechevsky not only cites research that is more than 20 years old but also does not challenge the Reggio educators' unquestioning acceptance of the observed differences between girls and boys engaged in group work.

According to the documentation produced in Reggio Emilia pre-schools it would appear that girls and boys tend to prefer to work in single-sex groups. Girls also prefer smaller groups than do the boys, and girls tend to discuss and collaborate from the start rather than, as the boys do, work independently before working collaboratively. Furthermore, boys are more easily distracted than girls (Rankin 1998; Bartoli et al. 2000; Piazza and Barozzi 2001; Strozzi 2001; Vecchi 2001). The focus of girls' projects seems to differ from that of boys'. When they were working on a project of the city of Reggio Emilia it became clear that girls' ideas of the city were located within the context of relationships and the real lives of the people who live in the city. The boys focused on functional aspects of the city, such as sewers and electrical systems, and connections, such as the train stations and roads (Piazza and Barozzi 2001). Similarly, a group in another pre-school worked on a castle project. Again, the comments, recorded and published in the book *Castelli* (Bartoli et al. 2000), suggest that the girls were interested in understanding the castle in terms of daily family life, and they described rooms such as the kitchen, living room and bedroom and talked about washing plates in the river because there were no sinks. The boys discussed the castle as a means of defence, with descriptions of the inside of the castle linked to rooms such as the armoury and the prison.

The documented differences between the girls and the boys should raise issues for practitioners keen to ensure that their provision supports gender equity. The first issue is that the validity of the girl/boy divide is never questioned. Reggio educators, therefore, appear to start from the premise that girls and boys are different. Furthermore, not only is it accepted that girls and boys are different; there also seems to be a view that there is nothing that educators can do about these differences except document them and accommodate the differences in future projects. This would suggest that Reggio educators view these differences as innate. Others who have reflected on gender issues in the 'Reggio approach' have also felt uncomfortable about the lack of critical thought about observed gender differences:

> I don't see the conversation goes beyond, well that what's girls and boys do, there's nothing about why that might be and so on. I have the impression that that is something about Italians, that that's not something that they see as an issue . . . it's . . . it's, that's how it is, you know?
>
> (University Lecturer, female)

This view was substantiated by the comments of a non-Italian parent who is married to an Italian and has children in Reggio pre-schools. When asked about equal opportunities in relation to gender she mused:

> Parent: Maybe as a culture we are little behind in that they still dress the girls in pink and the boys in blue right from birth.
> Interviewer: Because I was wondering, because they talk about encouraging the children not to accept things and to ask questions but when it comes to gender issues or sexism I've not seen any evidence of that being questioned.
> Parent: It's not an issue.
> Interviewer: You mean they don't see it as an issue?
> Parent: It hasn't become an issue, nobody has made it an issue.
> Interviewer: Are you saying that it is an 'equal' society?
> Parent: No. I'm not saying that because I'm from a different society and I see it differently.
> Interviewer: Yes, but looking in . . .
> Parent: Yes . . . there are some things, like yesterday everybody was commenting that it was the fathers picking up the children from school and no, we probably don't analyse things as much here . . . I think we are about ten years behind America. In America women all went out to work because it was the thing to do and now they are staying home because it's fashionable. So we're still all going out to work here but in ten years . . . The issues will come here but about ten years later, it's just taking more time. We have a lot of more cultural issues ingrained . . . I mean my daughter has blond hair and blue eyes and the amount of people who comment on how beautiful she is and how beautiful her hair is and I say 'And she's clever too' but no Italian would think of saying that.
>
> (Mother of two children in pre-schools in Reggio Emilia 2003)

Within Reggio pre-schools there does not appear to be any interest in the reason why there are observable differences between girls' and boys' interests, methods of problem-solving and collaborative skills. Despite the rhetoric about not 'normalizing' individuals, when it comes to gender the Reggio educators appear to have a very clear idea about what constitutes a 'normal' girl and a 'normal' boy, and the documentation merely proves the case.

It could be argued that the lack of thought about gender issues has implications for the culture of the school. In the UK anxiety has been expressed about how the culture of schools and early years settings tends to value and promote what have been traditionally viewed as 'feminine' traits (e.g. the ability to concentrate, helpfulness, lack of aggression, ability to work collaboratively). It is therefore interesting to note that the culture of Reggio pre-schools may also be similarly gender-biased. In considering how children approach problems Krechevsky (2001) has noted that girls and boys seem to adopt somewhat different approaches. When a group of three boys were asked to draw a single bicycle each boy drew a bicycle and the drawings were then compared and contrasted and the boys decided on which parts of each of the drawings should be used to compose a single bicycle. A group of three girls drew only one bicycle, and started off by discussing what needed to be done and negotiating who drew. Krechevsky asserted that when a problem is a familiar one boys tend to adopt the girls' strategy, but is uncertain about why this should be the case. She has suggested that:

> perhaps when a problem is new, children choose a more immediate approach that tends to be characteristic of the boys' style. But when the problem is presented again, the approach is more reflective and *the school culture of negotiation and working together is more likely to emerge.*
>
> (Krechevsky 2001: 251; emphasis added)

Clearly, then, the girls' strategies and approaches to problem-solving are closer to the school's culture. If a culture is being created within the school by all those involved (children, parents and teachers) it seems somewhat strange that the prevailing school culture is more female-orientated than male-orientated. Until very recently, however, in Italy men were prohibited by law from working with very young children and the overwhelming majority of adults in the municipal infant and toddler centres and pre-schools are consequently women. This, coupled with the apparent absence of debates about gender equity issues, may partially explain why the culture of Reggio pre-schools may be 'feminized'.

Conclusion

The 'Reggio approach' has much to offer educators around the world, not least in that consideration of the approach can be a useful catalyst for more in-depth reflection on current practice and the images we have of children as learners. The 'Reggio approach', however, provides few clues about how to support gender equity and reflection on some of the practice would suggest that the unwillingness to engage in a critical analysis of gender issues with the children simply serves to support the existing social status quo and gender power relations evident within society as a whole.

4 Girls' and boys' understanding, playing and talking about gender

Gender is not an issue in the nursery, the children don't really notice things like that.

(Nursery teacher, female)

Young children's ideas about who they are and their perceptions of what it means to be a girl or a boy are placed centre stage in this chapter. How children perceive girls, boys, women and men in terms of 'appropriate' behaviour, interests and life possibilities is examined. Young children's play is analysed, since it is a powerful medium for young children's exploration of 'femininities' and 'masculinities', what it means to be 'feminine' and 'masculine' and coming to understand the gendered nature of society.

This chapter draws on discussions with children aged 3 to 6 in early childhood settings. Listening to what children have to say provides an insight into what concerns children, how they are making sense of the world and how they are situating themselves and others. It was very apparent from conversations with the young children concerned that they were conscious of gender and as practitioners we need to be sensitive to and acknowledge how children's ideas about gender impact on how children position themselves and are positioned by others in the early childhood setting.

Gender identity or gender identities?

A common thread running through discussions in this book is the notion that what is usually referred to as our identity is not fixed and unchanging. Instead we are in a continuous process of constructing, revising and amending our ideas of who we are and of our place in the world. Furthermore, our understanding of who we are, our identity, is composed of a variety of 'selves'. In other words, each of us does not have a single, unified identity but instead we each have a range of identities, we have multiple identities. This multiplicity of identities enables us to adopt a variety of positions and roles in the various social contexts in which we find ourselves every day. These multiple identities do not arise and develop spontaneously. Children's developing sense of who they are and their place in the world is not merely a result of maturation and does not occur within a social vacuum (Davies 1989a,b; Dowling 2000; McNaughton 2000). We come to know who we are and how we can position ourselves as a result of our learning to make sense of our social interactions and experiences and through our engagement with a variety of discourses. The term discourses is here used to refer to 'the emotional, social and institutional frameworks and practices through which we make meaning in our lives' (McNaughton 2000: 50). It is important to remember that the various discourses a child has access to do not all provide the same 'world view', and discourses may conflict with each other. The gendered positions that children can take up will vary between discourses. Although a child can be said to be socially constructed (or positioned) I would argue that she also has a degree of control over how she constructs or positions herself. A child is constrained by the range of experiences she has and her access to alternative discourses that would provide her with further options, but

> she none the less exists as a thinking, feeling, subject and social agent capable of resistance and innovations produced out of the clash between contradictory subject positions and practices. She is also a subject able to reflect upon the discursive relations which constitute her and the society in which she lives and able to choose from the options available.
>
> (Weedon 1987: 125)

The term 'subjectivity' has increasingly been used (Davies 1989a; McNaughton 2000) instead of identity because it highlights the process by which our multifaceted identity is created. The term subjectivity serves to remind us that we are considering an individual's personal and social identities that are created through a process that involves her being made a subject or subjected to other people's readings of her and her positioning within society. She simultaneously makes highly personal decisions about the satisfaction she gains from, and the desirability of, the various ways in which she is able to position herself within society. This process is therefore not passive, in that 'individuals negotiate cultural understandings about femininity and masculinity, in shaping and reshaping their own sense of themselves' (Wearing 1996, cited in Rowan et al. 2002: 67). I would argue that it is possible to continue to use the more familiar term identity provided we are conscious of the process by which we create our identities, so that we think in terms of multiple identities rather than a single identity and are aware of the unstable nature of our concepts of 'self'.

Children learn about gender and develop their gendered identities through their interactions with others and through their experiences of positioning themselves within society and being positioned by others. When we observe young children and listen to what they have to say about themselves and others we are witnessing a small part of the ongoing process by which the children are developing ideas about who they are rather than observing a 'finished product'. Talking to children about gender provides us with an insight into their developing understandings of gender. It is important to hear what children have to say because it helps to clarify how children are categorizing themselves and others, highlights the discourses to which the children appear to have had access and helps to identify which discourses appear to provide the children with positive emotional feedback. Gaining an understanding of the signs and symbols that produce the social representations of gender that the children are exploring or aligning themselves with helps educators to comprehend the reasons and motives for children's behaviours, attitudes, concerns and interests. It also helps educators to understand the discourses of gender and of femininity and masculinity with which the children are engaging. Unless we know where children are coming from and what it is that appeals to them we cannot hope to effect change.

Girl or boy?

For children growing up in Britain one of the core elements of their identity is whether they are a girl or boy, female or male. From birth children are categorized as female or male. One of the first questions new parents are asked is 'Is it a girl or a boy?' The 'fact' of the existence of a binary divide between females and males is etched into the languages, social practices and institutions of the cultures and society that make up Britain today. A child grows up being labelled a girl or a boy. Being identified as a girl or boy is not the end of the story. What British society requires is that children must learn not only to correctly identify themselves as girls or boys but also to identify others correctly as female or male. How children come to do this is interesting because, although the dominant discourse relates gender to biological sex, in British society children are not able to rely on observable physical differences between females and males. Instead children must learn what the signifiers of gender are. Cealey Harrison and Hood-Williams (2002) have cited the work of Kessler and McKenna, which revealed how young children will look for signs such as hair length, eye shape and activity to help them to decide whether someone is female or male. Kessler and McKenna (in Cealey Harrison and Hood-Williams 2002) have argued that children's learning of the rules for attributing gender is a developmental process. Children initially provide idiosyncratic reasons (e.g. 'It's a girl because it's got red hair') but through interaction with older children and adults gradually learn what are regarded as appropriate and relevant signs.

Through learning how to identify people as female or male children are also learning that gender is a dichotomous category: one can be either female or male but not both. Furthermore, in gender terms, there is nothing a person can be other than female or male. There is no word in common usage for someone who is not female or male. This binary divide has implications for early years educators because it makes the notion of a gender continuum difficult. Instead, the dominant discourse pushes us and the children we work with towards creating a sharp distinction of people into two categories, female and male.

Children also learn that one's gender is invariant. A child cannot be a girl one day and a boy the next. A third 'fact' children learn, therefore, is that people are classified as girls and boys or women and men and an individual's gender attribution remains constant; they must remain in one category because ultimately it is determined by one's biology. There has been an increasing body of research that calls into question the validity of biological distinctions (see, for example, Cealey Harrison and Hood-Williams 2002: 42–50) but there is not space here to examine these arguments in depth. Attributing gender, however, is made harder by the fact that there are various ways of 'being' a girl or a boy. Gender is not simply an alternative word for sex. Thus, even were one to ignore the current discussions about the validity of assigning people into one of two groups, female and male, on the basis of their biological sex, gender remains a complicated concept. This is because gender needs to be conceived of in terms of individuals developing an understanding of what it means to be female or male, learning 'appropriate' behaviours and understanding the complex dynamics of the relationships between females and males at both individual and societal levels.

Children's ideas about themselves and others

All the children spoken to during the course of the research for this book were aged between 3 and 7 and every child was absolutely clear about whether she or he was a girl or a boy. Furthermore, it was apparent during the course of conversations with these young children that they had all managed to categorize the other children in the setting as either girls or boys. The children were also clear that their gender is invariant. When I asked girls whether they would like to be boys and boys whether they would like to be girls it was clear from the children's spoken responses and body language that they did not think the question was valid, as the choice was not feasible. Despite the children knowing that they could not change gender there was a marked difference between the girls' and boys' responses to the question. Most of the boys' responses were adamant and unequivocal:

Interviewer: Would you like to be a girl?
All three boys: No! [Firmly and frowning]
Robbie: No way!
Interviewer: Why?
Robbie: Don't like them.
    (Interview with Ashok aged 5.0, Robbie aged 4.6 and James aged 4.4)

These boys did not believe that it was possible for them to become girls but clearly the mere suggestion itself was unwelcome. It would appear that these young boys, and the other boys who responded in a similar way, had not only learned to categorize people but were already positioning themselves as boys and seemed to have an emotional investment in being boys rather than girls. The girls I interviewed tended to laugh a little at the suggestion before saying that they would not like to be a boy. The girls seemed to be less perturbed by the question, although they too stated that they did not want to be boys. It would appear that the young children interviewed had already developed an awareness of the binary nature of gender categorization and also of the invariance of gender.

It is interesting to reflect further on the girls' and boys' different responses to the question. When answering the question the boys did not look at each other before responding and their tone of voice was both incredulous and somewhat outraged. In view of this it is possible to suggest that for most of the boys the style of masculinity they were constructing and their current level of understanding of what it means to be a boy precluded any contemplation about wanting to be a girl or more feminine. The suggestion was an affront to them. Of course, it is possible that the boys may not have been as quick to reject the idea of being a girl had they been interviewed on their own or in a different context.

In contrast, the girls seemed less troubled by the question and most of them looked at each other and laughed before replying to the question. The girls may have been less uneasy about the question because they had encountered discourses of femininity that 'allowed' a degree of masculinity. Parents, for example, seem to be more tolerant of their young daughters engaging in 'masculine' activities than of their young sons engaging in 'feminine' activities (Thorne 1993). The issue of children engaging in non-stereotyped 'feminine' or 'masculine' behaviour is examined in more depth later in this chapter.

It could be argued that another explanation for the different reactions of the girls and the boys to the question may lie in the patriarchal nature of British society, which not only values masculinity more than femininity but also results in unequal power relationships between males and females. Although there have been changes in British society over the past three decades, patriarchy remains: 'the "change" of which there is so much awareness is not the crumbling of the material and institutional structures of patriarchy. What has crumbled is the *legitimation* of patriarchy' (Connell 1995: 226; emphasis added). The boys' strong negative response to the question may have been because they were unwilling to contemplate giving up their status and power, and hence their vigorous denial of the desire to be a girl. The girls, on the other hand, appeared to enjoy playing with the possibility of wanting to be a boy, which was evidenced by their laughter and exchanged looks. It is feasible that the girls found the thought of becoming someone with more power intriguing and attractive and, unlike the boys, did not feel threatened by the suggestion.

There may, however, be problems with using patriarchy to provide an explanation for the different responses of the girls and boys. As will become apparent later in this chapter, the problem does not lie in the children's lack of awareness of the existing unequal power relations between groups of children. Instead, the problem is that in this context the concept of patriarchy may be too blunt a tool. Walkerdine has argued that patriarchy is not 'a monolithic force which imposes socialisation on girls ... [instead it] produces the positions for subjects to enter' (Walkerdine *et al.* 1989: 205). It is necessary to bear in mind the notion that there are multiple discourses of masculinity and femininity that are shaped by the interaction of factors such as 'race', class and sexuality. The concept of multiple and diverse masculinities and femininities serves to remind us that we need to be sensitive to the relationships that exist between the different styles of masculinity and femininity. Thus, although in society as a whole the pattern of power relationships, both at a personal level and at an institutional level, benefits boys and men rather than women and girls, the locus of power may shift somewhat in the early years setting. Children's experiences of power in early years settings will vary depending on how they are positioning themselves and how the discourses they are using are viewed by others in the setting, both adults and children. Not all versions of masculinity are accorded the same status and imbued with the same degree of power in gender relations. It is possible that some of the boys interviewed adopted styles of masculinity that did not automatically accord them a higher status than girls and perhaps allowed for more 'feminine' positionings than are possible in more 'traditional' styles of masculinity. If this were the case, fear of loss of status and power would not be the reason why these boys showed such a strong negative reaction to the idea of being a girl and we would have to look for an alternative explanation.

Children's friendship patterns: 'Boy games . . . girl games'

This section explores what children say about who their friends are and the reasons for their choices. When talking to young children it is obvious that gender-based friendship patterns are a feature of life in early years settings. Listening to the children it became apparent that the majority tended to play in same-sex groups for most of the time that they were in the early years setting:

> Interviewer: And who do you play with?
> Emma: Bella.
> Interviewer: Bella? Is Bella your special friend?
> Emma: [Nods]
> Interviewer: Yes? And who else do you play with?
> Emma: Zareena, Chelsea . . . er . . .
> Interviewer: Do you ever play with Neil?
> Emma: Nah! I don't play with any boys.
> Interviewer: You don't play with any boys?
> Emma: I play with girls.
>
> (Interview with Emma aged 4.0)

A small group of boys were equally clear about whom they would play with:

> Interviewer: When I asked who you liked to play with you only mentioned boys. Do you not like to play with girls?
> Robbie: No.
> Interviewer: Why?
> Robbie: 'Cos I just don't.
> James: Just boys.
> (Interview with Ashok aged 5.0, Robbie aged 4.6 and James aged 4.4)

Not all children displayed a rigid gender divide in terms of their choice of friends. Stephen's choice of friends stands in contrast to that of Robbie, James and Ashok, as he happily named both girls and boys when asked about his friends:

> Interviewer: So, you play with Casey [a boy]. Who else do you play with?
> Stephen: John Wood, Neil . . . John White . . . Rochelle. That's all my friends that I've got in this nursery but I've another friend who goes to another nursery who used to go here.
> Interviewer: And what are they called?
> Stephen: Her name is Molly and she's about 5.
> (Interview with Stephen aged 4.2)

As with most research with young children it was important to have fairly lengthy conversations with the children before drawing any conclusions. This was because some of the children did not always immediately say what they really thought, saying instead what they thought that I, as an adult in the setting, wanted to hear. When I asked one teacher-selected group of girls and boys who their friends were they each listed the other children in the group and it was only later that it became apparent that the friendship patterns were very different. In a different early years setting, Jimel, when asked about his special friends, named the two girls in the teacher-selected interview group but later in the interview only mentioned boys when talking about what he played and whom he played with.

Many of the children were able to articulate clearly their reasons for their gender-based pattern of friendships. Interestingly, none of the children's comments hinted at parental or explicit peer group pressure (i.e. fear of being bullied). Most of the children identified differences in interests as the reason for not playing with certain children:

Interviewer: Why don't you play with any boys?
Emma: Because I don't want to run about I just think of playing with girls . . .
Interviewer: Sorry . . . What do you mean?
Emma: Because they just play boy games.
Interviewer: They just play boy games? What sort of games do they play then?
Emma: Like fightin' and I don't like playing it. I like playing girl games. Girls just like playing dogs, cats. I just like playing cats and dogs.
Interviewer: So boys play fighting games and girls don't?
Emma: [Nods]
(Interview with Emma aged 4.0)

Neil was also able to explain about how he thought girls' and boys' interests differed and the effect this had on his friendships:

Interviewer: The list of children you said you were friendly with, they are all boys. Do you ever have any girls playing with you?
Neil: [Shakes head]
Interviewer: No girls? Why do you think? Why don't girls play with you?
Neil: Because I'm not their friend.
Interviewer: Do they like playing the same things as you?
Neil: No. They don't like playing Power Rangers. I play Superman, Power Rangers and Batman and that's why I don't want to play with them.
Interviewer: So what do they play instead?
Neil: Dolls.

Interviewer: So you wouldn't want to play with them?
Neil: No.

(Interview with Neil aged 4.6)

The views and attitudes of these young children were echoed by slightly older children who, when asked whether girls and boys liked playing with different things responded with comments such as:

Boys like Power Rangers, football, tennis and cricket.

(Boy aged 6.2)

Girls like playing with Barbies and My Little Pony. Boys play with scary things and cars and trains.

(Girl aged 6.2)

Most boys like football. I don't really know what girls like.

(Boy aged 6.1)

Yes of course! Girls like pink stuff and yellow and Barbie and Sindy and boys like bluey [sic] stuff and Action Man and cars and trains. I like Power Rangers . . . I like the pink one. Boys and girls can play *together* like with Pokemon.

(Girl aged 6.5)

Girls like Barbie and things. Boys like Batman.

(Boy aged 5.9)

I found it somewhat chastening to hear children saying the same sorts of things that other children had said to me more than 12 years ago. The children's comments about 'boy games' and 'girl games' were a very clear echo of children's views more than a decade ago about certain toys and activities being 'girls' stuff' or 'boys' stuff' (Browne and Ross 1991: 39). Clearly, if educators are to make any headway in developing gender equity in their settings they need to know more than simply with whom and with what children play.

The consistent patterns of play preferences exhibited by very young girls and boys could be seen as evidence for a biological basis for the observed differences: it's 'natural' for girls to play with Barbie and boys to enjoy being Batman. Such a view is unsustainable in view of the research into brain development and the effect of hormones (see Chapter 2 of this book). Recourse to biological explanations is also untenable if we accept the notion of multiple femininities and masculinities, since this involves reducing these multiple femininities and masculinities to two categories of gender, feminine and masculine, which are then conflated with the dichotomous categories of biological sex: female and male. The end result of this is that gender categories are viewed as binary, mutually exclusive, polarized and natural (Letts 2001). Furthermore, a reliance on biological explanations does not take into account the impact of factors such as social class and ethnicity.

The view that girls and boys learn what is 'acceptable' or 'appropriate' for them to play with as girls and boys through observing others and absorbing social messages is weakened by the fact that children clearly do not uncritically learn or accept patterns of appropriate behaviour. This is evidenced by the lack of success educators and parents have had in changing gender-based patterns of children's play, and the way in which children will sabotage educators' strategies aimed at involving children in less gender-stereotyped activities or in activities they would not normally choose (Browne and Ross 1991).

It seems likely that children's choices of playmates and activities are part of their exploration of different styles of femininity and masculinity. Strategies used in the past that were aimed at encouraging boys to play in the home corner and girls to play with construction toys were only effective on a super-ficial level, so clearly they did not tackle fundamental issues. The question then is: why do these styles seem not to have changed over the past two decades, despite the implementation of equal opportunities strategies in early years settings and in wider society? The conversations with the children provided some clues as to what is happening.

Dealing with gender 'deviance'

As previously discussed in this chapter, the dominant gender discourse places females and males as different and in opposition to each other. Hegemonic masculinity is the term used to describe the dominant form or culturally accepted form of masculinity within a setting or society (Connell 1995, 2000). Hegemonic masculinity emphasizes, among other things, men's (and boys') superiority to women (and girls), competitiveness, physical strength and rationality. Other styles of masculinity can coexist with the hegemonic form but it is the dominant form of masculinity that determines what it means to be a 'real' man or boy. The prevailing conceptualization of gender in binary and polarized terms means that femininity is not masculinity and vice versa, and hegemonic masculinity is complemented by 'emphasized feminity', which reinforces male masculine power and emphasizes 'compliance, nurturance and empathy' (Connell 1987: 187–8)

Davies (1989a) has argued that the language we use perpetuates the social structure and in passing on language to our children we are also passing on a 'relative entrapment in the social order, including those elements of the social order we might well want to move beyond' (Davies 1989a: 1). Embedded within the English language, for example, is the 'fact' that people are either female or male and children hear adults talking about 'the opposite sex' and 'the weaker sex'. This point is important because the categories female and male are not 'natural' and children have to learn how to behave and relate to others in gender-appropriate ways through interaction with others and through gaining access to and understanding of the dominant gender discourse.

The girl/boy divide is not innate and the power relations between women and men and girls and boys are not 'natural', yet dominant discourses are construed as providing us with taken-for-granted 'truths' about the world. In order to retain a sense of psychological and intellectual equilibrium and maintain the 'reality' constructed by the dominant discourses, children (and adults) need to develop strategies for dealing with instances when they themselves, or others, deviate from the 'norm'.

One strategy is to ignore the deviations in order to retain a clear distinction between girls and boys or women and men (Davies 1989a). This ability to categorize clearly according to binary gender divisions while simultaneously ignoring contradictions and deviations is evident in the following comments made by a 5-year-old girl: 'Boys like Action Man and Spiderman. Girls like soft animals, they like Pokemon but it's really a boy thing.' Operating effectively within the dominant discourse provides high, positive emotional feedback to children, as they are 'correctly' positioning themselves and others, which itself is likely to attract overt praise ('What a good little girl!) and enables them to relate unproblematically and unambiguously, in gender terms, with others. In view of this it is not surprising that strategies aimed at encouraging children to deviate from the 'norm' have not proved to be successful. Furthermore, providing children with models of adults or children who 'do' gender in a way that diverges from the dominant norm has had limited success for three main reasons. First, insufficient account has been taken of the processes by which children learn to position themselves as girls and boys. Second, there has been little acknowledgement of the emotional investment in these positions. Third, children's tendency to ignore or discount instances of deviations from the norm and to 'other' those who cross the gender boundaries has been disregarded.

Another explanation for the difficulty adults experience in broadening children's play choices and playmate preferences could lie in the tendency in young children to conceptualize gender in terms of clear, and sometimes extreme, categories. Paley has noted:

> Kindergarten is a triumph of sexual self-stereotyping. No amount of adult subterfuge or propaganda deflects the five-year-olds' passion for segregation by sex. They think they have invented the differences between girls and boys and, as with any new invention, must prove that it works . . . [The doll corner] is not simply a place to play; it is a stronghold against ambiguity.
>
> (Paley 1984: ix)

When I asked children what girls and boys liked to play it was interesting to note how the majority talked about girls liking Barbies and playing mummies and daddies and boys liking cars, fighting and superhero play, which seem to be concrete illustrations of hegemonic masculinity and emphasized femininity. Only a few children mentioned activities that both girls and boys enjoy:

> Jemma: Girls and boys can play together.
> Interviewer: With what?
> Jemma: Um . . . Pokemon . . . I like Power Rangers.
>
> (Interview with Jemma aged 6.6)

Jemma also seemed to be conscious of the fact that liking the Power Rangers was not common among girls and she was careful to make a distinction between Pokemon, which, in her experience, both boys and girls in general liked, and Power Rangers, which was viewed by many of her friends as something only boys like. It is possible that Jemma was happy to adopt both 'feminine' and 'masculine' positions but was aware that this was not common and was therefore somewhat tentative about making statements about girls and boys in general, preferring instead to talk about what she herself liked.

It was very rare to come across a child such as Poppy who seemed willing to countenance the possibility that gender may not be the best indicator of a child's play preferences, and was able to express her view with confidence and clarity:

> Poppy: It depends what genes they have.
> Interviewer: Do you mean the jeans you wear?
> Poppy: No, the other sort of genes.
> Interviewer: Oh, I see.
> Poppy: And how old they are, sometimes it depends what colour the toy is, some boys like pink . . . so you never know.
>
> (Interview with Poppy aged 6.5)

Although Poppy's comments seem to look for a biologically based explanation for children's play preferences, she has at least moved beyond identifying biological sex as the key determining factor.

Kohlberg's cognitive-developmental theory provides an explanation for young children's rigid views about gender appropriate behaviour. Children, according to Kohlberg, are able to identify themselves as girls or boys by the age of 3 but it is not until the age of 5 or 6 that the concept of gender constancy is established. It is only around the age of 10 that children understand that gender roles are social rather than biological or 'natural' constructs. According to this theory, in order to maintain a stable gender identity young children tend to adhere to what they perceive to be 'gender-appropriate' behaviour and show disapproval of 'gender-inappropriate' behaviour in others (Marcus and

Overton 1978; Meyer 1980). This theory, however, does not explain why older children and adolescents may hold very rigid views about what is gender-appropriate. Furthermore, cognitive-developmental theory sits uneasily with theories of multiple femininities and masculinities because it takes as given the binary nature of gender. The theory therefore fails to take adequate account of the range of styles of femininity and masculinity a child may adopt and the power of different discourses in determining, in the child's mind, what is 'gender-appropriate' and what is 'gender-inappropriate'. I would argue that young children's rigid views about gender-appropriate behaviour are not as much a search for a stable personal identity as an expression of participation in a joint enterprise with others in society that is aimed at clarifying and maintaining gender categories. Since the binary gender divide is not 'natural', children have to learn the social practices and signifying systems in circulation in society as a whole that delineate 'female' and 'male' in order to position themselves and others successfully. Furthermore, the categories female and male exist and are perpetuated by the dominant gender discourse, and the drive to 'get things right' leads us all into finding ways of maintaining the categories even when our own or other people's behaviour refutes the existence of these categories. Adopting a fairly rigid view of what is gender-appropriate reduces the degrees of uncertainty surrounding gender categories and in so doing upholds the essentially arbitrary categories that have been constructed through the dominant discourse.

When talking to Jerome I got the sense that he, in common with many of the other young boys I spoke to, was very determinedly adopting a position in which his style of masculinity was unambiguous:

Interviewer: Why don't you like the home corner?
Jerome: Because I don't like it. [Frowns]
Interviewer: You just don't?
Jerome: Yeah.
Interviewer: There must be a reason. Is it maybe because of who else plays in there?
Jerome: Yeah.
Interviewer: Who else plays in there?
Jerome: I'm not gonna tell you.
Interviewer: I won't tell them.
Jerome: I'm not gonna tell you.
Interviewer: You don't have to say their names you can just say if they are girls or boys . . .
Jerome: [Crosses his arms and frowns]
Interviewer: So do your friends play in the home corner?
Jerome: [Shakes head]
Interviewer: None of your friends?

Jerome: Sometimes.
Interviewer: But you never do?
Jerome: I never?
Interviewer: Play in the home corner?
Jerome: No. [Shakes head]
Interviewer: Do you ever play things like mummies and daddies outside in the playground? Because when I was talking to Leena and Kelly they seemed to like playing mummies and daddies. Do you ever play with them?
Jerome: No.

(Interview with Jerome aged 4.4)

Many of the girls interviewed were equally clear about the position they were adopting, a position described by Davies (1989a: 121) as the 'home corner' girls. These girls talked about 'playing houses' and mummies and daddies, and Parveen, one 4-year-old, informed me that 'girls like to play teenagers', which involved playing with their make-up box.

Maintaining the binary gender divide and upholding the dominant styles of masculinity and femininity leads to what Davies (1989a: 28) has referred to as category maintenance work and McGuffey and Rich (2001: 73) refer to as negotiations within the gender transgression zone. Children who deviate from the norm are likely to experience disapproval from both adults and other children. This category-maintenance work is not confined to older children: even very young children will tease or criticize other children who do not conform and who seem to have disregarded the gender categories (Davies 1989a; Browne 1999). When talking about children's play preferences Lizzie demonstrated one way in which category maintenance work occurs:

> I should think girls like to play with Barbies and Polly Pockets and boys like Pokemon gameboys and Pokemon cards. I like Pokemon too. I think only boys might like to play with Knex [a construction toy]. If they like Barbie they must be gay.
>
> (Interview with Lizzie aged 6.5)

In this instance Lizzie was ignoring her own deviation (liking Pokemon) but was condemning any boy who might like Barbie. The condemnation took the form of calling into question their heterosexual masculinity. I am not certain whether this child fully understood the meaning of the word 'gay' but she knew enough to use it to insult boys who transgressed the gender boundary or deviated from the norm. Lizzie has an older brother aged 12 and it is possible that she has heard him using the word 'gay' to describe boys who have shown signs of 'feminine' behaviour. The message in such a comment is that boys who like Barbie have failed to live up to the standards of hegemonic heterosexual masculinity and are more 'feminine' than is socially acceptable, and as such are to be rejected. McGuffey and Rich quote Lehne (1992: 389) in arguing that the threat of being called gay is used as a means of 'enforcing social conformity in the male role' and is used to define the limits of 'acceptable masculinity' (McGuffey and Rich 2001: 82). Girls appear to be more tolerant of other girls who deviate from the norm (Browne 1999: 156; McGuffey and Rich 2001). Lizzie, quoted above, certainly seems to feel that admitting that she likes 'boys' toys' is unlikely to result in criticism and does not seem to think that it calls into question her femininity.

Davies (1989a) has argued that adults engage in category maintenance work with girls. During my research, I found that although girls did not rigidly enforce gender boundaries, adults would engage in gender category-maintenance work with young girls. An example of this occurred with two girls in a nursery where playing with guns and other weapons was not discouraged by the staff. The two 4-year-old girls were showing me something they had constructed out of two pieces of wood, and the following interchange took place:

Bella: [Showing me what she has in her hand, two pieces of wood nailed together to form a cross] A sword!
Interviewer: [Taking it and examining it] Is this a sword?
Emma: No! That's a gun!
Nursery assistant: I don't think so. I thought it was an aeroplane.

Despite attending a nursery where staff had decided that children should be allowed to engage in imaginary play involving toy guns and other weapons, it would appear that these two girls were being told that playing with guns and other weapons was really something for boys and that their interest in such activities suggested that the girls had not 'correctly' positioned themselves.

Connell (1987) has argued that this difference in tolerance levels of girls and boys towards those who flout gender-appropriate boundaries is evident because hegemonic masculinity subordinates other forms of masculinity (and all forms of femininity). Those boys engaging with this particular discourse have a higher status and more power than other boys and girls and therefore there is a high price to pay if the gender boundaries constructed by hegemonic masculinity are weakened. Girls, on the other hand, know that power resides with the boys and men and therefore there is 'no pressure to set up or negate or subordinate other forms of femininity in the way hegemonic masculinity must negate other masculinities' (Connell 1987: 187). Given the complex nature of the different styles of femininity and the interaction of 'race', social class and sexuality, I would suggest that if we accept that 'differences in female status [are] overdetermined by race and class' (hooks 1994: 124) then a hierarchy of femininities must also exist. Those, for example, who have access to discourses of power and privilege because of either their 'race' or their social class have the opportunity to adopt a style of 'femininity' in which they position themselves as having power over other girls. Davies (1989a) has argued that some children who adopt certain forms of 'femininity' attain a high status and are protected from criticisms and rejection due to having 'got things right'. These high-status forms of 'femininity' and 'masculinity' can be defined as those that do not challenge either the notion of a binary gender or the power relations between men and women (Davies 1989a). However, a hierarchy exists between these high-status ways of being:

> If you adopt one of these styles, you've made it. Rough, tough princesses and sirens are higher status than the 'home corner' girls . . . All are nonetheless unequivocally 'feminine' and are preparing the ground for some variant of oppressive gender relations.
>
> (Davies 1989a: 127)

Girls as young as 5 seem to be aware of some of the different forms of femininity and their status. A 5-year-old girl illustrated this point when she spoke about 'girly girls' in a disparaging tone of voice: 'Boys, lots of boys, like to play with Pokemon Game Boys. Girly girls like playing with Barbies, but I don't. I like playing with our dolls' house' (interview with Helen aged 5.11).

Not all boys adopt a hegemonic style of masculinity. Stephen, quoted earlier, was one such boy. He was very articulate and cheerfully spent a long time talking to me about his interests and his friends. He told me that he liked playing tennis and doing jigsaw puzzles. He also talked about playing at pirates and explained why Hercules was his favourite video: 'Um . . . 'cos he's very strong and I pretend to be strong. 'Cos I've got big muscles as well as him [flexes muscles] . . . but I'm not as strong as him.' He also talked about having girls as friends and was at pains to correct me when I suggested that he seemed to play only with boys:

Interviewer: What about . . . because there are a lot of girls out there I've noticed and you've only mentioned boys haven't you? So do the girls play things like pirates?
Stephen: Ah! I haven't just mentioned boys, you know Rochelle . . .
Interviewer: Rochelle, you did mention Rochelle.
Stephen: Rochelle's a girl.
Interviewer: Yes, you did mention Rochelle. What about the other girls? Do you play with them?
Stephen: Mmm . . . Tara. Tara usually plays with Leena and Kelly . . . she doesn't play with other children she just plays with Leena and Kelly.
Interviewer: What do they play? Do you know what they play?

Stephen: They play quite a lot of the time mums and dads. They like playing that quite a lot of the time and Leena, when I was playing with them, Leena was the grandma.
Interviewer: And what were you?
Stephen: I was the big brother.

(Interview with Stephen aged 4.2)

Stephen appears to be a good example of a child who, having rejected total adherence to the hegemonic style of masculinity, is successfully negotiating the various positionings that are an inherent part of different styles of masculinity and femininity. He is able to do this by ensuring that he engages in activities that are associated with hegemonic masculinity (for example, superhero play) and is friendly with boys who have clearly positioned themselves as 'real boys'. This means that his masculinity is not an issue and that he is free to engage in more 'feminine' activities such as playing mummies and daddies.

In view of the ruthless way in which the categories are maintained, children, especially boys, may pay a high price if they move away from the norm. This could explain children's resistance to strategies aimed at enabling boys to participate in activities traditionally associated with girls, and vice versa. There is no easy solution to this situation because of children's emotional investment in the positions they adopt but also because, in the case of the boys, they are unlikely willingly to give up their powerful place in the gender order.

Ensuring that children have access to a wider range of discourse (ways of seeing the world and ways of being) is a necessary aspect of work aimed at disrupting gender divisions. Children may decide to explore new roles and different positions that do not conform to accepted models of 'femininity' or 'masculinity' and in these instances children who are deviating from the current gender norms need to be supported. Davies and Banks (1995: 67) have argued that:

> for those who are engaged in resisting the dominant discourses on gender, the reactions of others to that resistance may be far less painful if understood as category maintenance work which shores up their own storylines and the gender order in which they are embedded.

Davies and Banks have also argued that introducing children to the notion of gender equity, developing non-sexist curricula and providing role models that challenge the existing gender order will not result in children rethinking their ideas about gender. What is needed is for children to be 'liberated from the burden of the unitary self and the limiting story lines that some of them are caught up in' (Davies and Banks 1995: 67). McNaughton has taken up this theme and has suggested that teachers will need to:

work hard to provide boys with understandings of masculinity in which dominance is not always seen as positive. They will need to work equally hard to provide girls with understandings of femininity that enable them to assert their rights.

(McNaughton 2000: 125–6)

The following chapter explores children's imaginative role play, especially superhero and weapon play, as this appears to be one way in which children explore the various gender positions available to them.

5 Mummies and superheroes

In my conversations with young children it was very apparent that there was a sharp gender divide in terms of imaginative role play. The girls talked time and again about playing mummies and daddies and the boys told me about their games of Batman, Superman, Spiderman and the Power Rangers. This echoes the findings of numerous other researchers (e.g. Paley 1984; Thorne 1993; Jordan and Cowan 2001). In the past boys have been discouraged from toy weapon and superhero play but in recent years concerns about boys' under-achievement at school and the ways in which early years settings were not meeting boys' needs have led to a reconsideration of the value of such play (Gurian 2001; G. Jones 2002; Holland 2003). There is not space here to rehearse all the arguments surrounding this aspect of children's play but this chapter aims to highlight some of the motivations for superhero play and explores the possible outcomes of such play. Educators' responses to superhero play and weapon play are examined in the following chapters.

Do children need superhero play?

The anxiety about boys' underachievement at school has resulted in a per-ceptible shift in many educators' response to superhero and gun play in early years settings. Such play is now being tolerated, and in some settings encour-aged, rather than being forbidden. The justifications for this shift in approach are numerous. One argument is that the high levels of physical activity that characterize superhero play and weapon play are what young boys 'need'. Gurian (2001), for example, has argued that the brain structure of small boys results in them playing rough, vigorous, competitive and aggressive games that involve bodily contact, tumbling and occupying more playground space than do girls (Gurian 2001: 35–6). There are obvious problems with this view because it relies on a belief that observed disparities in the behaviour of girls and boys have a purely biological basis, in that the differences are linked to differences in the brain structure and pattern of brain development of girls and boys (see Chapter 2).

Another justification is that superhero play enables boys who are learning English as an additional language to develop relationships and play with their peers (Holland 2003). This raises three issues. First, we ought to be convinced about the value of superhero and weapon play for children generally, and ought not to have any reservations about encouraging such play before considering whether it is helpful for children learning English as an additional language. Second, why do we not advocate superhero and weapon play for girls who are 'new' to English? Is it because it is mainly boys who engage in superhero play? If so, surely we need to consider the reasons for this gender-based difference? Third, to argue that superhero play and weapon play provides boys 'new' to English with an easy route into role play with their peers implies that much of the superhero and weapon play may be lacking in complexity and may be very formulaic, as it requires little complex or creative verbal interaction. Research has suggested that superhero play based on television characters and programmes tends to be very limited in terms of variety of plot, situations and dialogue, which leads to rigid playscripts (Cupit 1996). While the rigidity or predictability of the playscripts would enable participation by children who are familiar with the characters and stories, in other words children who have watched superheroes on television or video, it could be argued that the play itself is of limited value due to its repetitive nature. Surely educators should not be encouraging impoverished play merely to facilitate the involvement of boys who are learning English as an additional language? I would argue that all children deserve more than this.

A third justification for superhero and weapon play is that such play develops children's self-confidence and social skills:

> Wrestling, roughhousing, make-believe violence acted out with the whole body smash anxieties and wrestle fears to the floor. Pretended savagery lifts kids out of shyness and knocks down barriers to closeness. Games involving chasing, pillow fighting, squirt guns, and mock combat help kids learn how to judge dangers and take appropriate risks. Jumping willingly into those pretend dangers and coming out unhurt helps kids distinguish fantasy from reality.
>
> (G. Jones 2002: 67–8)

Again, it is worth remembering that it is mainly boys who engage in the types of activities Jones has written about. If Jones's view is valid then we should be asking why we do not encourage girls to engage in these types of play activities.

Psychoanalytical theory crops up in discussions of superhero play and is frequently drawn upon to explain or justify children's 'need' for imaginative role play and experience of stories in which good is pitted against evil, as they provide children with the chance to explore and eventually conquer their fears and anxieties. Bettelheim has argued that fairy tales deal with universal fears and anxieties and therefore play a vital part in young children's emotional development (Bettelheim 1978). Although Bettelheim was unconvinced about the value of modern children's literature and the superhero stories on television, others have extended his argument about fairy tales to include stories about Batman, Superman and other superheroes. Boyd, for example, has argued that 'superhero play offers a sense of power to children in a world dominated by adults' (Boyd 1997: 25) and that through superhero play children can work through fears about their own safety.

G. Jones (2002) urges parents and educators to 'trust the child's desires' when it comes to allowing children to experience action entertainment that may be violent and misogynistic, and makes a somewhat spurious comparison between children's desire for this type of entertainment and their desire for sugar:

> In the 1970s some spotty research linking sugar to hyperactivity, attention deficit disorder, and other illnesses and maladies touched the nerves of millions of parents; the studies were soon debunked but fear of its effects still lingers. Sugar does present challenges . . . but children crave it for very good reasons.
>
> Action entertainment is similarly appealing to kids . . . we feel a similar threat from it and look for danger signs in research. But children also crave it for very healthy and legitimate reasons . . . A kid who feels powerless knows that the video game industry is noticing his desire for power, if only by creating fantasies to sell to him. His desire to feel more powerful is healthy, and so is his desire to have it seen and acknowledged.
>
> (G. Jones 2002: 189–90)

The various arguments outlined above make it hard for educators to continue to be critical of activities that supposedly develop children's confidence, social skills, language and emotional resilience. There is, however, a need to examine the issues more closely, as the arguments tend to refer to 'children' and in so doing mask the gender dimensions of the issues. It is interesting, for example, to note that in the above extract, G. Jones (2002) moves from writing about children in general to male children in particular, yet this shift in focus is not explicitly acknowledged.

Who wants to play Batman?

Who are the children who engage in play fighting and superhero play? In the vast majority of cases they are boys (Holland 2003). If, however, we accept the argument that children, both girls and boys, 'need' such play it is not clear why there is a discernible gender divide in weapon and superhero play. If all children need this type of play why is it boys rather than girls who persist in finding ways to be Batman or shoot pretend guns in settings that have a 'zero tolerance' to such play? Jerome and Charlie were typical of many of the young boys I spoke to, in that they continued to play superhero games that involved fighting despite the fact that they were punished when their play attracted the attention of adults:

> Jerome: I pretend to be Batman.
> Charlie: I pretend to be Batman as well.
> Interviewer: Are you allowed to play Batman at school?
> Jerome: Yeah, but only if . . .
> Charlie: If you're fighting then you're on the list and you have to go and
> sit on one of the chairs near the wall.
> (Interview with Charlie aged 5.0 and Jerome aged 5.4)

It could be argued that girls learn the rules of setting earlier than do boys but this would not explain why it is boys rather than girls who engage in super-hero and weapon play in settings where such play is not outlawed (Holland 2003). The clear gender divide suggests that we need to question whether superhero and weapon play is 'needed' by all children or whether it is a type of play that is fulfilling for certain children, particularly some boys.

When we reflect on some of the dominant themes in children's imaginative role play there is little doubt that 'good' overcomes evil and fears are con-quered. Young children feel strong, empowered and secure through pretend-ing to be good fairies defeating wicked witches or 'flying' to the rescue as Batman, or pretending to be brave princesses chasing monsters or Spiderman imprisoning 'baddies' with a magic web. The various possible roles and stories, however, do not seem to appeal equally to all children. The vast majority of girls that I spoke to were adamant that superhero and weapon play was not something they did:

> Emma: I don't like Power Rangers.
> Interviewer: Why?
> Emma: Because it's a boys' thing.
> (Interview with Emma aged 4.0)

Much of the girls' imaginative role-play seems to draw on fairy tales:

> Erin: I'm a witch.
> Interviewer: You're a witch?
> Erin: Yeah.
> Interviewer: I'd never have guessed.
> Erin: I'm a good witch.
> Interviewer: Ah ha! So what can you do as a good witch?
> Erin: I can help people. If somebody's fallen into the water I can go in it then save them.
> Interviewer: Mmmm . . . So as a good witch you can save people?
> Erin: Er . . . mmmm . . . Yes, from the bad witch.
> (Interview with Erin aged 4.6)

Another girl, aged 5, made it clear that her fantasy play was based around romance and marriage and certainly did not involve guns:

> Interviewer: What about you? Would you like a toy gun?
> Sameena: No, 'cos girls don't play with toy guns.
> Interviewer: Why?
> Sameena: I don't know. 'Cos they don't like it 'cos they not boys.
> Interviewer: So who would girls pretend to be?
> Sameena: Sometimes . . . sometimes I be Sleeping Beauty's mother and then the princess sleep for a hundred years and great big forest grew around and some prince came and chopped the forest away. So then they would get married.
> (Interview with Sameena aged 5.0)

The vast majority of boys, on the other hand, seemed to take on superhero roles in their imaginative role play:

> Jamal: I be Batman. Batman flies to . . . at night and not on a sunny day and Superman come in a sunny day and Superman doesn't like night time.
> Interviewer: What do Batman and Superman do?
> Jamal: They find baddies to kill them.
> Interviewer: What do they kill them with?
> Jamal: With the gun.
> Interviewer: Do you have a toy gun?
> Jamal: No.
> Interviewer: Would you like one to play with?
> Jamal: Yes.
> (Interview with Jamal aged 5.0)

Interviewer: Why do you like playing Spiderman?
Orlando: Because we all of us like it.
Interviewer: All of the children you play with?
Orlando: No. Finlay, William and Toby.
Interviewer: What's so good about playing Spiderman?
Orlando: I don't know.
Interviewer: What do you do when you play Spiderman?
Orlando: We get baddies . . . there's nothing else.
Interviewer: What do you do when you've got them?
Orlando: Tie them up, that's all.

(Interview with Orlando aged 5.0)

A few boys mentioned other characters that they pretended to be but these characters were always male and were usually heroes, if not superheroes:

Stephen: I usually be Robin Hood or Peter Pan or Hercules.
Interviewer: Would you say Robin Hood's a hero?
Stephen: Yeah, he's a hero quite a lot.
Interviewer: What does he do?
Stephen: He shoots bows and arrows.
Interviewer: Mmm. So anybody who shoots bows and arrows or saves
    people is a hero? Or not?
Stephen: Yeah, quite a lot . . . yeah they are heroes.

(Interview with Stephen aged 4.6)

The tendency for girls to draw on fairy tales for their imaginative play-scripts and for boys to draw on superhero televisual texts may be explained by Zipes's argument that, contrary to Bettelheim's view, fairy tales may not encapsulate all of the unconscious and conscious desires and anxieties of humankind (Zipes 1986). This would mean that some children would be searching for stories other than fairy tales to fulfil their emotional needs. This explanation has some merit but it does not adequately explain the gender divide, with girls seeming to be drawn to fairy tales while boys are attracted by modern-day superhero stories.

A possible explanation for the differences in the imaginative role play of girls and boys lies in the fact that imaginative role play does not only function as a means through which children can explore and overcome fundamental fears and anxieties. Imaginative role play or dramatic storying is also a way in which children can explore who they are, what and who they would like to be and how they would like others to see them and position them. Explorations of who one can be are culturally embedded, in that the children can only make sense of themselves and others by drawing on the discourses available to them. In view of this we ought not to be surprised that young children's imaginative role play will show evidence of children exploring the different gender roles and positions that have been made available to them through the discourses they have experienced.

Who can be a superhero?

From talking with the boys it soon became very apparent that superhero play is about the exercise of male power and the celebration and exploration of hegemonic masculinity. The following extract is from a transcript of a conversation with three boys aged 5 and contains ideas and views that were representative of many of the boys I spoke to:

Interviewer: Do you know what a superhero is?
Otis: Yeah!
Michael: Yeah!
Interviewer: OK, Otis, you tell me what you think a superhero is.
Otis: Um, the person who saves the world.
Michael: I think the same thing. They can fight all the world. They help the baddies not to fight all the world.
Interviewer: Are superheroes always boys or men?
Otis: They can be girls or boys.
Interviewer: Can you give me an example of a superhero who is a girl?
Otis: Catwoman. I don't know anyone else. I know only one but I can't remember her name . . .
Otis: A superhero has got special powers.
Michael: Yeah.
Otis: Yeah! They are really strong and really fast.
Interviewer: So could a baddie be a superhero?
Otis: No! They can't . . . No! They fight the baddies.
Interviewer: Why do you think they should fight baddies?
Otis: Because the baddies can take over the whole world.
Interviewer: What about in your game Akil, what do they fight with?
Akil: With their feet and their hands.
Interviewer: What about Spiderman? What does he fight with?
Otis: He fights with his web and his hands.
(Interview with Otis, Michael and Akil, all aged 5.0)

Stephen, aged 4, explained to me why Hercules is a hero and provided me with his definition of a superhero:

Stephen: Um . . . 'cos he's [Hercules] very strong and I pretend to be strong. 'Cos I've got big muscles as well as him [flexes his muscles] . . .

but I'm not as strong as him . . . and at the end he proves himself a
true hero.
Interviewer: How? What does he have to do to prove himself a true hero?
Stephen: He has to get a girl called Meg from a bad person called Hades . . .
Interviewer: Are superheroes just the same as heroes, is it just another
word to describe them?
Stephen: Well . . . superheroes are . . . it means they are the best.
Interviewer: So would you say that Hercules was a superhero?
Stephen: Yeah. He's quite a lot a superhero.
Interviewer: So could you be really horrible and be a hero? Could you be
really mean and nasty and shoot bows and arrows and things and still
be a hero?
Stephen: No you couldn't.
Interviewer: Why?
Stephen: Because they're no heroes . . . the bad people aren't . . . no . . .
Interviewer: The bad people aren't heroes?
Stephen: Only good people can be heroes.

(Interview with Stephen aged 4.6)

These boys were working hard at developing an understanding of what it
meant to be a superhero, and although they felt it was possible for a woman to
be a superhero, they were hard pressed to name more than one. They were
clear that superheroes are strong, are physically agile, are morally 'good', will
use violence to achieve their ends and are powerful enough to 'save the world'.
Stephen clearly felt that strength and bravery were key indicators of heroism
and that superheroes are simply the most heroic of heroes. The characteristics
these young boys highlight are remarkably similar to those characterizing
hegemonic masculinity. At this point it is worth noting that it would appear
that the young girls I spoke to had not thought much about superheroes, and
although they could name a few superheroes they found it hard to recognize
the essential characteristics of superheroes:

Interviewer: When I was talking to some of the other children they were
talking about superheroes and things, do you think a witch is a
superhero?
Bella: No.
Emma: No.
Interviewer: Because . . .
Emma: Erm . . . ummmm . . .
Interviewer: When I was talking to some of the other children they said
things like 'Superman is a superhero' and 'Hercules was a superhero'
and I asked whether girls can be superheroes and they said yes, but
didn't tell me who could be a superhero. So when you were describing

> the witch and what the witch can do I thought that that was very
> brave and thought maybe that a witch could be a superhero . . .
> Emma: [Shakes head]
> Interviewer: But you are saying no? Do you think girls can be superheroes?
> Bella: [Shakes head]
> Interviewer: You don't think so Bella? What about you Emma?
> Emma: No.
> Interviewer: No? So can only boys be superheroes?
> Emma: Yes.
> Interviewer: Why?
> - Emma: Because they like boys' things . . . I like ballerinas.
> Interviewer: So what does a superhero do?
> Bella: Like flying like Batman.
> Interviewer: But Wendy in Peter Pan, she flies! So could she be a
> superhero?
> Bella: Maybe.
>
> (Interview with Emma and Bella)

Interesting research into older children's analyses and understanding of traditional folktales in Canada (Mello 2001) has shown that older children also
defined male heroes as brave and physically strong. Female heroism was not
linked to physical prowess but to effort, creative problem-solving and endur-
ance. Mello has argued that the children's comments revealed much about
how they saw themselves in gender terms:

> The hero's ability to battle monsters and mythical beasts seemed to be
> connected to the boys' attitudes and understandings of their relation-
> ship to aggression and power, and their sense of self. Knowing and
> enjoying violence was seen, by most students, as being part of the
> male gender role.
>
> (Mello 2001: 552)

Heroines, in contrast, were less limited than their male counterparts in terms
of the range of roles they could adopt:

> For example, students agreed that a heroine could be both a
> homemaker and a soldier. Heroines were valued as both passive
> housekeepers and aggressive warriors, *as long as these female characters
> acted in service to social need, such as rescuing another person or helping a
> parent, or as long as they got married at the end* . . . However, caring
> kindness, 'being smart' and being responsible, was not considered the
> same as being powerful. The problem with the role of the heroine was
> that although acting in a caring manner reaped great rewards (jewels,

land, freedom and honour), it did not increase social status or social authority.

(Mello 2001: 553; emphasis added)

Male heroes and superheroes seem to encapsulate the essential character-istics of unambiguous and traditional 'masculinity', while heroines, despite their brave deeds and resourcefulness, remain essentially 'feminine' in that they are kind and caring. This certainly resonates with Erin's comments about the good witch 'saving people'. It would seem, therefore, that the stories chil-dren have experience of and the imaginative role play that arises out of these stories can have far-reaching consequences for how children position them-selves as 'feminine' and 'masculine', what they understand as characterizing the positions they adopt and the emotional satisfaction they experience from these gendered positions. In Mello's study the boys talked about their conflict-ing feelings about war and violence but also talked about how reading about and fantasizing about physically active heroism 'felt good' (Mello 2001: 551). The boys that I talked to did not explicitly talk about superhero play mak-ing them 'feel good', but it was clear from their keenness to discuss what they did when pretending to be Batman or Superman or one of the Power Rangers and the animated way in which they narrated various superhero storylines that this was definitely an activity that not only captured their interest but also excited them. The emotional satisfaction the boys experienced through such play may help to explain why many boys seem willing to risk punishment in order to engage in banned superhero play.

As stated earlier, none of the girls I spoke to expressed a desire to partici-pate in superhero play. It is probable that even if the girls did want to become involved in the boys' superhero play the boys would resist their involvement, and certainly would not allow them to be a superhero or have any real power or authority within the game. It would seem that superhero play is something that boys do:

Robbie: Girls have to be them. [Pointing to a picture of the Powerpuff Girls]
Interviewer: Can girls pretend to be Batman?
Ashok: No.
Robbie: Yes . . . girls can be Batgirl.
Interviewer: So can't girls pretend to be Batman?
Robbie: No way.
Interviewer: Would you pretend to be the Powerpuff Girls?
Robbie: No way.
Interviewer: Why?
Robbie: I don't like them.
Interviewer: You don't like them?

Robbie: No. Just boys.
Interviewer: What about Spiderman? Can girls pretend to be Spiderman?
Robbie: No. Spiderman has a girlfriend.
Interviewer: Can Spiderman's girlfriend do what Spiderman does?
Robbie: No.
Interviewer: So who can girls pretend to be if they want to be pretend to be really strong?
Robbie: Mummy.
Robbie: Batman can be a Daddy!
Ashok: Girls can be a baby.
[The boys laugh]
James: They [points to a picture of the Powerpuff Girls] can pretend to be Batman 'cos they can fly but they're not really Batman . . . they are fairies.
(Interview with Ashok aged 5.0, Robbie aged 4.6 and James aged 4.4)

This conversation was fascinating, as it revealed not only that the boys did not think girls could be superheroes but also that they perceived mothers to be 'really strong'. This accords with the views of Walkerdine and Lucey (1989), who argued that it is only in the domestic context that women are seen to have any real authority. The boys' comments would suggest, however, that they could not tolerate the thought of the girls being placed in a powerful position and instantly added that Batman could be the Daddy, thus effectively reducing the girls' power as 'mother'. After all, what sort of a match for Batman is a mother? Ashok diminished the girls' power still further with his suggestion that the girls could pretend to be babies. Robbie acceded that girls could pretend to be the Powerpuff Girls but the Powerpuff Girls, who appear to have superhero powers, did not impress James, who very effectively neutralized their power by locating them in the 'feminine' world as fairies. Girls, it would seem, can be girlfriends, mothers, babies or fairies. The boys' view that girls could be Bat*girl* rather than Bat*woman* is also revealing, as they were assigning the girls a less powerful role than that of a woman. The boys themselves never pretended to be Bat*boy* or Super*boy*. If, as Davies (1989a) has argued, language perpetuates existing social structures, the young boys' positioning of young girls as girls rather than women in fantasy play, while positioning themselves as men, serves to preserve boys' superior status.

When one considers the manner in which boys talk about their superhero and weapon play it becomes more evident that the play is inextricably linked with their exploration of 'masculinity'. From talking to children about super-heroes it was very noticeable not only that the boys had thought carefully about what constituted a superhero but also that they became very animated and physically active when discussing what superheroes do:

Interviewer: Would you like to pretend to be them if they did? If they killed the good guys would you still like the blue Power Ranger?
Nathan: Yes.
Interviewer: So would you say the Power Rangers are good?
Nathan: [Nods]
Interviewer: So they are the good guys? Who are the bad guys?
Nathan: I know one's Ivan Ooze.
Interviewer: Ivan Ooze? What does he look like?
Nathan: He's a big purple guy and a flying one in my videos and he has special powers in his fingers and he goes PSHEWW! [Shouts last word] And they start fighting the Power Rangers and one day when he's not on his power he gets the man with his dog and kicking it in on the track. POW [punches air with fist] into space and he jumps over, he jumps on his head and he kills him when he jumps over the rocks and he kicks the can [kicks out with feet] and he gets it and then throws it in the docks and so the Power Ranger kicks it on his head.
Interviewer: And then what happens.
Nathan: I forgot. I forgot what else happens.
Interviewer: Is that the end of it?
Nathan: It's not the end of it . . . Ivan Ooze makes some new friends who's evil and he makes a new monster robot and he makes an ant one and a dragon one and they both have powers and they both have red eyes.
(Interview with Nathan aged 4.0)

When talking about Hercules, 4-year-old Stephen flexed his arm muscles, while numerous other boys I talked to leapt up from their seats and adopted superhero stances and demonstrated how their favourite superhero moved and fought as they talked excitedly about their superhero play. Such behaviour, I would suggest, is a prime example of the process of bodily inscription. One's adoption of particular forms of 'masculinity' and 'femininity' is not merely something that occurs inside one's head. From a young age one's ascribed sex (i.e. the sex you are assigned on the basis of your observed biological sex at birth) becomes inscribed on your body and this is evident in the way one stands, sits and moves. Grosz (1990: 62) has argued that the body is inscribed by cultural practices, social norms and values. The fact that dominant discourses currently emphasize a binary view of gender means that bodily inscription reveals how an individual has positioned themselves as either 'feminine' or 'masculine'. A major way in which we indicate our gender position is through how we use and present our body. It is possible to argue that young boys are exploring and learning a particular form of 'masculinity' through adopting exaggeratedly 'strong' poses, flexing their muscles, running, leaping, occupying large amounts of space with their bodies and engaging in physically aggressive, albeit playful, episodes. The bodily inscription that results from such activity serves as a potent signifier of gender and as such not only influences how others begin to position the boys but also develops the boys' understanding of what their bodies have the potential to do and what their bodies can and should do to reflect their positioning as 'masculine'. Girls' imaginative role play involves the girls in different types of physical activity and leads to them developing a different understanding of how they can and should physically interact with the environment and with other people.

Guns and magic wands

Much of the superhero play involves the use of an array of weapons that include guns, lasers, swords, light sabres and knives. As with superhero play, the issue of whether to allow young children to play with toy weapons has recently become the subject of debate. As Holland (2003) has shown, from around 1960 to the early 1990s early childhood settings in Britain adopted a 'zero tolerance' approach to weapon play. Holland has argued that allowing interested children, the overwhelming majority of whom are boys, to engage in play scenarios involving imaginary weapons does not encourage violence and aggression. She has documented how in some of the settings in which the 'zero tolerance' to such play was relaxed the boys' play became more imaginative and in none of the settings was there an increase in violence.

When talking to young boys it is clear that they are aware of the difference between their toy guns and real guns:

Interviewer: Do you ever play with guns?
Neil: Yes.
Interviewer: What do you play when you are playing with guns?
Neil: I shoot people . . . I got a James Bond gun.
Interviewer: A James Bond gun? Is it a special gun in some way?
Neil: No.
Interviewer: Just an ordinary gun?
Neil: It's a toy gun.
Interviewer: A toy gun. Can you tell me what it looks like?
Neil: It's a short one and you have it like that and you have plastic missiles and you shoot it when you press the trigger and you pull the thing on the top, pull it back until it clicks and then you fire it 'cos when you pull it back until it clicks it loads.

(Interview with Neil, aged 4.0)

One child, however, rather chillingly, seemed to be aware of the fact that even pretend guns could be mistaken for real ones:

Interviewer: Is it OK to point your toy gun at somebody?
Robbie: No, not at a policeman. They might take their real gun and point it at you.
James: If he had a shield that would be better, if he had a shield.
Interviewer: When you are playing with your toy guns do you like to pretend to shoot other people?
Robbie: Yeah, but not policemans [*sic*].
(Interview with Robbie and James, aged 5.0)

While children seem to be aware of the difference between toy weapons and real weapons the fact still remains that weapons, especially guns, are seen to be signifiers of male power, not in any Freudian 'phallic' sense but merely because the majority of male heroes and superheroes rely on weapons to vanquish their foes. Heroines, in contrast, tend to rely on other means, such as magic. Girls from a very young age associate guns with boys and the vast majority of the girls I spoke to claimed to have no interest in playing with weapons, on the grounds that guns were 'for boys'. It has been argued that toy guns empower and 'embolden' the children who play with them (G. Jones 2002: 53). The majority of children who play with guns are, however, boys. The question we need to ask ourselves is: what merit is there in encouraging boys to rely on imaginary weapons to injure or annihilate their 'enemies' when they could be encouraged to think of more creative ways of overcoming their foes and fears? Running around shooting down your enemies may be exciting and emotionally satisfying in the short term but does such play enable boys to face the underlying issues? Paley has observed that:

> Boys' [play] has already masked sensitive issues. Storytelling for them is primarily a recall of superhero themes. When something makes a boy sad, he simply becomes a more powerful superhero. He is not compelled to act out confusing events, face to face, as are the girls.
> (Paley 1984: 111)

In encouraging boys to deal with difficult experiences and emotions by whipping out a toy gun surely we are inhibiting boys' opportunities to acknowledge and deal with their emotions at a deeper, more fundamental level.

It has been argued that magic wands should perhaps be viewed in the same light as guns, since they can inflict fantasy pain and even death (Holland 2003). The difference between guns and magic wands lies in the fact that magic wands can be instruments of 'good' as well as destruction and, furthermore, are not gender-specific. A child pretending to have a magic wand does not have to be a superhero or to be engaged in any fantasy involving violence. The child with a magic wand may choose to overwhelm imaginary enemies by using magic to make their foes disappear, or neutralize them by turning them into something harmless or less threatening, and may also choose to use their magic wand to 'magic' themselves away to a different place or possibly to 'magic' the appearance of a friendly animal. A child with a toy gun can only pretend to injure or kill their imaginary adversaries. Magic wands, therefore, are less likely to reinforce unequal gender-based power dynamics within the classroom and in the playground.

G. Jones (2002: 49) has asserted that 'most kids find the gun to be a far more exciting form of magic than the wand'. In his view, the children who prefer wands to guns tend to be girls rather than boys. These children 'seem to have internalized adult anxieties about guns and aggression and prefer to project their fantasy into a more unreal realm' (G. Jones 2002: 49). Alternatively, could it be that the girls Jones writes about have not as much internalized adults' anxieties about aggression and violence as experienced and participated in gendered discourses in which violence and aggression are seen as 'right' and 'natural' for boys but not for themselves, as girls?

Consequences of superhero and weapon play

I would suggest that many educators' unhappiness about boys' superhero play is not because it is violent, as children rarely hurt each other when playing (Holland 2003). What educators may find unsettling is the realization that superhero play is essentially a display of hegemonic masculinity, and therein lies the appeal for some boys. Recurring episodes of superhero play enable boys to experience repeatedly a specific type of masculine power and the emotional high that goes with this experience of power.

While the boys are experiencing power the girls and women are experiencing being dominated. The boys' superhero play, for example, reduces the girls' access to a safe area to play in which they are not at risk of being knocked over by a gang of Power Rangers intent on saving the world. Adults may also be affected by this display of masculine power. An experienced nursery assistant told me that she sometimes felt 'intimidated' by the boys when they were running around in a group and 'shooting' at her and other children from the top of the climbing frame. The question educators have to face is how to deal with this superhero play, and in the following chapters educators' views are explored in more depth.

An interesting question is whether boys 'grow out' of such play and if so, why? Jordan and Cowan (2001) have argued that most boys do indeed move away from what they have termed 'warrior narratives'. This is not because they have eschewed hegemonic masculinity but because masculinity as expressed through the warrior narratives is replaced by a different form of masculinity, but one that carries with it power and status within modern-day society. Power in modern society requires men to embrace rationality and responsibility, and boys need to learn that relinquishing emotionally satisfying warrior narratives is the price they must pay to achieve power and status in society. This particular theory is interesting and needs to be considered by those who dismiss boys' superhero play as harmless on the grounds that they grow out of it. It is possible that all that happens is that those boys who appear to grow out of it replace one form of powerful masculinity with another. The gender divide and the power relations remain intact and unchallenged.

Conclusion

It could be argued that boys' fascination with superhero play is simply a very visible manifestation of their exploration of a particular form of masculinity, which will include developing judgements about the desirability of adopting such a form rather than another. Work on developing an understanding of multiple 'femininities' and 'masculinities' with young children will free them from the 'burden of the unitary self' referred to by Davies and Banks (1995). This work will entail talking with both girls and boys about which forms of 'femininity' and 'masculinity' they find appealing and helping children to understand and come to terms with the contradictions that arise when adopting different ways of being a girl or a boy. It will involve helping children to understand the power dimensions of the different positions they choose to adopt and to consider who benefits and who suffers.

6　Reflections on what we do

This chapter focuses on 75 early years educators and their reflections on their own practice, with particular reference to how they promote and foster equality in the current context. The comments and opinions of the group cannot be interpreted as representative of early years educators throughout Britain but they do provide an insight into what some early years practitioners are currently thinking about gender issues.

'Equal opportunities': what it currently seems to mean

It was very noticeable when interviewing educators about their views and ideas about equal opportunities that they all began by focusing on the 'underachievement' of boys and how early years settings need to change and adapt their curriculum and practice to accommodate the needs of young boys. This was in marked contrast to the conversations I had with educators from the 1970s to the mid-1990s, when the emphasis and focus was on minimizing the inequalities within society and the educational system that impacted negatively on girls' achievement. When I told one headteacher that I was carrying out research on gender equity she instantly opened the conversation with comments about the boys in her nursery setting: 'We've got that big group of older boys, which is . . . quite challenging' (Nursery headteacher, female).

The concern about boys' 'underachievement' has led to boys being moved to centre stage in most discussions on gender equity. This shift in focus is a reflection of the 'moral panic' about boys' underachievement (see Introduction). That the government has taken this issue seriously is evidenced by government-supported research projects. The Department for Education and Skills (DfES), for example, funded the Raising Boys' Achievement project, a three-year project which was launched in June 2000 with the aim of identifying the 'strategies schools have employed to raise the educational standards for boys (and girls)' (DfES 2002a). The concern about boys has also been evident in media reports (Foster *et al.* 2001), although it has not only been the popular press that has promulgated the 'fact' of boys' underachievement. Professional newspapers such as the *Times Educational Supplement*, a weekly paper read by many teachers in England and Wales, have also carried articles that have high-lighted how boys are now supposedly disadvantaged by the educational sys-tem. One such article, emotively entitled 'Cowed boys and Amazons', made the claim that:

> Classroom dynamics have utterly changed. Boys are now quieter than girls – that zest for life they once had barely produces a pulse now-adays . . . [since the 1970s] we have championed the academic aspir-ations of girls, encouraging them to assert themselves. Encouraging girls in this way has led to social change – but, in the classroom, it is a change too far.
>
> (Milln 2003)

Whilst it is the 'underachievement' and perceived failings of older boys that have been of particular concern to policy-makers and wider society, educators working in early years settings have felt the backwash of these concerns. Many seem to have responded by taking a fresh look at their curriculum, their peda-gogy and their views about aspects such as superhero play and weapon play.

This shift to focusing on the boys' needs is a manifestation of the domin-ant gender discourses, which not only understand and describe gender in bin-ary terms, as 'male' or 'female', 'masculine' or 'feminine', but also place 'female' and 'male' as opposite and in opposition to each other. An extension of this conceptualization of gender categories is that 'gains' made by one group are perceived as 'losses' made by the other. In educational settings this has meant that satisfaction with the strategies implemented to improve girls' aca-demic achievement is tempered by concern that these strategies may have been 'too successful', in that girls are now achieving at the expense of the boys.

Early years educators also seem to be more willing now than they were a decade ago to contemplate the possibility that girls and boys are 'different' and articulate the view that equality strategies ought to take account of the differ-ences between girls and boys: 'I used to believe it was possible to have all that sort of equal opportunities and make sure that everybody did the same. Now we much more openly talk about how we are going to engage the boys' (Nur-sery school headteacher, female). A nursery teacher made clear that her per-ception of equal opportunities was on a more individualistic level, although when she was considering children in groups it was the boys that seemed to be uppermost in her mind:

> Nursery teacher: Equal opportunities? It's ensuring that every child is given the opportunity to develop the skills they have and to achieve

their maximum potential and believe in themselves and think they are learners and that wherever they go after they have got that in-built feeling that 'I will achieve'.

Interviewer: That's the outcome [of equal opportunities strategies]?

Nursery teacher: Yeah, so therefore we have to ensure that we actually know every child as an individual and, er, address their needs and extend their potential and make sure we develop them whether they are boy, girl, Bengali or West Indian.

Interviewer: So do you tend to look at children as individuals?

Nursery teacher: Mmm, I do. But also as groups showing common interests.

Interviewer: So what sorts of groups show common interests?

Nursery teacher: It's really strange really, it's the boys usually who show the strongest interests, I mean as an entity.

(Interview with a nursery teacher, female)

This could mean that the girls tend to be viewed as individuals with diverse interests, whereas the boys are viewed as more as part of a homogeneous group. Alternatively, since this teacher was talking about planning for children's interests, her comments could mean that planning for boys' interests is beginning to occur. Further discussion certainly seemed to suggest that while planning explicitly addressed groups of boys' interests there was less explicit planning for the girls' interests:

Interviewer: So can you tell me how this theme was chosen?

Nursery teacher: Because they were really interested in Peter Pan and telling the story and listening to the story Peter Pan and being Peter Pan which was a lot to do with jumping around and flying and fighting with swords.

Interviewer: So the 'they' is?

Nursery teacher: The group of boys who run around outside. And it was a way of anchoring them and extending their play . . . And developing an interest which they showed and we have a lot of articulate and linguistically able boys so we were looking at all the kinds of stories that go with it . . . and it's been quite successful but it's flagged a bit.

Interviewer: I'm playing devil's advocate here but what about if I was to say that that it's a very 'boys' thing' and what about the girls?

Nursery teacher: But I think the girls are really interested in playing as well. We did a lot of things that would cater . . . um . . . that got the girls really interested, like looking at fish and going to the Cutty Sark and visiting and going down to the canal and looking at barges and the environment around canals and rivers. This is difficult because we really don't think of them in terms of boys and girls although we *did* choose that topic.

(Interview with a nursery teacher, female)

Some educators adhere to the view that it is individual children who need to be considered and not their gender, 'race' or class. A very experienced nursery headteacher, for example, talked passionately about how she and her staff approached the issue of equal opportunities:

> I think our approach is very individualistic in that each child is unique and even identical twins are unique and have different needs and it's not 'one size fits all', they are not graded grains, they are not milk bottles that will all come out the same – it would make life so boring and the challenge, the excitement of working with children, having worked with primary and secondary, having started with secondary, is that you sometimes have the privilege, at this age, of seeing their minds work, because they will put into words what is going on in here [taps head] and I think sometimes you can see these dilemmas happening and they don't know where they should go and some of them, because of their nature, will just plod on and go their own way and others will just hang around and hang back and not always get involved. So it is not always about their gender, some of it is about their personality. I think of my own children and I know that is true. So, most of the time I try not to think about it, equality of opportunity. I just try to think of 60 different individuals with 60 different curriculums.
>
> (Nursery headteacher, female)

As discussed in Chapter 1, the notion of the individual has exerted, and continues to exert, a powerful influence on early years practice and this is reflected in how many early years educators attempt to facilitate gender equity. Not all educators, however, agree that viewing children as individuals is the best way forward when considering issues of gender equity:

> Interviewer: Many people say that gender is important but they always consider the individual. What would your response to that be?
> Nursery advisor: Um . . . it's a cop out. Because we send huge messages out to children about gender but we don't deal with it because we haven't got the language to deal with it and we might think we are being very liberal but actually we are not – just in terms of what people do . . . We all play with tools but that's not the reality of the world so again I don't know again whether we're trying to change the world.
>
> (Interview with nursery advisor, female)

It is clear from this last quote that some educators are aware that in order to implement effective strategies aimed at gender equity it is necessary to understand individual children by placing them within their social and cultural contexts and, in so doing, to take into account the various discourses that have an impact on children's developing sense of who they are. In mentioning the lack of language to deal with gender issues it would seem that the nursery advisor quoted above is hinting at the critical role language plays in shaping our understanding of what 'should be' and what is 'right' in terms of gender (see also Chapters 1 and 7). In talking about the 'reality of the world', this nursery advisor could understand 'reality' to be something that exists independently of language and discourses and is therefore simply acknowledging this 'reality'. On the other hand, her comment could be interpreted as meaning the 'reality' as constructed by the dominant discourses, in which case it becomes a very important point for educators to consider. If the latter interpretation is accurate, the comments made by this nursery advisor suggest that gender equity will only be achieved if children and educators are introduced to alternative discourses, discourses that enable us to look at the world through a different lens, which may, for example, lead us and the children to question the notion that girls and boys are opposite and in opposition to each other.

Educators' views about girls and boys

Work on gender equity is influenced by how educators view children in general and, more specifically, how girls and boys are perceived. A diverse group of 75 educators were interviewed face-to-face or filled in a questionnaire with the aim of discovering their views about gender issues. The group had a wide range of experience in the early years field: some were experienced practitioners, while others were students who were new to the field and some were also parents. Some of the educators were working in maintained nursery schools or classes and reception classes; others were working in the private sector as childminders or as teachers or assistants in private nursery schools or early years classes. The settings in which these educators worked ranged from multicultural inner-city nurseries in London to relatively rural, less culturally diverse settings in parts of the south-west and south-east of England. There was a wide spread of ages within the group, ranging from 18-year-old BA (Ed) students through to teachers, child-minders and nursery assistants who were in their 40s and 50s. There was only very a small group of male educators, but this reflects the proportion of men working in the field (see Chapter 8).

Given the fairly heterogeneous nature of the group it was interesting to note that the overwhelming majority of the 75 educators who answered questions about differences between girls and boys in terms of their behaviour and interests stated that there were observable differences that were related to the children's gender. Only three of the 75 educators felt that there were no observable differences in the early years and two of these commented that differences between girls and boys did not become apparent until the children were older.

The differences the educators highlighted were fairly consistent. An 18-year-old student teacher noted:

> As a norm, boys are more physical than girls and are more reluctant to sit at tables and do teacher-directed activities. As a norm, girls are more willing to express themselves in writing and drawing and do more passive activities.
>
> (BA (Ed) student teacher, female)

More experienced early childhood educators echoed this student's views. A nursery nurse with five years' experience commented that:

> Boys seem to be more practical, more energetic and take part in aggressive play. Girls are more subtle in their approach to learning and more tolerant . . . Girls can also be more academic [than boys] in the sense that they enjoy writing and reading.
>
> (Nursery nurse, female)

The nursery nurse did not explain what she meant by the girls being more 'subtle' and 'tolerant'. It is possible that she felt that girls are more tolerant of other children and less likely to become aggressive or, as her final comment suggests, that the girls are more able to tune into the curriculum and tolerate the restrictions imposed by the curriculum and classroom life. The view that boys may be less amenable than girls was expressed by a male student teacher who stated that: 'Boys are more competitive, aggressive and confrontational. Boys are more interested in competition, mathematical and logical activities. Girls are more interested in interpersonal communication and aesthetics' (student teacher, male).

Differences in girls' and boys' willingness to settle to activities, especially adult-directed activities, were commented upon by a number of respondents. An experienced child-minder observed:

> Boys generally are more physical when they interact with their peers. Girls generally are more sensible and organized, enjoying reading, writing and drawing, organizing activities and mothering younger peers.
>
> (Child-minder, female)

A student who had just embarked on her postgraduate (PGCE) training certainly believed that girls were more willing to settle to an activity than boys: 'Generalizing, the "rough" children in a classroom tend to be boys. Boys generally seem more energetic and less likely to start an activity' (student teacher, female). Many of the of the educators commented on children's ability to concentrate or their attentiveness, and all of those who chose to highlight this aspect of children's behaviour felt that girls' concentration skills were better than those of boys: 'Boys are more boisterous and interested in being noisy and running around. Girls are more able to sit and concentrate' (nursery assistant, female).

An experienced male nursery teacher commented on the differences he noticed between girls' and boys' play:

> Boys tend to, once they have detached from you as an adult, in the process of settling in they become attached to you and then become involved in their free play over a matter of weeks or months . . . I tend to see the boys in a lot of the role play, you know, superhero role play and construction. But like that's like a phase they seem to go through and again they springboard into different activity areas, particularly the sensory activities, water, sand and er . . . the girls it tends to be more a sit down or on the carpet type of activity but there is role play involved within there as well, in the home corner.
>
> (Nursery teacher, male)

Another very experienced nursery teacher also commented on gender differences in children's play:

> The boys, I think, I always see it in terms of schemas. They are more interested in where things are going, trajectories, things *going*, their bodies *going*, in things they are throwing, *going*, and they are really interested therefore in things that are going around. They need . . . they *seem* to need to expend a lot more energy and the girls will be lot more sedate and work on scenarios that they build together, they build characters and it's quite elaborate and it is based on language.
>
> (Nursery teacher, female)

It is perhaps worth noting at this point that although educators were simply asked whether 'there are any discernible differences in girls' and boys' behaviour', the majority of the respondents began by commenting on the boys. This suggests two things: that boys are uppermost in people's minds when considering gender equity issues or that boys' behaviour is understood to be the 'norm' and girls' behaviour is judged against this 'norm'.

Origins of differences between girls and boys

Although there appeared to be widespread agreement that there are discernible differences in young girls' and boys' behaviour there was no such consensus about the origin of the observed differences. A small proportion, approximately 25 per cent, of the educators that I spoke to or who filled in the questionnaire felt strongly that observed differences between girls and boys were attributable to innate factors. A young student teacher noted: 'Girls seem to have a more caring side to them, which seems to come naturally (possibly hormones and/or genes)' (student teacher, female). An experienced childminder echoed the view that gender differences have a biological base: 'A girl's motherly instinct and organizational skills [are innate], boys are built stronger for more physical work' (child-minder, female). The head of a pre-school told me that her experiences of working with young children had led her to conclude that there were natural differences between girls and boys, not least in their 'need' for physical activity and noisy play:

> We have to open the doors in the afternoon and let the boys outside. It's a nightmare when the weather is wet, the boys are running around and shouting. I don't care what people say about equal opportunities, in my experience it is natural for boys to run around, that's how their brains are made.
>
> (Head of a pre-school, female)

The majority of early years educators, however, seemed to believe that most of the differences between girls and boys were not innate and were the result of socialization or, as one respondent expressed it, 'the way they are treated at a young age'. Many educators referred to the influence of the media, family and society in general: 'I believe that behaviour is learned from those around us. Girls from their mothers and boys from their dads' (classroom assistant, female). A nursery nurse stated that differences were due to: 'how we mould our children, their environment, etc. Parents behave differently towards boys and girls' (nursery nurse, female). Other educators felt that observed behavioural differences between girls and boys might be the result of the interaction of innate influences and environmental influences:

> I think that society and the mass media have an influence, you know Barbies are for girls and Action Man for boys. And it is a Barbie *doll* and an Action Man. I have read that innately girls nurture and boys hunt but I don't know if I agree.
>
> (Early years classroom assistant, female)

The view that differences between girls and boys are a mix of innate and environmental factors has been put forward by writers such as Gurian (2001, 2002), who has used neurobiology, evolutionary and socialization theories to support his argument that male and female brains are essentially different:

> In order for the human species to survive [this] divergence of sex roles was necessary. Until about ten thousand years ago . . . humans were hunter/gathers, males being responsible for hunting (a very spatial occupation) and periphery protection and war (very aggressive occupations); females were responsible for gathering roots and other vegetation and most child care . . . Both the brain and its hormones . . . came to differ with gender . . . Human environmental socialization tended to enhance these tendencies in those cultures that required greater difference.
>
> (Gurian 2001: 39)

The validity of Gurian's assertion must surely be brought into question by the fact that he is happy to draw on two conflicting theories, evolutionary theory and creationist theory, in order to support his argument:

> Evolutionary biologists believe our brains differ by gender because it has been necessary in human evolution for humans to divide up tasks by gender. If your personal religious convictions make evolution distasteful to you, then the evolutionary theory can be changed into 'God created us this way'.
>
> (Gurian 2001: 38)

Although only a quarter of the educators I surveyed felt that differences between girls and boys were innate, this, from my personal experience, is a higher proportion than those who expressed such a view in the 1980s an early 1990s. At this point it is worth reflecting for a moment on the possible reason for the increase in educators who believe that the observed gender differences are innate. A conversation with a very experienced nursery teacher provided a clue as to why some early years educators who had previously been very committed to 'equal opportunities' have become somewhat disheartened about this particular aspect of their work.

Interviewer: Would you say, since you talked about boys' *need* to run around and you've talked about *boys'* energy levels, do you think that it is something innate?
Nursery teacher: I've grown to think it is.
Interviewer: Could you tell me what you used to think and why you've changed your mind?

Nursery teacher: Well I've always thought that girls and boys were exactly the same and it was a cultural thing, the way mothers handled them etcetera but looking at . . . I've got two daughters and they were very much into those things we talked about, small role play . . . But anyway, I've seen boys of friends, my friends have actually bought dolls for their boys and were going to educate them in a completely feminist way and the same thing happened. The boys were into Batman and rushing around, doing this kind of thing, having swords and guns and wanting to hit at things and . . . um, I think, this is going to sound really sexist!

Interviewer: No, no, no, I was just interested because I think there is an increasing move towards the view that perhaps culture isn't the explanation but I was just wondering how far back we can go in terms of culture. Because you say that parents treat children differently and they treat them differently from the day they are born and others treat them differently . . .

Nursery teacher: Yeah, I'm sure . . . it's difficult, it's really difficult . . .

Interviewer: I'm really trying to get to grips with this thing of just how innate it is or what the balance is or whatever.

Nursery teacher: And also all this so-called brain research is showing that boys and girls are different as well, and that's just putting more mud in the pond isn't it?

Interviewer: So are you keeping up to date with the brain research.

Nursery teacher: Very vaguely. And all that business about boys producing more adrenaline and the hunter. [Laughs]

Interviewer: You're laughing – do you not agree with the view?

Nursery teacher: I don't know, I think because it is brain research it is taken terribly seriously and actually it's the same as any old research and we should be quite wary of it and wonder who is doing it and why they're doing it.

Interviewer: So why do you think they might be doing it?

Nursery teacher: I don't know because I think the men are, at the moment are feeling really threatened in society because of the way that women actually are taking a much greater role . . .

(Interview with nursery teacher, female)

This conversation is particularly interesting because it illustrates how, and why, experienced educators may begin to change their minds about the validity and effectiveness of their work on gender equity. For this particular teacher, observations of children led her to conclude that even if the parents were trying to adhere to 'feminist' principles, the children seemed to sabotage the adults' efforts and engaged in stereotypical gender-specific play. These observations, coinciding with the growing respectability of the notion of biological determinism, seem to have led her to question her previously held view that culture and socialization played a key role in determining and maintaining stereotypically gendered ways of being. Furthermore, although by her own admission she is not up to date with the scientific research into brain differences and is somewhat sceptical about the work itself and the underlying motives, she has none the less been influenced by it.

This nursery teacher was not alone in her disenchantment with past approaches to equal opportunities, as the following extract from a conversation with a nursery headteacher illustrates:

Headteacher: I used to think you could put all children together and provided you gave them the same experiences and dressed them all in pink they would all love Barbie but you know, all those things about how you use language you pick up a baby girl and say, 'Isn't she beautiful?' and you pick up a baby boy and say, 'Isn't he strong?' which you know goes on . . . so there are real cultural differences. And I see children here by 3 are completely identified by gender and the notion that you can do much about that is pretty hard, not realistic I think.

Interviewer: So you do you think the identification by gender is something the children come to learn because of the way they are treated rather than something to do with their brains or . . .?

Headteacher: I don't know enough about their brains. I think there has been some research about that . . . but I don't think you have to know huge amounts about research to know that there are differences in the way children approach their learning. So I suppose sensibly one would think there must be something neurological because people have tried very hard to be, you know to change that, with their girls, to make sure they are playing with trains, which is all gender typed anyway but those sorts of things and it's just not on. So all you can do is work with it.

(Interview with nursery headteacher, female)

Recourse to biological explanations does not satisfy many educators who have been working on equal opportunities and who have felt that the work has not been successful. One nursery advisor talked about the lack of clarity felt by many of her colleagues when she reflected that:

you sort of get the feeling that everyone wants everybody to be the same which is not realistic either. We want them [children] to be the same but people are also saying that boys and girls are very different so that's where I think, 'What do we think really?'

(Nursery advisor, female)

Gender equity strategies

The views that educators hold about the range, flexibility, universality and cause of observed differences in the behaviour of young girls and boys will obviously have an impact on the gender equity strategies that individual educators feel comfortable about implementing and will also have an impact on the gender equity policies of settings. For example, educators who believe that gender differences are innate, in other words those who have adopted a biological deterministic approach, will have little interest in developing strategies that enable girls and boys to position themselves in a variety of ways and explore a range of 'femininities' and 'masculinities'. Such educators, however, are likely to view deviations from accepted gender norms as a cause for concern.

In contrast, educators who believe that children learn about gender through mimicking those around them and receiving positive reinforcement and 'moulding' are advocates of the sex-role socialization theory, and may decide to adopt strategies that include providing non-stereotypical role models (e.g. female teachers at the woodwork bench and male teachers in the home corner), ensuring that books and other resources show girls and boys and women and men engaged in a broad variety of occupations and activities, many of which are 'non-sexist', and expressing a wide range of emotions. These educators are also likely to argue strongly for the need to employ more men in early years settings to provide good male role models, especially for those children who do not have such a male role model at home (see Chapter 8).

Those educators who argue that children learn about gender through the discourses to which they have access will probably believe that the aforementioned strategies are likely to be unsuccessful in the long run. This is because the strategies fail to take account of how children position themselves and are positioned by others through engagement in different discourses. Furthermore, the aforesaid strategies do not acknowledge the emotional investment children have in taking up particular forms of 'femininity' or 'masculinity' in different contexts – in this instance the early years setting.

Reflecting on how educators respond to enduring issues within the early years setting, such as language use and children's friendship patterns, provides a deeper insight into the educators' views and also highlights possible ways in which to move forward regarding gender equity in early years settings.

Language and gender

The issue of language use in the early years has been examined in the past (Browne and France 1985) but strategies aimed at modifying how we talk to children and how we talk about children have had only limited success in furthering gender equity. This is because, although language plays a major part in constructing the world, creating categories and ways of thinking about and analysing one's experiences, a focus on language alone can fail to take account of the relationships and interactions that take place within specific discourses. It is these interactions and relationships that add depth to the meaning of words and help to determine children's emotional attachment to different 'ways of being'. Thus, talking about 'children' rather than 'boys', as many do when discussing the issue of superhero play (see Chapter 7), does not change the gender-based power relations that operate through such play activities – it merely serves to conceal the existence of the exercise of power.

The classroom assistant who talked about how Barbie dolls are always described as 'dolls' whereas Action Man dolls are described as Action 'men' had begun to explore the role that language plays in creating a 'reality' in which the power relations between girls and boys, women and men, are unequal. Not only are boys not 'supposed' to play with toy dolls but the toy figures that the children play with emphasize the power differential: males are powerful, muscular, aggressive men and females are pretty women but essentially nothing more than dolls.

Early years educators described girls and boys in very different ways. Words and phrases used to describe girls included 'chatty', 'eager to please', 'interested in neat presentation', 'calm' and 'attentive'. Boys were described as 'noisy', 'boisterous', 'find it hard to sit still', 'physical', 'competitive', 'interested in exploring things' and 'liking sports'. This finding suggests that the majority of the educators involved in this piece of research hold the view that girls and boys are not only different from each other but also opposites. The gender binary divide shines through clearly in the educators' language. Educators clearly have to consider very carefully how the gendered discourses they are drawing on to interpret children's behaviour may influence not only what is 'seen' but also the nature of the strategies they put into place in an effort to ensure gender equity within the setting.

Children's friendship patterns: the adults' views

In Chapter 4 the children's views about playmate preferences were explored, and the issue of educators' attitudes towards young children's friendship patterns is worth considering here.

Conversations with educators and the written responses to the survey questions revealed how most of the adults were placing children on either side of the binary divide, in other words categorizing them as either girls or boys and highlighting the 'fact' that girls and boys are different from each other. Children's play partner preference was one way in which this binary divide was exemplified. Children's play partner preferences were also seen to validate the view that girls and boys are different from each other. A teaching assistant who felt that children only showed a preference for same-sex friends at around the age of 6 or 7 attributed this pattern of friendship to: 'the way they [children] think, the games they play, how they interact and the beginnings of the realization that boys and girls are different' (teaching assistant, female).

When I was researching for this book, I asked practitioners about the age at which children started to play with children of the same sex as themselves. It was interesting to discover that half of the respondents believed that this gender-based pattern of playmate choice does not begin to happen until after the age of 5. A small group of practitioners asserted that this gender-based pattern of friendship is not apparent until the children were 6 or 7 years old. The majority of the remaining half believed that children begin to prefer same-sex friends at around the age of 3 to 4. A very small minority felt that children under the age of 2 show a preference for same-sex playmates. There was a diversity of opinion among practitioners with regard to the reasons for the children's preferences for same-sex playmates. A commonly expressed view was that the children's choice of same-sex playmates was due to their growing awareness of their gender identity: 'They start to define themselves by what groups they are in – "I'm a girl" – and they notice differences between children' (student teacher, female). Some felt that girls and boys have different interests and argued that children were more likely to choose a same-sex playmate because, as one classroom assistant wrote, 'Maybe they perceive they have the same interests.' A very experienced nursery nurse commented. 'Boys' and girls' interests are different. For example, boys like the superhero type play and girls like the fantasy play, princesses and mummy and baby role play' (nursery nurse, female).

A student teacher who had worked as a nanny for two years felt that the friendship patterns might be due to the impact of organizational factors in early years settings:

> At this age [5 to 6 years old] in school children are made aware of the fact that their class (single sex schools excluded) is made up of two groups: boys and girls. They wear different uniforms so children prefer someone who is 'one of them'.
>
> (Student teacher, female)

Another student teacher who believed that same-sex playmate preference was not evident until the end of Key Stage 1 (i.e. around the age of 7) felt that children's playmate preferences were influenced by cultural and social pressures: 'Children begin to realize the differences between themselves and others and often due to stereotyping certain activities are geared towards one sex only and therefore they play with children of the same sex' (student teacher, female). Other educators mentioned the impact of other people's responses to children's personal choices: 'They probably show a preference for same-sex playmates because otherwise they would probably get bullied or teased by others' (student teacher, female). The issue of the role language plays in maintaining gender divisions was only mentioned very occasionally, and no comment was made about how language and interactions (i.e. discourse) created gender division in the first place: 'They can empathize with those with similar physical characteristics and parents and society perpetuate gender division in everyday talk and actions' (student teacher, male).

Research into young children's play partner preferences tends to suggest that from around the age of 3 children seem to prefer same-sex play partners (Thorne 1986; Lloyd and Duveen 1992; Macoby 1998; Martin and Fabes 2001). In the late 1980s research by Macoby and Jacklin highlighted young children's preferences for same-sex playmates (Macoby and Jacklin 1987, cited in Macoby 1998). This piece of research showed that at the age of 4 and a half children will spend three times as much time playing with children of the same sex as with children of the 'opposite' sex. By the age of 6 and a half children will spend eleven times as much time playing with same-sex playmates as those of the 'opposite' sex. More recently, Martin and Fabes (2001) investigated the same-sex peer interactions of 61 children aged from 3 years to 6 years in three pre-school classes. They found that 90 per cent of the girls in their study played more with girls than with boys, while 45 per cent of the girls played almost exclusively with other girls. Similar patterns were found among the boys, of whom 82 per cent played more with other boys than with girls and 35 per cent played almost exclusively with other boys.

The educators' comments would seem to suggest that adults were conscious of the children's play patterns. Furthermore, the adults also seem to believe that these play patterns not only demonstrate that young children categorize themselves as either girls or boys but also that the children see the two groups as being very different from each other. Moreover, the adults' comments suggest that they think that children believe that membership of one group precludes membership of the other. The children I spoke to were very clear that one could be either a girl or a boy (Chapter 4), but it could be argued that the children's world-view was being shaped and influenced by the discourses to which they had access. Research by Lloyd and Duveen (1992) showed that gender is used regularly by teachers as a social category, which leads to the gender marking of activities, spaces and behavioural styles. Even more interestingly, they found that teachers' use of the terms 'girls' and 'boys' provided young children with rather confusing messages about the salience of gender as a social marker. So, for example, teachers will say 'Boys! Stop shouting!' but then will tell the children: 'We don't have girls only tables.' If the adults who work with young children, through their use of language and their day-to-day interactions with the children, convey the message that gender is an important distinction and furthermore is a binary category with no move-ment between the two sub-categories, female and male, it ought not to sur-prise us that young children may begin to develop the same view of gender. None of the educators mentioned strategies that they used to encourage girls and boys to play together, although many talked about the need for girls and boys to play with non-stereotyped toys and to engage in non-stereotypical activities. One educator stated: 'In an "equal opportunities" society all chil-dren should be encouraged to take part in all activities whatever stereotyped label it may have' (early years classroom assistant, female). This suggests that there is a belief that the division by gender is natural and harmless, but what is important is that children are encouraged to engage in activities traditionally associated with the 'opposite' sex.

Educators, such as the one quoted below, who appear to find Kohlberg's cognitive-developmental theory persuasive are likely to believe that girls are motivated to play with girls and boys with boys because it helps them to develop their gender identity: 'It has been well researched that no matter what practitioners and adults do, gender-stereotyped play will continue. It's about role modelling, girls like to be like Mummy and boys like to be like Daddy and it is innate' (reception class teacher, female).

It is worth considering the implications of single-sex play within the con-text of furthering gender equity. Martin and Fabes (2001) have argued that their research findings suggest that children who spend more time with same-sex peers have more opportunities to engage in 'gender-related' behaviours and, furthermore, children who spend more time with same-sex peers experi-ence more pressure to conform to gender-related behaviours. In addition, they have argued that play in same-sex peer groups serves to intensify the segrega-tion of girls and boys. In other words, the segregation by sex becomes a self-perpetuating cycle because the children's play experiences serve to encourage the children to develop behaviour patterns that 'the other sex' finds uninteresting. As a result, girls and boys become less likely to interact with one another:

> for both boys and girls, playing with same-sex peers contributed to tendencies to engage in gender-typed behaviours that went beyond the initial individual tendencies to do so . . . The findings support the conclusion that the experiences children have with same-sex peers have later consequences for how they behave and interact. Time spent with same-sex peers sets powerful forces in motion that affect children's subsequent development.
>
> (Martin and Fabes 2001: 444)

While it is clear that Martin and Fabes appear to accept that gender is a binary category, as is evidenced by comments such as 'the other sex', it is possible to reflect on how their research findings map on to the theories that focus on the way in which discourses enable children to make sense of who they are and their position in the world. The 'powerful forces' that Martin and Fabes refer to may not be socialization forces in that the children are simply socialized by their peers into adopting specific behaviours. The 'forces' could be the discourses to which the children have access while engaged in playing with their same-sex peers. A group of friends who are girls, for example, may be coming to understand what it means to be a girl through their involvement in discourses in which 'femininity' is signified by certain clothes, an interest in domestic play and being kind and caring. If these girls continue to play only with other members of the friendship group they may lack access to alternative discourses with alternative conceptualizations of 'femininity' and few opportunities to explore other ways of being a girl that may be emotionally satisfying. The result will be not only that this group of girls will not have to question their understanding of 'femininity' but also that their emotional investment in this particular gender positioning will be high. Furthermore, it could be argued that in this particular case the girls would come to understand that power for females resides in the domestic sphere, perhaps located in the mother. For these girls the female/male divide will remain unchallenged, as will the power relations between girls and boys. These girls will not have had the opportunity to position themselves as girls in a wide range of other ways.

In essence, children's friendship groups may have a powerful effect on their developing understanding of gender, in that involvement in particular groups may open up children's access to a range of discourses, some of which will be contradictory and challenging, or alternatively may close down access to certain discourses. Since we can only understand ourselves and others through the discourses we experience, educators need to consider whether children's friendship groups are limiting or broadening access to alternative discourses. Duveen (1993) has argued that the positions children adopt at any one point in time have consequences for their gender identities in the future. This argument is particularly pertinent when one considers research findings that show that, in the first year of schooling, same-sex peer grouping is less likely to occur when children are engaged in adult-organized activities and that boys are more likely than girls to spend time in same-sex groups (Lloyd and Duveen 1992). These research findings, coupled with theoretical explanations of the ways in which gender identity develops, suggest that early years educators should seriously consider whether same-sex peer grouping should be accepted as a fact of life, encouraged and facilitated. Alternatively, adults may have a role to play in helping children to gain access to alternative discourses and 'ways of being' by judiciously and sensitively disrupting the customary patterns of same-sex peer groups. The unwillingness to 'interfere' in young children's play is rooted in the dominant pedagogical early years discourse that places great emphasis on children developing 'naturally' but, as discussed in Chapter 1, what is termed as developmentally appropriate practice is often not conducive to the exploration of gender issues.

This chapter has explored educators' views about 'equal opportunities', their ideas about the differences and similarities between groups of girls and boys and their views about children's friendship patterns. The following chapter looks in more depth at educators' ideas about certain gender equity strategies and the changing attitudes towards superhero and war and weapon play in early years settings.

7 'Recuperative masculinity' strategies and superhero play

This chapter focuses on a certain category of gender equity strategies, those that are referred to as 'recuperative masculinity strategies'. It explores how facilitating superhero, war and weapon play in early years settings can be viewed as a 'recuperative masculinity' strategy, and the implications of this for gender equity within early years settings.

Boys' underachievement became a burning issue in the mid-1990s, leading to a 'moral panic' (Foster *et al.* 2001). Central government became involved in the debates and boys' underachievement became the focus of gender equality issues in schools and policy documents (Foster *et al.* 2001). In the summer of 2000, David Blunkett, Education and Employment Secretary, commented that the 'gap that has opened up between the sexes at school is a long-standing one and an international problem for which there is no quick fix, but I am determined that our boys should not miss out' (DfES 2000b).

It is not the intention here to discuss the validity of the claim that boys are 'underachieving', as this has been explored in great depth by others (e.g. Epstein 1998; Foster *et al.* 2001; Rowan *et al.* 2002). What is of interest here is the response to the anxiety about boys' achievement at school in the light of debates about the causes of this 'underachievement'. Epstein (1998) has discussed how the cause of boys' 'underachievement' has been linked with three dominant discourses about boys: 'poor boys' or 'laddishness', 'boys will be boys' and 'failing boys, failing schools'. It is the first two discourses that have particular relevance to early childhood settings.

The 'laddishness' alluded to by Blunkett (DfES 2000b) or 'poor boys' discourse views boys as victims who are 'underachieving' as a result of the impact of feminism on society and developments in pedagogic practice aimed at achieving greater educational equality for girls. In addition, the 'femininity' of early childhood settings are seen to favour girls and impede boys' progress, an issue that is discussed later in this chapter and in the following chapter.

Within the 'boys will be boys' discourse, boys are understood in traditional ways, in that they are seen to be different from girls, not least in their levels of aggression, their physicality and their interests. Boys' behaviour is characterized by high levels of activity and noisiness, a tendency towards aggression, the need for competition and short-term goals. Such stereotypical views about boys owe much to the view that girls and boys differ because of innate differences (see Chapter 2). The weakness in this view is that it relies on biological determinism and there is a tendency to perceive boys as a homogeneous category. As with the 'laddish' discourse, the 'boys will be boys' discourse positions boys as victims in an education system that is best geared to the needs of girls.

One response to both of these discourses has been to introduce strategies that draw on boys' interests in order to motivate and involve them in learning. Such strategies have been described as 'recuperative masculinity' strategies (Lingard and Douglas 1999), in that they seek to reinstate a particular form of 'masculinity'. Furthermore, 'recuperative' approaches are positioned in opposition to feminist strategies (Ailwood and Lingard 2001).

One resource for older children that has resulted from 'recuperative masculinity' strategies is a book entitled *The Chelsea Bunny* (Blum 2002). This book was written to support the literacy development of older 'reluctant readers', particularly boys. The publicity states:

> the stories are a quirky satire on the 'macho values' that a lot of boys and increasingly, some girls, bring into the classroom with them . . . [and is] especially suitable for reluctant readers who have given up hope that they would ever read anything that dares admit to the bravado and violent swagger of their adolescent sub-culture.

The rabbit in question has poor reading and writing skills and

> flicks paper at his mates, reads his book upside down and shouts out the names of all his favourite footballers, rather than getting on with his work.
>
> In his spare time he's out at matches, brawling with other teams' supporters . . . Every time he loses his temper, which is almost on every page, he head butts the nearest object. Floors, walls, tables and other football supporters come in for some rough treatment!

One problem with such resources lies in the fact that they appear to treat boys as a uniform group in assuming that their interests will be the same, in this case football. Furthermore, such resources seem not to acknowledge the concept of multiple and diverse 'masculinities' and instead utilize a traditional view of 'masculinity': violent, aggressive and confrontational. One can also not take it for granted that the boys reading such books will understand the satire, in which case it will seem to the boys, and girls, that such 'macho' behaviour is not merely accepted but also celebrated. After all, when all is said and done, 'boys will be boys'. While the books may amuse some boys and motivate them to learn to read, we need to ask hard questions about what else they, and their peers who are girls, are learning about 'masculinity' and 'femininity'.

There are possible parallels between resources such as *The Chelsea Bunny* and the moves to facilitate superhero and weapon play in early years settings. It could be argued that facilitating such play draws on both the 'boys will be boys' and 'poor boys' discourses, in that it could be seen as an example of how early years educators are introducing changes to their early years provision in order to engage the boys.

When I discussed superhero and weapon play with a male nursery teacher it was clear that he had few doubts about whether or not boys should be allowed to engage in such play:

> Teacher: I have my own personal views about that sort of thing. Children . . . *boys* should pursue it because it's their needs and their interest and they want to pursue it and step outside of it and come back into it again.
> Interviewer: Why do boys need it?
> Teacher: Erm . . . probably, they . . . are spending a small amount of time with us and maybe the environment they are in at home or amongst cousins or other friends where that is . . . er . . . not so much encouraged but the environment is right for those boys to do it. They might have the swords and the knives which may come down from parents or as gifts whereas in school we wouldn't have those as such, a child would have to use a toilet roll as a dagger or a Lego gun, they are not mirroring but extending what is happening outside.
>
> (Nursery teacher, male)

This teacher could have meant that boys need superhero and weapon play because 'that's how boys are', and while the outside school environment simply recognizes the essential nature of boys, the school tends to attempt to deny or ignore it. It is also possible to interpret the teacher's comments slightly differently. It would seem that while this teacher has stopped short of stating that boys are biologically pre-programmed to need such play he is none the less hinting that early years settings should take account of the interests that boys bring into the setting. He does not talk about 'discourses' but his comment that 'the environment is right for the boys to do it' could imply that the discourses within which the boys are situated outside the school environment encourage them to engage in superhero and weapon play, as it is 'right for those boys'.

Those who treat the biological explanations with caution argue that educators need to acknowledge and value children's home experiences (e.g. their cultural heritage, their patterns of interaction with parents and how early experiences within the family may influence young children's play prefer-ences). Research by Macoby and Jacklin (1983) into how parents played with their 45-month-old children revealed that three times as much rough play occurred between fathers and sons as between mothers and daughters. Macoby concluded that the findings of this study were consistent with the research findings of others (e.g. Leaper and Gleason 1996) who had indicated that parents play more roughly with boys than with girls and offer them 'sex-typed' toys, which maintain 'sex-appropriate' play themes (Macoby 1998: 125). There is, however, only minimal evidence to support the assertion that children's experiences with their parents 'will lodge in the child's psyche as a stable personality trait called masculinity or femininity which in turn shapes a child's play with her or his peers' (Macoby 1998: 126). In view of these findings it is not possible to argue convincingly that girls and boys come to early childhood settings already socialized into preferring 'sex-appropriate' play themes, in this instance superhero and weapon play for boys. I would argue that the research of Macoby and Jacklin (1983) and Leaper and Gleason (1996) supports the view that young children's understandings of 'femininity' and 'masculinity' are not set in stone by the time children enter early years settings, and therefore early years educators need to consider how to broaden all children's horizons by offering alternative ways of being 'feminine' and 'masculine'.

Recently, some of the liveliest and most revealing conversations I have had with educators were those that involved discussion of superhero and weapon play. This is possibly because debates about this particular aspect of early years practice are relatively new and involve educators in having to consider carefully their views on gender. Boys' involvement in superhero and weapon play, for example, could be an example of how a group's play may limit the exploration of different forms of 'masculinity'. A nursery advisor seemed to be aware of this when she was asked whether boys' desire to engage in superhero play was a phase that they simply grew out of:

Interviewer: So would you imagine that boys, if they were allowed to engage in superhero play, gunplay, whatever, would eventually come through it and not want to play it any more or do you think they would want to play it throughout their childhood?

Nursery advisor: [Long pause] It depends on so many things because some of them aren't allowed to play anything else either. People like to see them playing that because that's what boys are supposed to do and they get strong messages that they are not supposed to play with the dolls, and people thought that was less so these days but I'm not too sure about that.

Interviewer: You mean outside school?

Nursery advisor: Yes, parents and family. They say 'Does he play with any boys?' If boys are playing with girls, they do not like it at all and I think there is a really big homophobic part to it as well and I think that is what a lot of it is about. So parents don't like their sons to be that kind of 'masculine' but I'm not sure what they want, or what *we* want boys to be at all. More gentle or something. We don't like violence but on the other hand we are not helping them either, we don't give them any images. You know how you say does your mum have a saw at home? 'No, my dad does.' It's very difficult to get over those strong stereotypes because that's what they see.

(Interview with nursery advisor, female)

Although this nursery advisor talked about 'images' it is also possible to understand her comments in relation to discourses. This educator, like the male teacher quoted above, was suggesting that, for some boys, the principal discourses within which they are situated are those in which 'masculinity' is understood in terms of being strong, tough, non-nurturing and heterosexual. She seemed to be suggesting that for these boys, the absence of other 'images', for which I would substitute discourses, makes it difficult for the boys to adopt or explore other forms of masculinity.

Educators are clearly endeavouring to make sense of the various theories about the process of gendering and the range of discourses that give rise to diverse 'femininities' and 'masculinities'. This is illustrated in the following extract from a conversation, which is worth quoting at length as we see the nursery teacher articulating her ideas about the issue of power and super-hero play and grappling with some of the contradictions in her own thinking.

Nursery teacher: Maybe that's why they [boys] need the large group play, because they feel secure and powerful as part of a group. And running around is not something that adults do either so they are doing their own thing and therefore being in charge and considering their own power in that way.

Interviewer: So, if I was to play devil's advocate here and say that you've acknowledged to a certain extent that it could be to do with an exploration of power . . .

Nursery teacher: Mmmm.

Interviewer: And that in running around in big groups they are developing that notion of power. Are you not then supporting the idea that actually boys are powerful?

Nursery teacher: No, because I think a little girl playing in the home corner and doing the washing up and playing with a doll and being a mother is exploring power in that she sees her mother's power over her and over the family as the household's most powerful person, because I think women tend to be. Because they are in charge of all the machines, they are in charge of what comes into the house and feeding the family etc., which is an awfully big source of power. So they're exploring power in the same way.

Interviewer: But that's very domestic, isn't it? A very small sphere. These boys, you could say, are exploring power in a much bigger sense, on a wider canvas, and isn't that what . . .

Nursery teacher: No, I actually think that the girls playing in the home corner exercise more power than the boys running around outside and that if boys and girls play together in the home corner, which they do, the girls are always in charge and telling who's going to be who and what's going to happen and devising the scenario.

Interviewer: Okay, so in the home corner the girls are very powerful.

Nursery teacher: And outside as well . . .

Interviewer: If they are playing that kind of role . . .

Nursery teacher: Yeah.

Interviewer: If it's say Power Rangers that the children are playing and a girl wants to join in, who exercises the power then as to whether or not she can join in?

Nursery teacher: I think they are all fairly equal. The girl who would actually come in and play would be an equal. I think the way Sarah would be . . .

Interviewer: Do you think Sarah was unusual?

Nursery teacher: Yes . . . she would also be the leader actually.

Interviewer: So she was unusual. But the 'average' girl, if we can talk about an average girl, what do you think would happen?

Nursery teacher: They either don't get involved or they just come in on a par with the other children.

Interviewer: So coming back to this exploration of power, because I think it's really interesting, because it's one of the big issues isn't it, this notion of who exercises power on a big scale, I'm not talking about the domestic front, but who is it that actually exercises power in certain workplaces, politics, the world?

Nursery teacher: Yeah, so the boys are practising that role you think, running around and . . .

Interviewer: Or do you think that's too far fetched a view? I mean they don't know they're practising it . . .

Nursery teacher: But if you see the Houses of Parliament as that kind of 'big, all boys together' as a group . . . that's the same thing . . . I would tend to agree.

Interviewer: So, if you think that . . .

Nursery teacher: Do we agree that is a genetic thing? Is it something that is built in?

Interviewer: If it's a genetic thing, *if* it is, does that mean we're going to be like this for ever more so we might as well not bother and we just need to accept that when we talk about what an individual's achieving, what they are capable of, we need to say, 'Yes, but capable of as women . . . capable of as a man'? Or do we say it's not genetic and it's cultural or whatever else and we don't know where it's coming from but, for whatever reason, we are just going to go along with it and it will just go on to repeat itself in the next generation and the next generation?

Nursery teacher: But the thing is I've worked trying *not* to let boys work in that sort of way and it doesn't seem to work . . . it sounds really sexist.

Interviewer: No, no, no it's very interesting.

Nursery teacher: And when you allow them to develop those things they seem to explore it for a long, long time.

Interviewer: Do you think they grow out of it? I'm thinking about age . . . is 3 to 5 a key age for this?

Nursery teacher: Possibly, it would be interesting to follow children and see what they play but it's skewed because in the primary school they are not allowed to explore any of their interests, so looking at their play in the playground would be the only time when they could actually . . . but then they might go into football or something which is actually the same thing as Power Rangers . . .

(Interview with nursery teacher, female)

In this conversation this nursery teacher is striving to clarify her own thinking and in so doing uncovers some ambiguities and contradictions, which she then tries to make sense of. She starts by considering the possibility that boys' attraction to superhero and weapon play may be attributable to their search for security and feelings of power that they gain through playing in a large group, which, in her nursery, characterizes this type of play. Her view was echoed by a nursery advisor who, when talking about boys engaged in superhero play, said: 'They [the boys] obviously needed something emotional, maybe it was about male bonding, I don't know' (nursery advisor, female). This observation is particularly interesting in view of the final statement made by the nursery teacher, in which she reflects on the possibility that as the boys grow older they simply replace superhero play with football, which is 'the same thing as Power Rangers'. The nursery teacher's ideas about the transition from superhero play to sport is important, as it reflects current thinking about the link between the physical expression of masculinity in both superhero play or 'warrior narratives' and sport.

'Warrior narratives' have been described as those in which the use of violence by males is viewed as legitimate in the struggle between forces of good and evil (Jordan and Cowan 2001). The males in these 'warrior narratives' are frequently superheroes, 'goodies', who are often supported in their mission by a loyal group of supporters who will help in the fight against the criminal, monster or other such 'baddie'. It has been argued that the type of masculinity that is expressed through warrior narratives is also expressed in many male-dominated sports (Messner *et al.* 1999; Jordan and Cowan 2001; Messner 2001). While this view does not clarify whether the boys' 'need' for superhero play is innate, Jordan and Cowan's arguments highlight the possibility that many boys learn that 'the deeply appealing masculinity of the warrior narratives can still be experienced through symbolic re-enactment on the sports field' (Jordan and Cowan 2001: 114).

It could be argued that sport is a healthy activity and one that we should be encouraging children to engage in. While on one level this is undoubtedly true we also need to consider the discourses of sport and what versions of 'masculinity' and 'femininity' tend to prevail. Analysis of sports programming in the USA highlighted the consistent use of military metaphors and warlike language to describe sports action involving men and boys (Messner *et al.* 1999). Furthermore, sports programmes on television carry the message that a 'real man' is aggressive, combative, strong and willing to fight other men (Messner *et al.* 1999: 11). There is insufficient space here to discuss sport and 'masculinity', but the nursery teacher's comment about the link between Power Rangers and football suggests that early years educators are conscious of a possible association between superhero play and sport. Educators may feel that this link becomes more apparent when they reflect on how boys' football games in the primary school playground can occupy most of the space available and compare this to the effects of superhero play in the nursery garden:

> that's the really interesting thing as well, the way that the boys actually physically dominate the space outside . . . but this is really difficult because at the moment we have a really large group of boys and only about four or five full-time girls , and the group of boys we have at the moment are very interested in those games [superhero play], all the time.
>
> (Nursery teacher, female)

This physical domination of space is an illustration of the unequal gendered power relations.

The foregoing discussion suggests that adopting 'recuperative' strategies and not introducing children, both boys and girls, to discourses in which 'masculinity' and 'femininty' are constructed in other ways may mean that the version of 'masculinity' that characterizes superhero play is not overtly challenged and does not disappear, but merely rematerializes in the playground in the form of football games. Jordan and Cowan claim that 'The mantle of the warrior is inherited by the sportsman' (Jordan and Cowan 2001: 105). Why should there be a problem with this? Is it not 'safer' for boys to engage in sports than to continue to be fascinated with superhero and weapon play? The answer may be yes if sport were an apolitical activity that played no part in maintaining the existing patterns of gender relations. Messner (2001), however, has argued convincingly that organized sport is not only a 'gendered institution' that reflects 'dominant conceptions of masculinity and femininity' but is also a 'gendering institution', in that it contributes to the construction of the current gender order by, for example, the ' "masculinizing" of male bodies and minds' (Messner 2001: 97–8).

We need to help children to become conscious of the diverse forms of masculinity and acknowledge that certain activities, while enjoyable for those engaged in them, may also have much to do with gender issues and discourses of power. In view of what has been noted earlier about the impact of same-sex peer groups, it is possible to argue that the facilitation of a form of play that tends to encourage same-sex groups needs very careful consideration. With this in mind it is worth noting that all the early years educators who responded to questions about the desirability of gender-stereotyped play stated that such play should not be encouraged (although a very small minority seemed to suggest that it was inevitable). When these same educators were asked whether superhero play should be permitted in early years settings many of those who had made strong statements about the need to discourage gender-stereotyped play seem to take a completely different stance, as the following comments illustrate:

> Superhero play should be allowed as they should be encouraged to use their own imagination. If this helps it should be allowed.
>
> (Nursery supervisor, assistant, female)

> This is a form of role play for them so should be allowed. Circle time can be used to explain about the behaviour in society as a whole.
>
> (Early years classroom assistant, female)

> I see no reason why boys and girls should not be allowed to indulge in this type of play. I know it is TV that influences this type of play.
>
> (Reception teacher, female)

The use of the word 'children' or 'they' was typical of the responses to this questions, and would seem to suggest that the overwhelming majority of educators glossed over the fact that such play is generally engaged in by boys. The only educator who explicitly mentioned both girls and boys had specifically stated earlier that: 'Boys and girls are different, boys like superhero play . . . girls like creative drawing . . . boys like superheroes' (reception teacher, female).

Much, although not all, superhero play involves the use of weapons of some description, and when educators were asked about war and weapon play it was revealing to note that those who were in favour of superhero play were less positive about play involving toy weapons and toy guns:

> I strongly disagree that children should be allowed to play with toy guns and toy weapons. These items represent things that kill adults and children and cause massive suffering to others.
>
> (Pre-school supervisor, female)
>
> I do not have guns and weapons as such in my setting. It is difficult to prevent them making them out of Lego bricks or using their fingers. When this happens we discuss with the children about guns.
>
> (Reception class teacher, female)

A few educators were in favour of allowing children to play with toy weapons and guns but were unclear about the benefits and justified their stance by referring rather vaguely to research findings: 'Pilot projects on this have shown that children (especially boys) can gain a lot from this type of role play – that's what it is to them' (early years classroom assistant, female). Educators' difficulty in constructing a coherent argument in favour of superhero and toy weapon play suggests that this is an area of early years provision that needs very careful deliberation, especially when considering the ways in which such play may contribute to the maintenance of unequal gender power relations and 'traditional' forms of 'masculinity'.

The nursery teacher quoted in the extract above argued that there is no unequal distribution of power in gender relations, arguing that the power is merely expressed in different arenas, by women in the domestic sphere and men in the more public spheres. She acknowledged, however, that the grouping of boys and the exercise of power during superhero play parallel how power is seen to operate in the adult world (e.g. the male-dominated world of the Houses of Parliament). As the preceding discussion makes clear, for many boys the superhero play is replaced by sport, in which 'traditional' masculinity is valued. In the modern day world, however, the real power in society does not reside with sportsmen. The decision-makers, those with the power to affect the lives of others, are those who control the economy and the running of the state. Such men may enjoy sport in their private lives but know, for example, that it would be unacceptable to use personal physical violence to achieve their ends, although of course the state may (Jordan and Cowan 2001). The Members of Parliament (MPs) and others with power in this society have adopted a form of masculinity that is characterized by rationality and responsibility, and so it could be argued that there is no direct connection between MPs and superhero play. I think the teacher, however, draws a valid link between the two because, although the version of masculinity underpinning the actions and decisions of MPs is not the same as those of the 'warrior', there are similarities, not least in the unequal gender power dynamics.

The nursery teacher quoted earlier admitted that her professional and personal experiences have led her to consider the possibility that boys' 'need' for superhero play and the exercise of power that goes with it may be innate, biologically determined rather than socially developed or discursively constructed. It is clear that this teacher is trying to resolve the tensions that have arisen when she has considered gender equity and superhero play and, although she may appear to have opted for a biologically deterministic explanation, it is very apparent that she is not comfortable with adopting this view.

This nursery teacher was not alone in trying to grapple with the possibility that boys' superhero play was an exploration of power and a particular form of 'masculinity', coupled with a nagging discomfort with the idea that boys' 'need' for group play may be natural or innate. The nursery advisor quoted earlier commented that superhero play in large groups may fulfil 'something emotional' and suggested that the activity was a form of 'bonding'. She went on to say:

> They did need to be playing with what a 'boy' is and I think that was a problem for them [teachers] as well because they wanted to challenge this sort of kind of masculinity, which was why they had never allowed it in the first place, and that's what I had always felt, I don't want this as a masculine role model . . . but there was the feeling that somehow boys needed to do that just as girls were playing with the other extreme stereotype of what a female was and all the dollies and pink . . .
>
> (Interview with nursery advisor, female)

These comments raise the important issue of educators' ambivalent responses to boys' superhero play. On the one hand, if boys 'need' such play, either for their emotional well-being or because of innate factors, educators feel that they should facilitate such play. On the other hand, some educators feel uncomfortable about the extreme form of traditional masculinity that boys adopt when they engage in such play. One solution has been to intervene in the children's superhero and weapon play.

A nursery advisor who has worked in a number of nurseries and helped the staff to facilitate superhero and weapon play was clear about the importance of adult intervention:

> Interviewer: What would you say if someone were to say to you that by enabling or indeed encouraging gunplay you are helping to perpetuate stereotypes?

Nursery advisor: I would completely disagree. By allowing children to play like that we can question it . . .

Interviewer: Who can question it?

Nursery advisor: Well the practitioners can with the children so you can have a dialogue about the sort of things they are playing with, and if it does include their ideas of male and female and good and evil, fear and death, it gives them a chance to talk about it. So, I don't think that the nursery can be a little retreat away from the real world.

Interviewer: So would you say that that dialogue between the practitioners and the children is a vital element . . .

Nursery advisor: Yes. It's no good just allowing it and people not engaging with it . . .

Interviewer: So would you say then that the kind of dialogue that you had with children, was it led by them in the sense that they would ask you questions or would you see an opportunity to raise an issue . . . how interventionist was it, I suppose?

Nursery advisor: Well, quite . . . because we were using video a lot so I'd either play with them and bring up issues through playing so that it would sort of turn into a drama as well, where I'd deliberately bring out moral issues.

Interviewer: Right. So what you are really saying then, is that superhero play or gunplay is fine, from your standpoint, provided there is this dialogue?

Nursery advisor: You can't just ignore it or let it happen. I know one nursery where I'm visiting the little boys have been shooting for weeks and nobody ever dies and nobody ever acknowledges the fact that they have got guns and I think that is very poor quality and it would be better if they had no gun play at all, but they need somebody to react to the fact that they've got guns.

Interviewer: So what do you think would be the result of that kind of play?

Nursery advisor: With nobody getting involved? I don't think they are getting anything out of it because, apart from making noises and it helps them to feel safe, I don't know what value that has.

(Interview with nursery advisor, female)

Many early years educators may feel that involvement in superhero and weapon play is difficult for a number of reasons: the adults are unclear about their role, the superhero and weapon play often occurs outside and involves a great deal of running around and provides few opportunities for discussions with the children. This being said, if we are to help children to choose to adopt less 'traditionally' gendered positions we need to offer them alternatives. Those educators who decide that superhero and weapon play should be allowed a place in the early years setting need to consider how they will help the boys involved to develop other less aggressive and violent 'masculinities'. Participating in children's role play in order to provide them with opportunities to explore alternative 'ways of being' requires a light and sensitive touch on the part of the adult. Children will reject moves that require them to relinquish emotionally satisfying positionings. Many boys are also likely to react negatively to suggestions that involve surrendering their power, especially if there is no emotionally satisfying alternative position or version of 'masculinity'. The interventions should introduce boys to alternative forms of 'masculinity', versions of 'masculinity' in which courage and strength are not measured by the degree of violence, albeit imaginary, one is prepared to use against foes (real and imagined) or the willingness with which one approaches physical conflicts. Other strategies have been listed by McNaughton (2000) and include introducing boys to different stories, images and performances of masculinity and redefining what 'masculinity' means, talking with the boys about which masculinities they find appealing and why, enabling boys to explore alternative ways of being masculine (e.g. cooperative and caring) and helping boys to understand how 'traditionally' gendered positionings impact on girls.

'Feminization' of schooling

The notion of the 'feminization' of schooling has played a key role in the development of 'recuperative masculinity' strategies. In recent years the government and others have argued that the 'feminine' nature of primary and early years settings disadvantages boys (e.g. Gurian 2001; Mahoney 2001; Skelton 2002). There are three distinct but overlapping elements to the concept of the 'feminized' school (Skelton 2002). The first is statistical, in that there are more women teachers than men teachers in primary and early years settings. This is undeniably the case. One response has been to suggest that more men should be employed in order to provide positive male role models for boys so that learning and behaving well are not seen as 'uncool'. As discussed later in this book (Chapter 8), there are real problems with the whole concept of role modelling. However, this is a route the government has gone down and one with which many early years educators agree. The second element is cultural and is seen to be linked with the first element. It is been argued that the predominance of women has led to changes in the curriculum, valued learning styles, preferred teaching styles, routines and practices that favour girls (Gurian 2001). The third element is political, in that the supposed 'feminization' of teaching is used to attack feminism.

Some early years educators accept the arguments about the 'feminine' nature of early years provision, possibly because they understand gender identity formation as a straightforward product of socialization and role modelling, perceive gender in binary terms and do not ascribe to the view of multiple 'femininities' and 'masculinities'. Other early years educators are less happy to accept that schools have become 'feminized' and certainly do not accept any blame:

> I think we've been made to feel it's our fault because we're female and can't cope with boys and therefore it would be much better if there were more males in the profession, so there's all that guilt that's chucked at us and whether you are aware of it or not, I don't really accept that either.
>
> (Nursery advisor, female)

There is not space here to discuss this issue in great depth but it is important to consider whether or not the claims about 'feminization' of schooling have any validity, not least because the concept has influenced, and will continue to influence, gender equity strategies.

It has been argued that primary schools, rather than becoming 'feminized', have become increasingly 'masculinized' (Mahoney and Hextall 2000) as the discourses underpinning and shaping primary and early years provision have become increasingly 'masculinized'. One way in which this 'masculinization' has been marked is in the language now used in the early years field. We talk about the foundation stage rather than the nursery, we have the curriculum guidance outlining early learning goals, we have targets to be achieved, those working with young children are called practitioners rather than, for example, nursery nurses, teachers or child-minders. In this there is a sense that there has been an attempt to 'rationalize' and control early years provision and this control has even extended into people's homes (e.g. child-minders). Haywood and Mac an Ghaill have clearly outlined how the masculinization of schools is evident in their organization:

> High status has been ascribed to the 'hard masculine' functions of the accountant, the Key Stage tester, the curriculum co-ordinator and the Information and Communication Technology expert. At the same time, female teachers are associated with and directed into the 'soft' feminine functions of profiling and counselling.
>
> (Haywood and Mac an Ghaill 2001: 28)

A comment by a nursery headteacher provides an excellent example of what Haywood and Mac an Ghaill are writing about:

> And the other thing, if you have INSET on ICT or technology they come out of the woodwork, men. You know, there they all are, all the men because they're the ones who are given that responsibility in

school and if you are doing anything low status like social and emotional development out come the women.

(Nursery headteacher, female)

The emphasis on management of early years services, testing of children,
inspecting educators and settings and evaluating provision would suggest that
early years policy is becoming increasingly 'masculinized'. Jordan and Cowan
(2001: 112) argue that: 'Although teachers in the first years at school are predominantly female the regime they impose is perpetuated by male teachers
and this preference is endorsed by powerful and influential males in society at
large.' If early years settings are becoming increasingly 'masculinized' we need
to be wary of gender equity strategies, such as 'recuperative masculinity' strategies, that will hasten the process to the detriment of all children.

What about the girls?

The previous section has suggested that the revival of superhero play
and weapon play can be viewed as an example of recuperative strategies. An
alternative view may be that such play is valuable for both girls and boys.
Holland (2003) argues that relaxing the zero tolerance approach to superhero
and war and weapon play enabled boys to transgress the stereotyped gender
behaviour boundaries. She goes to on to claim that such gender boundary
crossing was also observed in some girls in settings in which the superhero
play was not only permitted but also involved the active participation of
female members of staff. Allowing such play, therefore, 'increased the range of
possibilities of what it might mean to be a girl' (Holland 2003: 26).

One of the nursery teachers I spoke to talked about how adult intervention influenced the girls:

Nursery teacher: Well, when I join in or any of the adults join in the girls
will *then*, for a little while but they don't sustain the interest . . .
Interviewer: Why?
Nursery teacher: I don't know. Odd isn't it? I don't know. We had one girl
last term. Or the term before and she spent the whole of her time
outside, and she's the only girl I've met so far like that, she'd play with
the boys all the time and be just dashing around, climbing, and she
was fantastic because she was all the female variants, she'd be the girl
lion in the Lion King and she'd always be like the girl Power Ranger
and she was very strong as a girl . . .
Interviewer: So she identified herself very much as a girl but . . .?
Nursery teacher: Yes, but she needed that kind of play.

(Interview with nursery teacher, female)

It was apparent from this conversation that, although a few girls occasionally participated in superhero and weapon play, the involvement was short-lived. This would suggest that in this particular nursery the girls' versions of 'femininity' did not map on to superhero and weapon play. There is too great a distance between the 'masculinity' of such play and the girls' own versions of femininity, making such play emotionally unappealing and unsatisfying to the girls. That girls perceive a disjunction between their versions of 'femininity' and the 'masculinity' of superhero play is intimated by the following observation:

> Yes, some of the girls joined in. In particular one girl but a few months down the line she said, 'I don't play with guns because boys do' but she was also very into pink and dolls then so that was her trying to figure out 'I'm a girl so I shouldn't be doing that', but she had played with it before but she decided it was time for her to stop.
>
> (Interview with nursery advisor, female)

It is interesting to note that the adults demonstrated a degree of ambiguity towards girls' involvement in superhero and weapon play, as the nursery advisor made clear to me:

Interviewer: So basically then you think that this kind of play is positive, particularly for boys but also, possibly, for girls?
Nursery advisor: Yes.
Interviewer: Would you actively involve girls in it?
Nursery advisor: Er . . . um . . . erm . . . I was trying to think. This video clip I've got, there's this little girl and she's made a gun but she can't join in because it's only boys so I said to her, 'Do you want to join in? Well, you could rescue someone', so I put a different angle on it so she thought, 'Oh yeah', so she could get straight into it. Some people thought that was encouraging her, which they didn't think was a good idea. But it was funny that she was only encouraged by something like rescuing. I know when people watched the video of her involved one person said it was a shame that, because gun play was allowed, she'd been sort of dragged into it, whereas if it hadn't been allowed she wouldn't have ever played with guns and they saw it as a sort of detrimental thing.
Interviewer: And yet they didn't think that for the boys?
Nursery advisor: Mmm . . . maybe it's my argument, 'cos you know Cupit analyses it saying that maybe it was boys who had a problem communicating or they've got English as an additional language or that it would happen in the afternoon when they were a bit bored and we saw that that was clearly the case and some boys, they were getting

a lot of benefit from playing that 'cos they made contact with other boys, so people could see the benefit of it like that. And the more they watched it they could see that the children weren't hurting each other really so they could see the benefits for the boys.

(Interview with nursery advisor, female)

It would appear that early years staff are willing to contemplate the advantages of superhero play for boys but are less sure about the involvement of girls. It is also interesting to note that the nursery advisor suggested that the girl pretend to rescue someone in order to gain access to the ongoing play scenario. Research by Mello (2001) suggests that children believe that heroines can be brave and adventurous but only in order to save or care for others, while believing that heroes do not need similar justifications for their aggressive and violent behaviour. The fact that the girl was happy to 'rescue' someone but not simply join in the play by brandishing her toy gun suggests that this 4-year-old girl showed an appreciation of the different codes of behaviour directing the behaviour of heroines and heroes. The adult's suggestion, although well meaning, could have had the effect of making it clear that although girls and boys can engage in superhero and weapon play there are different rules depending upon whether you are a girl or a boy. Involving the girls in this way does not challenge the unequal gender-based power dimensions of such play and, as suggested earlier, what are also needed are interventions that introduce girls and boys to alternative forms of 'femininity' and 'masculinity'.

As early years educators we need to be honest about our motivations for introducing changes to the setting (e.g. relaxing the zero tolerance approach to superhero play) and also need to think through the implications for all children, both girls and boys, of any such changes. From conversations with early years educators who feel that superhero play is a positive development it would seem that most are thinking of the advantages for the boys and accept that it celebrates a particular form of 'masculinity' (i.e. it is very much a 'recuperative strategy'). One nursery teacher described the boys' movements when playing superheroes:

Nursery teacher: And the movements are really important. I remember watching about 12 boys and being up high is important but it was a beautiful dance that I was watching. Fantastic. Jumping up and being together and moving around and I can't think of any other way they could do that in their play.
Interviewer: And the girls don't do that?
Nursery teacher: No, they don't. They run around a lot but not in the way . . . in that way they don't seem to be as creative as the boys were in their movements.

Bearing in mind that one's gender is inscribed on one's body (see Chapter 6), the teacher quoted above is clearly valuing the boys' development of certain types of movement and physical positioning. While the boys' mock combats may appear to be a 'beautiful dance', we need to bear in mind that the movements and postures reflect the boys' positioning of themselves as 'traditionally' 'masculine' (i.e. strong, aggressive, violent). We need to ask ourselves how this benefits girls and also enables all children to explore different ways of presenting their diverse 'femininities' and 'masculinities'.

The recent emphasis on meeting boys' 'needs' has resulted in girls being sidelined in discussions about equality and gender. Many early years settings tried a variety of strategies that they now felt were inappropriate: 'I remember the days when we'd have things like girls only construction and people thought that was good but we'd never do things like that anymore' (Nursery headteacher, female). As was made clear at the beginning of this chapter, some educators have found that strategies they had tried in the past were ineffective and have stopped using them. There has been relatively little debate within the early years field about why strategies based on the view that children develop a unified gender identity through socialization are likely to founder. In contrast, there has been discussion about brain development in relation to gender, the 'underachievement' of boys and the feminization of schooling. The result has been that many educators have dropped the equity strategies they had in place but have been unclear about how to proceed. The wider agenda of boys' underachievement has made it difficult to consider girls and gender equity because the focus is now squarely on the boys. This was reflected in a comment made by a nursery teacher:

> The girls are okay now. They can do whatever they want. I need to think about how to encourage the boys to read . . . they are not interested and can't wait for the door to the outdoors to open. I really worry because when they go into the next class they will be expected to sit still at their tables and they are not ready to do it.
> (Nursery teacher, female)

Another nursery teacher, working in a nursery that had been working hard on developing superhero play, was asked about the girls in the nursery:

> Interviewer: So what do you think is happening for the girls here?
> Nursery teacher: For the girls? I always think they have got stronger personalities anyhow and they will find their own thing and just pursue them, in the way that the boys find their own things and pursue them but in larger groups . . . I think there's a lot for them [girls] to do here . . . what do they do, they build some complicated scenarios and they really explore some interesting stuff . . . about what it is to be a

painter, so they go around and pretend to be a painter, they include also a lot of television characters, things like Buffy, so female role models . . .

(Interview with nursery teacher, female)

Both of these responses would tend to suggest that there was a degree of satisfaction with the provision being made for the girls. It was interesting to note, however, that in one nursery there seemed to be a very different response to the repetitive play of girls and boys:

Nursery teacher: That's an anxiety that we have as well because it [superhero play] is so repetitive but . . . there must be a need for that because they do that every day and if you let them it will just be all the time and they'd do nothing else . . . The group we have at the moment are into that play all the time and they would make the same artefacts, play the same games. And the other day it was the whole afternoon, just running and running and pow! Pow! Pow! So for us it becomes really boring and we try to introduce changes but that's you know, us . . .

Interviewer: Nothing to do with them?

Nursery teacher: Not really

Interviewer: But girls' play can be very repetitive?

Nursery teacher: Very. We've got a little girl who's been with us four or five terms and she's going around with a baby and bottle all the time and that's very boring as well.

Interviewer: Do you think people react to it in the same way?

Nursery teacher: I don't think they do because I keep on going on and on that she's got to put that baby down now and the others think at least she's not offensive and she's quiet.

Interviewer: So it's not offensive?

Nursery teacher: No, exactly, whereas the boys running around killing each other they find more difficult to accept.

This teacher was being very honest about what occurred in her nursery and discussion with other early years educators shows that this different response to girls' and boys' repetitive play is fairly common. If as early years educators we are convinced of the value of play it begs the question of whether or not girls and boys are being equally challenged and extended in their early years settings. Could it be that dealing with children, most of whom are boys, engaged in noisier, more boisterous activities takes up a disproportionate amount of the adults' time? If so, this has obvious implications for gender equity within early years settings.

Conclusion

This chapter has examined how the 'boys will be boys' discourse and the 'poor boys' discourse may be influencing the sort of initiatives being introduced within the early years, which are, ostensibly, concerned with gender equity. Careful analysis of new initiatives is clearly required if educators are to avoid implementing strategies that reinforce rather than challenge the notion of the oppositional nature of 'feminine' and 'masculine'. Gender equity strategies must also take account of the multiple ways of being 'feminine' and 'masculine'.

8 Are more men needed?

The shortage of male educators in early childhood settings is a well known and well publicized phenomenon. In recent years this lack of male staff has been framed as problematic and current debates about the gender imbalance of early years educators focus on children's need for male role models, boys' underachievement and the status of early years educators.

Balance of female and male staff in early childhood settings

There can be little doubt that in the early years and primary phases of education male staff educators are in the minority. In England, government statistics for maintained nursery and primary schools show that in 2001 men accounted for just under 16 per cent of the workforce in schools (DfES 2003c). Many of the men in the primary sector teach older children (i.e. Key Stage 2), so if the primary teachers are excluded the proportion of men working in the early childhood field is far lower, a mere 2 per cent (DfES 2002b). In Scotland the situation is similar, with females accounting for 92 per cent of staff in private and maintained primary schools (Scottish Executive 2001) and with 'nearly all' the pre-school teachers being female (Scottish Office Central Research Unit 1998). Recent research discovered that only 1.5 per cent of students on childcare courses in Scotland were men (Spence and Chisholm 2001). In Wales the pattern is repeated (General Teaching Council for Wales 2002). This gender imbalance is not peculiar to the UK. In Australia, for example, men account for only 3.3 per cent of childcare workers and 2.3 per cent of pre-primary teachers (Press and Hayes 2000). In Portugal the proportion of men is very low, with less than 1 per cent of early childhood teachers being men (Ministry of Education 2000).

There are a number of reasons for the low rate of participation by males in early childhood settings in a wide number of countries. One common thread is undoubtedly the fact that historically childcare and early childhood education have been seen to be the province of women. In Portugal, for example, a Ministry of Education report on early childhood care noted:

> Despite the progress attained in spheres of education and employment, women are still viewed as the main link for children between home and pre-school. There remains a cultural perception, even amongst women themselves, that a mother's primary role should be to care for her children and family . . . Men are generally viewed as providers not carers and educators . . . There are virtually no men involved in the professional care or education of young children, reinforcing these traditional division of gender roles.
>
> (Ministry of Education 2000: 165)

The link between mothers (i.e. women) and early childhood education is deep-rooted in other countries too. In England, the Home and Colonial Infant School Society was established in 1836 with the aim of training teachers to work with very young children aged from 2 to 6 years. The training courses were underpinned by Pestalozzian principles, which is relevant, as Pestalozzi believed that mothers were educators of their young children (Kamm 1965). Given the clear gender roles of the time it required only a small step to move from the idea of mothers as teachers to identifying women as most suited to the task of teaching very young children. Teaching in an infant school presented a new career opportunity to single middle-class women at a time when career opportunities for these women were still very scarce (Martin 1999). Opening up the career to women, however, minimized the likelihood that teaching young children would be seen as a suitable career for men.

Pestalozzi was not alone in believing that mothers, or certainly women, were better suited than men to early childhood care and education. Early years practitioners across the world frequently refer to the influence of Freidrich Froebel, but he argued strongly that:

> The destiny of nations lies far more in the hands of women – the mothers – than in the possessors of power [i.e. men], or those innovators who for the most part do not understand themselves. We must cultivate women who are educators of the human race.
>
> (Von Marenholtz-Bulow 1876)

The view has persisted that 'maternal' care is what is best for young children, preferably at home but failing that in a nursery setting. This view was not wholeheartedly shared by all. Margaret McMillan, the nursery pioneer, was adamant that young children need trained teachers and did not concur with the widespread view that 'any kind of nice motherly girl would do for a nursery-teacher'

(McMillan 1919: 15). Despite this comment, Margaret McMillan's vision of a nursery classroom was basically domestic and maternal (Anning 1997).

Throughout most of the twentieth century early years provision continued to be staffed mainly by women, and this was not seen to be a problem. The development of early childhood services in Britain has had a chequered history, which has been well documented elsewhere (see for example David 1990; Browne 1996), and during the twentieth century the main purposes of early years provision were determined by the prevailing social, economic and political conditions. At various points in time the prime aims have been variously identified as providing physical care, supporting early socialization, providing a safe place for young children whose mothers were at work and, in some cases, providing compensatory education. Throughout most of the twentieth century there was also a deep-rooted belief that it was 'natural' for women to provide this sort of early childhood care. The archives of primary schools in England often reveal clear gender-based differences in the staffing of the junior phases (i.e. that which is currently known as Key Stage 2) and the nursery and infant phase (Foundation Stage and Key Stage 1). Manchester Road Primary School in Manchester, for example, had three headmasters between 1907 and 1934, while during the same period the infant department had four headmistresses (Manchester Road School Archives).

In 1949 Dorothy Gardner, then Head of the Child Development Department at the University of London, wrote:

> The Nursery School teacher knows that she will often be called upon to act as a wise mother and is ready to give comfort and warm caresses at times of distress, as well as to respect the child's desire for independence when he [the child] feels happy and secure . . . The Nursery School also aims at providing those conditions for the best development which the busy mother is unable to provide during the hours when she must be absorbed in her domestic duties.
>
> (Gardner 1949: 14)

In the late 1970s Van der Eyken wrote that in comparison with the primary and secondary schools 'the pre-school is psychologically nearer the home environment' (Van der Eyken 1977: 204). It is not surprising then that early childhood educators have long been viewed as surrogate mothers. Steedman (1985) has argued that early years teachers are the ideal mother 'made conscious': early years educators have primarily been viewed as carers and the *educative* aspect of their role is nothing more than what a 'good' middle-class mother would do with her own children. In 1993 the British government retained and strengthened the link in people's minds between the 'maternal' and childcare when it talked of a 'Mum's Army' of early years teachers who would be able to teach nursery-aged and Key Stage 1 children (i.e. children from 3 to 7), but who would differ from teachers of older children in that their training would be different and they would be non-graduates (Browne 1996). This deprofessionalization and downgrading of early childhood educators' work continued through the 1990s. At the time of writing the government fails to make a distinction between the variety of adults who work with children in early childhood settings (QCA 2001). Consequently, highly trained graduate teachers are described as 'practitioners', as are other less well trained workers in the field, such as child-minders and poorly paid assistants in pre-schools. This new terminology plays a part in ensuring that work with very young children is seen to be of a lower status than other work (e.g. 'teachers' of Key Stage 1 and 2 children).

The construction of early years educators as carers and essentially maternal rather than well qualified professionals has had a number of consequences. First, the occupation's definition as 'women's work' has prevented the involvement of men. Second, in common with other occupations that are conceptualized as 'feminine', the status of early years educators is low and the pay is correspondingly low in the early years sector. Furthermore, the general view is that workers in the early years field need not be particularly intellectual. Margaret McMillan was conscious of the low status of nursery workers. It is a perhaps a measure of how deep-rooted gender roles are within society that words written by McMillan almost a hundred years ago still have meaning today. Margaret McMillan wrote that nurseries should not be 'viewed as the dumping ground for the well-intentioned but dull woman of today' (McMillan 1919: 16) and there is ample anecdotal evidence that academically successful youngsters are currently not encouraged to consider working with young children. Research by Blenkin and Kelly (1997) revealed that fewer than 40 per cent of staff working in 548 early years settings had a first degree, approximately 11 per cent had an MA and only 1.4 per cent had an MPhil or PhD. Do these figures simply support the view that early years educators are not particularly academically able or are they a reflection of other realities, such as the staff concerned having no time or money to pursue academic qualifications, the lack of opportunities for early years educators to further their own education once in post, the lack of opportunities for career progression or even, as Blenkin and Kelly point out, simply the fact that many diploma and higher degree courses do not meet the needs and interests of early years educators (Blenkin and Kelly 1997)? All the reasons listed here are clear reflections of the gendered nature of the early years field.

Is the absence of men a problem?

A diverse range of 75 educators were asked whether they thought employing men in early childhood settings was beneficial. Approximately half were very positive about the employment of men, while the other half felt that the sex of the early childhood educator was immaterial:

> As long as the teacher is conscientious and aware of giving equal attention to all pupils this [the employment of men] should not be an issue.
>
> (BA (Ed) student teacher, female)
>
> I think it's the quality of teaching the teacher provides that matters, not the sex of the teacher.
>
> (Nursery nurse, female)
>
> Because young boys and girls are at school to learn basic skills, reading etc., it's the attitude and personality of the teacher that counts, not the sex.
>
> (BA (Ed) Student teacher, female)

And a play group supervisor stated simply that she felt that 'Young children just need to know that you care and are available to them.'

A very small minority felt that the employment of men in early childhood settings would not be particularly beneficial for any of the children. One respondent with a 5-year-old daughter commented that: 'I feel that in general, a woman is more likely to be aware of the necessity to positively encourage girls to come to the fore. In the case of very young children I feel that the maternal element may also play a part' (BA (Ed) student teacher, female). A child-minder however, argued that while girls might benefit from a male teacher, boys would not:

> Young boys are generally used to being cared for a woman, so they may feel uncomfortable having a male teacher and more comfortable with a female teacher. Young girls enjoy the attention and time spent with a father; therefore they will be comfortable with male teacher and benefit from time spent with them
>
> (Child-minder, female)

Prospective primary school teachers seem to be even more convinced that the gender of the primary school teacher is unimportant. Skelton (2002) found that approximately 60 per cent of the PGCE primary students she surveyed felt that the gender of the teacher was 'irrelevant' in the primary school.

In recent years, however, the paucity of men in early childhood settings has increasingly been seen to be undesirable in the eyes of many educators and policy-makers. There are various reasons for the growing anxiety about the poor levels of male involvement in early childhood settings. One reason put forward is that the gender-related patterns of involvement in childcare reflect sex-stereotyped patterns of employment generally, which in turn diminish the possibility of gender equality within society. This is not a new concern, in that for the past 20 years feminist educators have argued for an increase in the proportion of men in early childhood settings (e.g. Browne 1986; Aspinall and Drummond 1989). In October 2001 the Equal Opportunities Commission (EOC) launched its 'What's stopping you?' campaign in an effort to tackle sex-stereotyped career choices and to foster equality in employment: 'We won't get true equality in the workplace unless measures are taken at school to encourage young people to pick from all the options available' (Julie Mellor, Chair of the EOC 2001a). The campaign received widespread support, not least from the Teacher Training Agency (TTA):

> Teaching needs men and women with high aspirations and the drive to make a difference in young lives. The more the profession reflects and represents the wider community, the better. It is not a career that can afford to waste talent. We say that, whether male or female, 'Those who can, teach'.
> (Ralph Tabberer, Chief Executive of the TTA, quoted in EOC 2001b)

It has been argued that the government's initiatives to increase the number of men employed in childcare should be welcomed, as they will help to ensure that the early years workforce will 'reflect the true diversity of society' (Skelton and Hall 2001: 7). Hugh Jones, Teacher Recruitment Advisor for Wales, stated that the drive to employ more male teachers was partly because of the desire for staff to 'reflect society as a whole' (H. Jones 2002).

Many early years educators, including students training to be early years teachers, have clearly thought about the issue, and some of their comments suggest that several of the students and educators would agree with Jones's view. One trainee teacher stated: 'Society is made up of men and women yet when children come to school they enter a female-dominated environment' (PGCE student, female). The same student went on to state that, in her view, employing male teachers was simply a way of redressing the balance in an 'artificial and unbalanced environment'. Another student also emphasized the issue of equality: 'I feel children should have a mixed teaching staff, to represent the idea of equality' (PGCE student, male). The drive for equality within the workforce in terms of numbers of women and men employed has not, on its own, been a sufficient motive to effect change. Possible reasons for the slow rate of change are discussed later in this chapter.

The changing nature of families and patterns of employment has led to a reconsideration of the roles of parents, both mothers and fathers. This, in turn, has played a part in altering people's perceptions about the role of men in childcare:

> Several competing strands of thought currently exist in Britain about
> fathers . . . [Some] focus more on the ways in which fathers are, or
> are not, changing their roles and becoming more nurturing and
> caring – in other words 'new men'. A minority view assumes that
> fathers are increasingly not relevant in the lives of their children.
>
> (Roberts, in Burghes *et al.* 1997: 7)

One example of this change is the concern expressed about parents' need to be
able to reconcile their family and working lives, and this has been cited as a
major impetus for the involvement of men in childcare (Cameron *et al.* 1999).
Support for fathers and other men came in the shape of the 1992 European
Council of Ministers Recommendation on Childcare, which was adopted
in 1996 (Council of Europe 1996). Article 6 of the European Council's
recommendation stated very clearly that 'Member states should promote and
encourage increased participation by men in the care and upbringing
of children' and so an unambiguous statement was made about the
importance of male participation in childcare (Council of Europe 1996). The
recommendations arose out of the recognized need to create 'effective equality
of opportunity and treatment for women and men workers' in order to abolish
discrimination between women and men in the labour market and,
importantly, to facilitate 'a more equal sharing of family responsibilities
within each family' (Council of Europe 1996: paras 1 and 16).

The recognition of the importance of fathers' involvement in the
day-to-day lives of their young children has led to a re-evaluation of the role
that men can play in the care and education of young children generally. It has
been argued that the concept of fathers as both providers and nurturers and
men as carers would gain credibility if there was an increase in male childcare
workers, as this would convey the message that childcare is not just mothers'
(or women's) work (Burgess and Ruxton 1996). Changing beliefs about the role
of fathers have certainly heightened concern about 'absent' fathers and the
effect this has on young children.

It has been argued that fathers are important since they:

> help young boys and girls develop conceptions of themselves in
> relation to men as well as women and encourage them to be
> comfortable with masculinity and maleness. It's about helping young
> people understand about the dynamics of relationships in general
> and close relationships in particular.
>
> (Roberts, in Burghes *et al.* 1997: 8)

Many fathers in England work more than 48 hours a week, which is much
more than other fathers in the European Union (see, for example, Ferri and
Smith 1996). It has been be argued that the long hours many men work have
resulted in fathers having very little time to spend with their children, leaving

mothers as the main childcarers. Children growing up in single-parent families may also find that their father is completely absent or plays only a limited role in their lives. The number of single-parent families has trebled since the early 1970s (Haskey 1998) and it is estimated that one-parent families account for nearly a quarter of all families (Office for National Statistics 2000). According to figures published by the charity Gingerbread only 11 per cent of single parents are men. Approximately half of these fathers have children of pre-school or primary school age, which means that the vast majority of young children growing up in single-parent households are being brought up by their mothers (Gingerbread 2001). It is clear that this demographic change has played an important part in changing people's ideas about the importance of male involvement in early childhood settings.

Male educators as role models

A recurring theme in the responses from those in favour of employing men in early childhood settings was that men in early childhood settings were of particular value to children, and more especially boys, being brought up by their mothers in single-parent families. An experienced primary classroom assistant felt that children would benefit from being taught by men because: 'Perhaps in today's society boys may need male role models and male input . . . girls would only benefit if there was no "daddy" around' (classroom assistant, female). This view was shared by a student teacher: 'Many young boys are being brought up by single mothers; therefore there is no male role model at home' (student teacher, female).

The following comments were representative of many of those who were questioned:

> I think that they [male educators] are of benefit for children that are from one-parent families, because then they have a male role [*sic*].
> (Student teacher, female)

> Boys may benefit [from a male teacher] but it depends if they already have a strong role model in their lives.
> (Behavioural therapist for autistic children, female)

> It depends if the boy has a male figure in his life. If not then it would benefit them to have a male teacher but if they do have a male figure in their life it wouldn't make a difference.
> (Nursery nurse, female)

Some respondents explored the theme of role-modelling a little further: 'Male teachers provide boys with strong role models inspiring them to achieve, especially if there is no father figure at home' (student teacher, female). A male student teacher, however, argued that male teachers were important for both girls and boys: 'A male teacher may be their only role model until secondary school. An omission of them (as such) is a lack of entitlement to a diverse social education' (student teacher, male). Another student teacher felt that the extent to which a boy would benefit from being taught by a male practitioner would depend upon the boy's attitude and behaviour and also: 'upon how strong a role model they have outside school – if none they would benefit'. A teaching assistant argued that constant female tuition may not nurture their masculine side. A highly experienced nursery school headteacher's comments placed the issue of men and role models within a wider context:

> I do believe that we need a variety of role models, men women, black, white, different backgrounds, different accents, different languages, we've got a disabled member of staff at the moment who is a man and another who is truly bilingual.
>
> (Nursery school headteacher, female)

Government initiatives in Great Britain seem to be based on the view that the provision of male role models is a pressing need: 'The recruitment of men into the childcare workforce should be actively encouraged, we need to establish a larger mixed gender base workforce. Children need role models drawn from all members of society' (DfEE 2000: 11, para. 3.15). A year later, in 2001, men were being targeted in the early years recruitment drive on the grounds that they could provide a 'positive role model' and 'a male figure in a child's life when there is none at home' (*TES* 2001a). It would seem that male practitioners are viewed as valuable in that they can provide role models to children. This is seen to be of especial value to children from one-parent families headed by the mother, and also seems to be particularly crucial for boys who lack positive male role models at home.

Many professional bodies concerned with early childhood care and education share this concern about children from one-parent families and the importance of providing a male role model. Young Minds, a children's mental health charity, is clear about the importance of the provision of male role models: 'We would also suggest that the issues of recruiting men into the childcare system be given careful consideration in the absence of male role models in the lives of many children' (Young Minds 1998: para 2.26).

Concern about children from single-parent families is not confined to Great Britain. In Finland, for example, the Gender Equality Unit noted:

> Apparently the most commonly used justification for increasing the number of male teachers in school is the claim that a school dominated by women teachers gives too superficial an image of men

to pupils. It is probable that many pupils go through their first six years of schooling without encountering a single male teacher. Because of the small number of male teachers it is thought that school does not offer boys enough models of male behaviour. Today many boys, especially the sons of single mothers, lack such models in their lives.

(Gender Equality Unit 1999)

In Australia the importance of male role models for boys has also been the subject of debate and in October 2002 the Education and Training Committee tabled its report, *Boys: Getting It Right*, which focused on the education of boys. Again, the importance of male role-modelling received attention:

it is important that we convey to boys that men value learning, not just later when you are in the workforce . . . but right now in that classroom in the early years. That is where we need to convince boys that men value learning. The best way to do that is to have men demonstrate that, obviously. You can imagine it is not quite as convincing for a female teacher to tell the boy that men value learning as it is for him to see men doing it.

(Education and Training Committee 2002: 160, para 6.92)

Educators and policy-makers appear to agree that early years settings and schools should be more 'balanced' in terms of the gender of the staff and that it is important that children living in single parent families with their mothers have experience of being cared for by men and are provided with positive male role models. It is perhaps worth pausing for a moment to consider the extent to which changes in family composition have resulted in children being without a male role model at home. Although proportions of single-parent families will vary from setting to setting, approximately 65 per cent of children live with both their biological parents and a further 10 per cent of children live with one biological parent and a step-parent (Office for National Statistics 2001). This means that approximately 75 per cent of children have a father figure as a male role model at home. With this in mind it is possible to argue that, while concern about children from single-parent families undoubtedly exists, the drive to employ more men in early childhood care owes more to concerns about boys' underachievement in school than the need for children to have access to a 'father figure'.

The issue of boys' 'underachievement' has played an important role in the development of initiatives to increase the number of male workers within the early years field. Within the 'poor boys' discourse, discussed in Chapter 7, boys from single-parent families (headed by the mother) attending early childhood settings staffed by women are seen to be victims, in that their needs, unlike the girls' needs, are not taken account of or even identified by the female staff. The government's strategy to narrow the gender gap in attainment has included 'tackling the laddish culture', which Blunkett claimed was responsible for the view among boys, particularly working-class boys, that it is cool to fail at school. Providing 'more good role models to challenge boys' resistance to learning' was seen to be of key importance in turning around boys' academic performance (DfES 2000b).

Within the 'boys will be boys' discourse (see Chapter 7), increased employment of men is seen to be one solution to the problem posed by schools, as men will have a better understanding of the needs of young boys and are more likely to be sympathetic towards and unthreatened by boys' macho behaviour. The widely read professional paper the *Times Educational Supplement* has carried articles that support the view that boys are victims:

> Schools unintentionally widen the gap [between girls' and boys' achievement]. They value the qualities that girls bring to their schoolwork – neatness, precision, perseverance – more than the energy and inventiveness that characterises, and distracts, the boys . . . Overwhelmingly, boys' first teachers are women. It is not surprising that that some boys pick up the message that learning is really for girls.
>
> (Duffy 2002: 16)

Parents too may perceive their sons as being stifled by the ethos in early childhood settings and the attitudes of the staff. A father of two young sons articulated this view very clearly when he explained how he felt that his older son had suffered through a lack of male teachers:

> He suffered because he had a lack of a male role model and the women teachers he has had have not been able to cope with boys' rough and tumble play and high levels of energy. The particular kind of teachers he has had have always been trying to create a 'safe' environment. Little girls can bring in their Barbies but the boys' Beyblades [battling spinning tops] have been banned. The only boys who are valued are those who want to be cuddled, those who are like girls.
>
> (Father of two sons)

Although there seems to be widespread agreement that men in early childhood settings offer something valuable to the children, in that they can act as male role models, there is not a consensus as to what exactly men should be modelling. Cathy Jamieson, the Scottish Education Minister, speaking in November 2002 at the Men in Childcare conference, mentioned how employing more men in childcare would help to break down stereotypes:

'Children should have a variety of role models when they are growing up . . . I would like to see more men working in childcare to help counteract the view that this is somehow "women's" work.' For many educators the value of male staff lies in their modelling of males in nurturing and caring roles, thereby challenging of some of the most common stereotypes. A nursery supervisor simply stated that 'Men teachers help teach non-stereotyped views.' An experienced nursery nurse, however, was more forthcoming regarding the benefits of male practitioners in early childhood:

> They [boys] will relate to the male role model – they will understand each other better. The child can aspire to be like them and it challenges stereotypes about men. Girls can see that men can be in a caring role. It will challenge the view that men have little to do with young children.
>
> (Nursery nurse, female)

A student teacher felt that young boys would benefit from being taught by men because the male teachers would provide 'positive role models of responsible and caring men', while girls would benefit because it would 'question their viewpoint of stereotyped males'.

When reflecting on what men bring to an early childhood setting, a headteacher of a school in inner London said:

> The role model . . . that men are not always abusive, as certainly here, for many of the children there's a huge amount of drugs and drink and abuse in the families. That role model of seeing a very big man changing children, and he's quite happy to do it, is important.
>
> (Headteacher, nursery school, female)

A father commented that it was 'Good to see men with that side to them . . . you know the nurturing and teaching aspect'.

In Australia positive relationships between women and men have been highlighted as an important focus for role modelling:

> the role modelling and teaching by males whose relationship and commitment to boys is genuine is the most important factor. We know that they watch us very closely, so the way we work with women, the way we talk to women, the way we can work as a colleague is something these boys are watching all the time because in the environment that they are from that is not the sort of relationship that they are used to seeing. We are very aware of that sort of thing, that what we display to the boys is what they want to take on board.
>
> (Education and Training Committee 2002: para 6.92)

For other educators the value in employing male staff lies in the belief that women and men are different from each other and men therefore will bring to the setting what it is to be a man (Murray 1996). Some feel this benefits children, especially boys, who have no male role model at home (Cameron *et al.* 1999).

Male practitioners may find that there is an expectation that they will model stereotypical male behaviour. A head of a private pre-school talked about why she valued her male volunteer staff:

> he comes in to help and work with the children. He's not a qualified teacher but is qualified to work with the children. And he will often work with them doing different things, and they are doing things like building blocks. I don't know but men will build things in a different way to women won't they? They'll have that different input and I think it's fantastic. Reading stories, they'll somehow read it differently. And the children love to see a man coming in. They really bond with him. So yes, as often as I can get a man to come into the nursery and help out with the children . . . the man might come in and play rough and tumble with the boys and the boys will immediately go for that . . . sometimes the boys, if they are feeling in a disruptive mood, if a man comes in with a sterner voice it can have more of an effect on them but then, you can have a girl running round who just needs a firmer voice too.
>
> (Head of private pre-school, female)

A nursery nurse who was training to be teacher also felt that male staff would help with discipline on the grounds that she felt that discipline is expected from the male and so 'they [children] will listen to him'.

Some educators felt that male staff could model 'maleness', while simultaneously challenging gender stereotypes:

> Men in the nursery are essential because they play differently than we [women] do and they've been through all those kinds of boys' games as well . . . we had a wonder worker called Michael and he was fantastic. It is difficult to say how but it's a really good balance and I think it is really good for the boys to see a man cooking or being a really good role model in that sense, telling stories, playing with babies and also being very human and saying 'I'll be your friend and I'll look after you because you're nice' . . . using this female thing. I think it's good for girls as well, possibly for some girls who don't have a male role model at home, because they [men] *do* relate differently to the children. Michael would be climbing up everywhere and taking

them on a ride on his bicycle and stuff . . . *and* be caring. So I think it's good for boys and girls in the same way.
(Deputy head of nursery school, female; original emphasis)

A nursery headteacher had a similar point of view but focused on the relationship aspect:

Children form different relationships with different people. So, as many different types of relationship that you can introduce children to are important. And it isn't simply that I think boys need a man at all. I just think that to have somebody in the nursery who is gentle and male and, in this case, um, it's actually important for children to understand that this isn't just a women's role and he *does* see things slightly differently.
(Nursery school headteacher, female; original emphasis)

This lack of clarity about exactly what men are supposed to be 'modelling' in an early childhood setting can create problems for male practitioners. On the one hand, they are expected to stand in for absent fathers but how this is to be achieved is unclear. Furthermore, there is no single way of 'being' a father: how men interpret what their role as a father is and how they operate as fathers are inextricably linked with a wide range of interlinked factors, such as their perceptions of gender, concepts of family and cultural values and expectations. If male educators are to provide role models the question arises as to which types of behaviours, attitudes and attributes they should be modelling. The caring, nurturing man? The physically active, 'typical' male? This raises questions about the validity of perceiving maleness or masculinity as reducible to a few key characteristics. One nursery headteacher commented on the complexities of expecting men to model 'masculine' behaviour:

What was interesting when Michael [male teacher] was here was that we were doing all that work around gunplay and he was *horrified* at the thought of gunplay. So that this notion that men who work in the nursery are necessarily going to do all the things that you want boys to do is nonsense because they're all individual as well, I mean Simone [a member of staff] is more likely to be out there shooting people dead than Michael or Marlon ever would be . . . So it's a nonsense, it's stereotyping to think that men are somehow going to be there for the boys.
(Headteacher of nursery school, female; original emphasis)

Cameron *et al.* (1999) discuss how one nursery worker was expected by colleagues and parents to model aspects of masculinity that were not only not part of himself but that he had made a conscious effort to reject (Cameron *et al.* 1999: 86–7) This raises the question of whether or not women's views about what men bring to the setting concur with what men themselves think. Furthermore, do men see themselves as providing a role model?

One male student teacher questioned the narrow justification for employing more men in nursery settings: 'It is based on the idea that they need role models for their "manhood". I really want to teach early years and feel that children should have a mixed teaching staff, to represent the idea of equality' (student teacher, male). A male deputy headteacher of a nursery was similarly loath to position himself as a male role model:

> I think it's only . . . I see myself in terms of a role model as an adult as opposed to being a man. But I see . . . erm . . . I can see that the point of view where there are families without a man or there may be several men who come and go so I can see that point of view but, to me . . . I didn't feel I was a male role model and that's what I have maintained all the way through.
>
> (Deputy nursery headteacher, male)

Problems with the concept of role modelling

The lack of any real consensus about what men should be demonstrating and modelling and the unwillingness of some male practitioners to present themselves specifically as male role models are two problems that beset consideration of role modelling. The third and major problem becomes clear when one looks beyond what adults are saying and doing and examines views about the relationship between role-modelling and the development of gender identity.

The emphasis on the provision of role models is based on a particular view of how children develop their gender identity. It has been argued that children learn what is 'normal' for girls and boys and for women and men through sex-role socialization, a process involving a combination of observing others (i.e. modelling) and social reinforcement. Children are therefore taught what it means to be a girl or boy. The problem with this is that children do not become what their parents and teachers want them to be. Many mothers will tell stories of how, despite all their best efforts at providing non-stereotypical role models and encouragement to engage in non-gender stereotypical activities, their young daughters still crave Barbie dolls and spurn the construction toys and cars. Teachers have noted how children will 'sabotage' their efforts and strategies devised to encourage non-gender stereotypical play patterns and behaviour (Browne and Ross 1991). Clearly there is more to the process of developing one's gender identity than merely accepting the messages given by parents, teachers and society as a whole. The 'sabotaging' should perhaps indicate that the children are more active participants in the construction of their gender identities than was previously thought.

Hekman (1991) created the term 'social duping' to describe the process of identity development through observation and social reinforcement. In terms of gender identity, if children accept and absorb uncritically what is presented to them by society, Hekman argues that they can be said to have been 'duped' into learning what society wants them to learn. This view of learning about gender and what it means to be a 'normal' girl or boy involves one-way traffic: messages about gender transmitted by the media, parents, schools, etc. are simply absorbed by the children. Within this framework, a male teacher 'modelling' a caring and nurturing male will lead to children unproblematically and uncritically accepting the view that both men and women can be carers, and boys will begin to see themselves as carers and nurturers. Similarly, male teachers modelling the view that 'learning is cool' should result in young boys with the same outlook. This view has been criticized (e.g. Davies 1989a, b) and anyone who has worked with young children knows that the process by which children develop their gender identity is much more complex.

To begin with, children receive a multiplicity of messages about gender and these messages are influenced by and embedded within a range of social and cultural contexts. Children have to make decisions about which of the messages and the underlying meanings they are going to use in constructing their gender identity. These decisions are not random and McNaughton writes about gender identity construction occurring as a process of negotiation within a 'controlled marketplace of ideas', where some of the meanings have more power due to their availability or because they are more pleasurable, desirable or easily recognized by others (McNaughton 2000: 24). Furthermore, one's construction of self is an ongoing process and one's identity cannot be said to be immutable, settled or unitary. As a result, 'who one is, is always open to question with a shifting answer depending upon the positions made available within one's own and others' discursive practices' (Davies 1989a: 229).

Adoption of this alternative view of identity construction provides early childhood educators with a different function. This function goes beyond ensuring that the children develop, once and for all, a sense of self that includes what the educators feel is desirable in terms of gender, through surrounding the children with 'correct' messages and providing role models demonstrating 'correct' attitudes, behaviour, interests and methods of interacting with others. Instead, the early childhood educator needs to help to make explicit to the child what decisions are being made, by whom and for what reason, and in so doing to help the child to understand themselves and others better. This involves discussion with children about what they enjoy doing, encouragement to share their personal feelings about being girls and boys and discussion of the different ways one can be female or male.

I would argue that the provision of a few male role models is not going to have a significant effect in terms of fostering gender equity. Furthermore, if the concern is with boys' underachievement, more fundamental changes in schools will be required than simply employing a few more men. Research by Harnett and Lee discussed in the *Times Educational Supplement* (2001b) called into question the government's view that more men in early years and primary schools will improve boys' performance, highlighting instead curriculum changes and teaching approaches as more useful strategies. Research by Thornton and Bricheno (2000) of Hertfordshire University has also challenged the accepted wisdom that more male teachers are needed to improve boys' performance. The government continues to ignore these research findings, perhaps because the alternative to more male teachers will involve changes in curriculum and pedagogy, a route the government is unwilling to take.

Employing more men

Status and pay

The English government, in common with governments as far apart as Australia, Finland, Denmark and New Zealand (Gender Equality Unit 1999; Education and Training Committee 2002; Ross 2003), has discussed the need for more male teachers. In England, in March 2001, an initiative was launched to increase the number of men working in early years settings. The government's initial aims were modest, as the target was to increase the percentage of men in the early years workforce to 6 per cent (TES 2001a). A year later the percentage of men employed in childcare had remained unchanged. As discussed earlier in this chapter, one of the reasons for low levels of male involvement in early childhood settings is the perception that it is basically 'women's work'. In common with other occupations in which women are predominant, issues of status, pay and career progression need to be taken into account when considering changing the gendered nature of the workforce. In England, central government is clearly aware of the need to change the widely held perception of early childhood care and education as the preserve of women. The link in employment between gender, status and pay is indisputable. In terms of teachers the government has acknowledged that the issue of pay cannot be ignored. Blunkett announced the launch of a £70 million initiative aimed at increasing teacher recruitment:

> The new pay system, which is being introduced, offers teachers the chance to earn up to £30,000 a year in the classroom. *That makes teaching a more attractive career choice.*
> In a competitive labour market with rising employment,

graduates are in high demand. So we need to ensure that those graduates who want to become teachers see teaching as an attractive career option.

The package will help us to improve recruitment in shortage secondary areas, to improve the pool of applications for all post-graduate teaching courses and to encourage more good graduates and *more male teachers to primary teaching.*

(DfES 2000c; emphasis added)

Approximately nine months later the first report of the Select Committee on Education and Employment (Early Years) was published (DfES 2000a) The report made for some very uncomfortable reading with respect to the status and pay of early childhood educators, in that it was stated that 'early years practitioners are working in circumstances where low wages and low status predominate', and it was pointed out that approximately half of pre-school assistants were paid half the minimum wage (DfES 2000a: para. 27). The Professional Association of Early Childhood Educators was quoted as urging that: 'Strong efforts must be put in place by policy makers to increase salaries and status in early years teaching so that, for example, male teachers are encouraged to work in the phase' (DfES 2000a: para. 28). The National Early Years Network had given evidence to the Select Committee and stressed that 'the issues around the gender balance within the workforce in the early education field need urgent attention' (DfES 2000a: para. 28). One of the recommendations from the Select Committee asked that the DfES research the reasons for the low recruitment of men and urged that 'strenuous efforts' be made to increase the recruitment of men (DfES 2000a: para. 38).

Since the publication of the Select Committee Report there has been a concerted effort on the part of policy-makers to increase the number of men working in the early childhood field by reframing the work as an attractive career option for men. The way in which this has been done has been not only to emphasize the contribution that men can make to the profession and to the children but also to publicize the opportunities for career progression that exist. The government targeted men in their childcare recruitment campaign.

In October 2002 the Teacher Training Agency sent 4500 mini sets of a construction toy to prospective male teachers as part of its 'Men into Primary' campaign (Shaw 2002). In December 2002 Charles Clarke, the Education Minister, emphasized the importance of increasing the number of men involved in early childhood care and education:

Male child carers play a vital role and valuable role and we believe that the childcare industry needs to draw on a wider pool of talent if it is to ensure that children continue to get the best quality childcare and education. I hope more men think about childcare as a career because they have so much to offer.

(BBC News 26 December 2002)

He went on to outline some of the attractions of a childcare career and highlighted the fact that there were opportunities for degree level training as well as management and business opportunities.

A few months later Baroness Ashton, the Minister for Early Years Education, appealed to men again by arguing that 'childcare is a demanding and rewarding career with real opportunities' (Hinsliff 2003). The Daycare Trust, a childcare charity, launched a campaign in June 2003 under the SAS-style slogan 'He Who Cares Wins', arguing that men can be just as good at the job as women.

Research (Lloyd 1999) has suggested that it may not be the status of the job as such that influences young men's career choices but the pay, and although young men may feel that childcare is essentially for women, a sizable minority of men express an interest in working with children. The message seems to be 'if it pays enough, and I could do it, I would' (Lloyd 1999). It is, however, difficult to separate pay and status. Research by the Teacher Training Agency would suggest that a combination of pay, status and conditions of work were the three key factors responsible for the negative impression of teaching as a career option (Carrington *et al.* 2001).

Some women practitioners feel strongly that employing more men is not the way to raise the status of the profession:

> It's a pointless exercise, I think there are much better ways of raising the status of nursery teachers than by putting men in there . . . Raise the status of *all* teachers, raise the status of the learning that goes on and if they [men] want to be involved in that, great . . . I think getting more men involved for young children I think is a good thing but that's about learning, but just as a way of raising the status, I'm not interested in it.
>
> (Head of nursery school, female)

Promotion

The emphasis on career progression and management opportunities in discourses about men in childcare has not passed unnoticed by women working within the field. Many feel that this is simply compounding the gender inequities that already exist within the field. One nursery headteacher commented:

actually I quite resent the fact that when you look around headteachers, for example, the number of men at the top compared to women teachers is extraordinary and I think that's not terribly 'equal opportunities' and it does make me quite cross . . . I think you want the very best people and *if* the very best person is a man only then should he be doing it.

(Nursery headteacher, female)

This headteacher's concerns about the inequalities in terms of promotion are not unfounded. Government statistics clearly show that women are under-represented in the senior posts within schools. In 2001, for example, 84 per cent of the teachers in nursery and primary schools were women and only 16 per cent were men. The percentage of male teachers who were heads was almost 40 per cent while the percentage of male teachers who were deputy heads was just over 25 per cent (DfES 2002b). This situation is not confined to England.

In Scotland it has been noted that although women predominate in the primary school sector, where they account for 94 per cent of the basic grade teachers, proportionally more men become headteachers. Furthermore, men are more likely than women to be promoted to senior management posts (Scottish Office Central Research Unit 1999). In Australia, where men account for a mere 3.3 per cent of childcare workers and 2.3 per cent of pre-primary teachers the trend is for men to move away from 'contact roles into management positions' (Press and Hayes 2000: para. 4.3.4).

Only one of the men interviewed alluded to the possibility that men may be advantaged in terms of career progression within the early childhood field. This particular practitioner had taken on an acting deputy headship post within 18 months of qualifying as a teacher and was then appointed as a permanent deputy headteacher. He said:

I expected, obviously, to be in the minority on the course [teacher training] and in future settings but that didn't hold me back . . . it wasn't an issue for me. I let people make the comments, as they do, about me being a man in the nursery and er . . . I can do the job as well as anybody and er . . . you know my promotions were through my own endeavours.

(Deputy head, nursery school, male)

Research by others has suggested that while women practitioners are often very aware of the gendered career advantages their male colleagues enjoy, the men concerned often do not appear to consider gender as an issue in their career development (Sumsion 2000; Thornton and Bricheno 2000).

The reasons for this gendered pattern of promotion are complex. Research for the Teacher Training Agency showed that male PGCE students tend to be slightly older than their female colleagues (Carrington *et al.* 2001). The average age difference is only two years and this is not sufficient to suggest that the male teachers will bring far more life experience and maturity to the senior posts than would their slightly younger female counterparts.

Research by Thornton and Bricheno (2000) suggests that male and female teachers tend to have different views about promotion. Of the male primary teachers with higher degrees half were seeking promotion and the other half were thinking of leaving the profession (for another job or to retire). Of the women who were equally well qualified, only 39 per cent were seeking promotion, while half were not seeking promotion (Thornton and Bricheno 2000). This could be because of differences in the reasons why women and men choose to take up a career in the early childhood field. Research has suggested that women are more likely to be attracted by intrinsic factors (e.g. work with children, feeling they are 'making a difference'), while men are more attracted by extrinsic factors such as status and pay (Edmonds *et al.* 2002). If this is the case, the only way in which men working within the field of early childhood will achieve their goal of a high-status job will be if they pursue a career path that leads them into a senior management position. Women practitioners, on the other hand, may feel that taking on a senior management role will remove them from the close day-to-day work with children that they value (Skelton 1991; Williams 1995). The different promotion prospects for women and men in the early years field cannot be explained purely in terms of personal aspirations. It is also necessary to consider which groups of workers within the early years field are particularly valued and to consider how this may support the realization of individuals' ambitions.

> The men are hard work. We do get them through the training but they are not very good. Some of them don't do the paperwork, they seem to think they can do the job without all that and the women in the nursery condone it. They let them get away with it.
>
> (Early years advisory teacher, female)

This comment resonates with a body of research findings (Williams 1992; Murray 1996; Penn and McQuail 1997; Cameron *et al.* 1999; Sumsion 2000) that highlights the way in which men are not only welcomed into the field of work but also treated preferentially in comparison with their female colleagues. This preferential treatment of men working in traditionally 'female' occupations has been graphically termed the 'glass escalator effect' (Williams 1992).

A headteacher of a nursery school talked about her black male nursery worker:

Head: He has the jargon, he has the language and he's funny and he's late every morning and he's not the most reliable in the world but I think it's important he's here.

Interviewer: But would you put up with that from somebody else?

Head: Well, for me it's about saying, 'OK you're ten minutes late but when you're here you're brilliant' . . . And he always comes and says sorry and he's paid very little as well.

(Head of nursery school, female)

The same head talked about how a male teacher's application form was 'absolutely appalling but he was a huge asset'.

It would be disingenuous to suggest that all men working in the early childhood field are welcomed with open arms. A minority of male practitioners have reported experiencing feelings of isolation and encountering difficulties linked with some colleagues' and parents' misgivings about men working with young children and wider anxieties about child abuse issues (Cameron *et al.* 1999). On balance, however, it would seem that men are valued in the early years field because of their rarity and because it is felt that they have something to offer that women do not. Furthermore, shortcomings such as unwillingness to 'do the paperwork', unreliability and poor punctuality, which, in the case of women, would be viewed as evidence of lack of professionalism or commitment, are overlooked in the case of men. If male practitioners' shortcomings are ignored and they are valued just for being men in a female-dominated field they are clearly an advantaged group. It is also worth noting that interview processes may favour men, especially in the case of maintained schools, where governing bodies, who may not have had any training in equality issues, make decisions about promotions (Cameron *et al.* 1999).

Clearly, if men are employed within the early years field as part of a wider move towards a more equitable society then it is important that issues such as men's overrepresentation in the management positions need to be openly discussed within a framework of gender equality. Encouraging more men to apply to work in early childhood care and education through financial inducements and the promise of bright career opportunities (TTA 2002) is not an effective strategy for ensuring that there is more equality within the field. Traditional views about the 'right' of men to hold authority need to be challenged, as do inequalities in the power relationships between women and men. Strategies to attract men to work in the early years need to be accompanied by strategies aimed at improving the representation of women in senior management roles. Strategies could include flexible work patterns, improved childcare availability and better and more appropriate training, particularly in terms of issues of management.

Conclusion

This chapter has explored the history of male involvement in early childhood settings. It has examined the validity of some of the arguments in favour of increased involvement by men in the early childhood field and has shown how the drive to reverse boys' 'underachievement', coupled with simplistic notions of gender identity development, has led to emphasis on the value of male staff as role models. From an examination of issues relating to pay, status and promotion it would seem that early years settings need to reflect on issues such as the extent to which the staffing profile reflects the gendered nature of power relations in wider society.

It has been argued that male workers may introduce a notably different pedagogical style, one that the predominantly female workforce may find disconcerting but that will be of benefit to the children (Holland 2000). Holland asserts that this outlook rejects modernist approaches, in that it acknowledges and values the differences observed in the pedagogical styles of some males and females (Holland 2000). A problem with this argument lies in the fact that it can also appear to be supporting an essentialist view of gender, as there seems to be little space for the view that there are multiple ways of being male and female and for the possibility that individuals can adopt a range of both 'masculine' and 'feminine' positionings.

If one is open to the posssibility of multiple 'masculinities' and 'femininities', what is required is more discussion and reflection on what it means to be female or male, and a greater understanding needs to be developed of what 'masculinity' and 'femininity' may encompass. This is relevant, as it could challenge the view that what is needed in schools is more men:

> Masculinity as a social gender refers primarily to activity-orientation, dominance, performance, asserting oneself and rationality, whereas femininity refers to community-orientation, emotionality, empathy and warmth. However, few men would recognise themselves as being purely masculine, similarly few women feel that they are merely [*sic*] feminine, This also applies to teachers. In fact, it may be said that school does not need more masculinity in the biological sense, but positive masculinity in the sense of gender. The latter can also be provided by women teachers.
>
> (Gender Equality Unit 1999)

The logical extension of this view is that in the same way that women can provide 'positive masculinity' men can provide positive femininity. Women, in other words, are not required to provide the 'feminine' element of early childhood care and education and men are not required to provide the 'masculine' element. We are then left with the situation that early childhood practitioners can be either female or male and neither is 'better' than the other, provided the practitioners are sensitive to the needs of the children and aware of what is required to promote gender equity within the setting.

Afterword

This book has not been written to provide 'right' answers or quick-fix solutions to the challenges and problems caused by gender inequalities. Instead I have aimed to introduce the reader to alternative ways of thinking about familiar issues.

Throughout this book I have challenged the validity of widely accepted 'truths' currently circulating within the early years field. In the first chapter, for example, the dominant pedagogical discourse, that of the 'naturally developing child', was scrutinized in relation to gender equity, and scientific 'truths' arising from scientific research were explored in the second chapter. A key idea that has permeated the book has been that it is possible to think about gender in a different way, in a manner that avoids placing 'female' and 'male' in mutually exclusive and oppositional categories. I have also discussed how diverse discourses generate different versions of what it means to be 'a girl' or 'a boy' and also how different versions of 'femininity' and 'masculinity' are privileged or marginalized in different contexts, which in turn results in varying dynamics of power related to gender. Thinking in terms of multiple 'femininities' and multiple 'masculinities' liberates us, and the children we work with, from the search for a single archetypal version of 'femininity' or 'masculinity'. The notion of multiple 'femininities' and 'masculinities' also reminds us that 'girls' and 'boys' are not homogeneous groups and gender equity strategies need to take account of the wide range of positionings girls and boys may adopt and of the emotional appeal of these different positionings. In addition, talking of 'femininities' and 'masculinities' is a reminder that these 'ways of being' are produced by discourses, rather than being 'natural'. All of this makes it more possible for early years educators to work with young children and bring about a degree of change through introducing children to alternative gender discourses.

We need to do more than simply 'offer' children alternative ways of being 'feminine' and 'masculine' because young children are frequently not able to make totally 'free' choices about how they position themselves. A headteacher made this point when she commented on children's imaginative role play:

> If you are [pretending to be] a fire-fighter or a ballerina there are certain bits of baggage that seem to come attached to it and some parents don't like boys dressed up in frilly dresses and tutus and some parents don't like their girls being fire-fighters . . . We really encourage them to think outside their own box but then if Mum or Dad comes in and they are caught in the other role, they've got to deal with it. And I feel sorry for some of them because I think sometimes we are creating a huge dilemma for them in that they know they can be anybody they want to here but outside they are not always allowed to be anybody they want to be. There are parameters.
>
> (Nursery school headteacher, female)

It is not just parents who maintain the gender boundaries; children and educators may also respond negatively to what is viewed as 'gender deviance'.

The promotion of gender equity within an early years setting requires the adults to be willing to look closely at their personal beliefs. bell hooks has argued that educators who aim to empower children will encourage children to take risks but will also be willing to take risks themselves (hooks 1994). In the context of promoting gender equity these risks will include the introduction of new strategies and new ways of working with the children, some of which may fail or be criticized by fellow educators, parents or indeed the children.

Educators also need to risk engaging in critical reflection on their own stance on gender equity issues and their understanding of how children learn and develop. A nursery advisor commented: 'It's very rare to find a class where children are encouraged to be critical thinkers . . . I think it's because teachers are not critical thinkers, because they've got lost in it [the day-to-day practice], they've not got time.' Throughout the book it has been suggested that encouraging children to think critically about widely accepted norms of behaviour and the different ways of being 'a girl' and 'a boy' is fundamental to advancing gender equity. We cannot, however, expect the children to become critical thinkers if we ourselves do not become more willing to question what has always been and reflect on the 'truths' circulating within the early years field. It could be, for example, that the concept of equal opportunities rather than gender equity is more comfortable for many early years educators, since it seems to sit more easily with the dominant discourse of the 'naturally developing child'. This particular discourse has led to beliefs such as the importance of 'free' choice and minimal adult 'interference'. Educators need to think through the implications of such as stance and ask a multitude of questions, such as: are children's play choices really 'free'? How does the concept of the 'naturally developing child' take account of the notion of discourses? If children develop 'naturally' does this mean that differences between girls' and boys' interests and behaviour are also 'natural', in other words biologically based?

We ought not to ask children to consider alternative discourses if we, as educators, do not also take the risk of doing so. For example, this book has been written at a point in time when anxieties about boys' 'underachievement' have been having a strong impact on gender equity work within schools and early years settings. The discourse of boys' underachievement has become so well established that research findings questioning its validity receive relatively little publicity. In 2000, for example, a study in Birmingham revealed that by the age of 7 some boys are indeed trailing seriously behind the highest achieving 7-year-old girls. Closer examination of the statistics shows that differences in attainment were due to a combination of factors, including season of birth, language background, economic status of the family, ethnicity and lack of nursery education. Ethnicity, poverty and season of birth, rather than gender, appeared to have most impact on children's progress (Budge 2000). Despite findings such as these, gender continues to be cited as a major, decisive factor in the underachievement of some boys, but ignoring factors such as ethnicity and levels of poverty has led to viewing boys and girls as being part of homogeneous and separate groups. As a result, the underachievement of *some* boys has been recast as the underachievement of *all* boys. This, coupled with the enduring view of gender as a binary category that places 'girls' and 'boys' as opposite and in opposition, set the stage for the 'moral panic' about boys' 'underachievement' and the growth of recuperative masculinity strategies discussed in Chapters 7 and 8. Educators need to ask themselves whether such strategies challenge or maintain existing gender inequalities.

It was clear from talking to educators that some were disillusioned about the progress of 'equal opportunities' in early years settings. One nursery headteacher appeared to be opposed to 'equal opportunities', arguing that:

> Equal opportunities . . . is stopping us developing and stopping children developing in that you can wrap something up and make it look pretty on the outside but on the inside it is still an empty box and children are wise enough to see.
>
> (Nursery headteacher, female)

I believe that as educators we have the responsibility to ensure that gender equity is not merely an attractively wrapped but ultimately empty box. This book has attempted to offer new ways of thinking about familiar issues and will, I hope, provide new starting points for ways of moving forward.

Bibliography

Abbott, L. and Nutbrown, C. (eds) (2001) *Experiencing Reggio Emilia: Implications for Pre-school Provision*. Buckingham: Open University Press.

Achiron, R., Lipitz, S. and Achiron, A. (2001) Sex-related differences in the development of the human fetal corpus callosum: in utero ultrasonographic study, *Prenatal Diagnosis*, 21: 116–20.

Ailwood, J. and Lingard, B. (2001) Endgame for national girl's policies, *Australian Journal of Education*, 45(1): 9–22.

Allen, L. S., Richey, M. F., Chai, Y. M. and Gorsski, R. A. (1991) Sex differences in the corpus callosum of the living human being, *Journal of Neuroscience*, 11: 933–42.

Anning, A. (1997) *The First Years at School*. Buckingham: Open University Press.

Anonkhin, A. P., Lutzenberger, W., Nickolav, A. and Birbaumer, N. (2000) Complexity of electrocortical dynamics in children: developmental aspects, *Developmental Psychobiology*, 36: 9–22.

Archard, R. (1993) *Children: Rights and Childhood*. London: Routledge.

Aspinall, K. and Drummond, M. J. (1989) Socialised into primary teaching. In D. de Lyon and F. Migniuolo (eds) *Women Teachers*. Buckingham: Open University Press.

Ball, S. (1994) *Start Right: The Importance of Early Learning*. London: Royal Society of Arts.

Bartoli, S., Paterlini, E. and Vignali, R. (2000) *Castelli*. Reggio Emilia: Scuola 8 Marzo, Reggio Children.

Berenbaum, S. (1990) Congenital adrenal hyperplasia: intellectual and psychosexual functioning. In C. Holmes (ed.) *Psychoneuroendocrinology: Brain, Behavior and Hormonal Interactions*. New York: Springer-Verlag.

Berg, S. J. and Wynne-Edwards, K. E. (2001) Changes in testosterone, cortisol and estradiol in men becoming fathers, *Mayo Clinic Proceedings*, 76: 582–92.

Berliner, D. C. and Calfee, R. C. (eds) (1996) *The Handbook of Educational Psychology, Volume 1*. New York: Macmillan.

Bettelheim, B. (1978) *The Uses of Enchantment: The Meaning and Importance of Fairy Tales*. London: Penguin.

Biddulph, S. (2003) *Raising Boys: Why Boys Are Different – and How to Help Them Become Happy and Well-balanced Men*. London: Thorsons.

Bilton, T., Bonnett, K., Jones, P. *et al.* (1996) *Introductory Sociology*. London: Macmillan.

Bland, J. (2001) *About Gender: The Fetal Environment* (www.gender.org.uk/about/04embryo). Accessed 12 December 2002.

Blenkin, G. M. and Kelly, A. V. (eds) (1994) *The National Curriculum and Early Learning: An Evaluation.* London: Paul Chapman.

Blenkin, G. M. and Kelly, A. V. (eds) (1997) *Principles into Practice in Early Childhood Education.* London: Paul Chapman.

Blum, P. (2002) *The Chelsea Bunny.* London: Learning Design Ltd (www.learningdesign.biz/new). Accessed 30 May 2002.

Bowlby, J. (1951) *Child Care and the Growth of Love.* Harmondsworth: Penguin.

Boyd, B. J. (1997) Teacher response to superhero play: to ban or not to ban?, *Childhood Education*, 74(1): 23–8.

Browne, N. (1986) Do the gentlemen in Whitehall know best? In N. Browne and P. France (eds) *Untying the Apron Strings: Anti-sexist Provision for the Under-fives.* Buckingham: Open University Press.

Browne, N. (ed.) (1991) *Science and Technology in the Early Years: An Equal Opportunities Approach.* Buckingham: Open University Press.

Browne, N. (1996) English early years education: some sociological dimensions, *British Journal of Sociology of Education*, 17(3): 365–79.

Browne, N. (1999) *Young Children's Literacy Development and the Role of Televisual Texts.* London: Falmer Press.

Browne, N. and France, P. (1985) 'Only cissies wear dresses': a look at sexist talk in the nursery. In G. Weiner (ed.) *Just a Bunch of Girls.* Buckingham: Open University Press.

Browne, N. and Ross, C. (1991) Girls' stuff, boys' stuff: young children talking and playing. In N. Browne (ed.) *Science and Technology in the Early Years: An Equal Opportunities Approach.* Buckingham: Open University Press.

Browne, N. and Ross, C. (1993) *Girls as Constructors in the Early Years.* Stoke-on-Trent: Trentham Books.

Budge, D. (1998) Contributing to a shortage of male teachers, *Times Educational Supplement*, 28 August.

Budge, D. (2000) Gender only 'small factor in boys' failure, *Times Educational Supplement*, 1 September.

Burgess, A. and Ruxton, S. (1996) *Men and Their Children: Proposals for Public Policy.* London: IPPR.

Burghes, L., Clarke, L. and Cronin, N. (1997) *Fathers and Fatherhood in Britain.* London: Family Policy Studies Centre.

Burman, E. (2001) Beyond the baby and the bathwater: postdualist developmental psychology, *European Early Childhood Research Journal*, 9(1): 5–22.

Cadwell, L. B. (1997) *Bringing Reggio Emilia Home: An Innovative Approach to Early Childhood Education.* New York: Teachers College Press.

Cagliari, P. (2003a) Observation, interpretation and documentation. Paper presented to the International Study Group, Dialogues on Education, Reggio Emilia, 19–24 January.

Cagliari, P. (2003b) Experiences of participation. Paper presented to the International Study Group, Dialogues on Education, Reggio Emilia, 19–24 January.

Cagliari, P. (2003c) The proposals of the Municipality for the elementary and secondary school. Paper presented to the International Study Group, Dialogues on Education, Reggio Emilia, 19–24 January.

Calvin, W. H. (1991) *The Throwing Madonna: Essays on the Brain*. New York: Bantam Dell Publishers.

Cameron, C., Moss, P. and Owen, C. (1999) *Men in the Nursery: Gender and Caring Work*. London: Paul Chapman.

Carrington, B., Bonnett, A., Demaine, J. *et al.* (2001) *Ethnicity and the Professional Socialisation of Teachers: Report to the Teacher Training Agency*. London: TTA.

Caviness, V. S., Kennedy, D. N., Richelme, C., Rademacher, J. and Filipek, P. A. (1996) The human brain aged 7–11 years: a volumetric analysis based on magnetic resonance images, *Cerebral Cortex*, 6(5): 726–36.

Cealey Harrison, W. and Hood-Williams, J. (2002) *Beyond Sex and Gender*. London: Sage.

Ceppi, C. and Zini, M. (1998) *Children, Spaces and Relations: A Meta Project for an Environment for Young Children*. Reggio Emilia: Reggio Children Modena Domus Academy Research Centre.

Coltheart, M., Hull, E. and Slater, D. (1975) Sex differences in imagery and reading, *Nature*, 253: 438–40.

Connell, R. W. (1987) *Gender and Power*. Stanford, CA: Stanford University Press.

Connell, R. W. (1995) *Masculinities*. Berkeley, CA: University of California Press.

Connell, R. W. (2000) *The Men and the Boys*. St Leonards: Allen and Unwin.

Constantino, J. D., Grosz, P., Saenger, P., Chandler, D. W. and Earls, F. J. (1993) Testosterone and aggression in children, *Journal of the American Academy of Child and Adolescent Psychiatry*, 32(6): 1217–22.

Corsi-Cabrera, M., Herrara, P. and Malvido, M. (1989) Correlation between EEG and cognitive abilities: sex differences, *International Journal of Neuroscience*, 45: 133–41.

Council of Europe (1996) *Recommendation No. R (96) 5 of the Committee of Ministers to Member States on Reconciling Work and Family Life*. Strasbourg: Council of Europe.

Cupit, C. G. (1996) Superhero play and very human children, *Early Years*, 16(2): 22–5.

Dahlberg, G., Moss, P. and Pence, A. (1999) *Beyond Quality in Early Childhood Education and Care: Postmodern Perspectives*. London: Falmer Press.

Dally, A. (1982) *Inventing Motherhood: The Consequences of an Ideal*. London: Burnett Books.

Darwin, C. (1871) *The Descent of Man and Selection in Relation to Sex*. New York: D. Appleton and Company.

David, T. (1990) *Under Five: Under-educated?* Buckingham: Open University Press.

Davies, B. (1989a) *Frogs and Snails and Feminist Tales: Pre-school Children and Gender*. Sydney: Allen and Unwin.

Davies, B. (1989b) The discursive production of the male/female dualism in school settings, *Oxford Review of Education*, 15(3): 229–41.

Davies, B. and Banks, C. (1995) The gender trap: a feminist postructural analysis of schoolchildren's talk about gender. In J. Holland and M. Blair (eds) *Debates and Issues in Feminist Research and Pedagogy*. Clevedon: Multilingual Matters/Open University.

Daycare Trust (2003) *Childcare Facts: About Employers*. (www.daycaretrust.org.uk). Accessed 28 May 2003.

De Lacoste-Utamsing, C. and Holloway, R. L. (1982) Sexual dimorphism in the human corpus callosum, *Science*, 216: 1431–2.

DfEE (2000) *Good Practice for EYDC Partnerships: Recruitment Strategies for Childcare Workers*. Nottingham: DfEE.

DfES (2000a) *Select Committee on Education and Employment: First Report*. London: HMSO.

DfES (2000b) Boys must improve at same rate as girls – Blunkett. Press release, 20 August.

DfES (2000c) Graduates to get £150 a week Training Salaries in £70 m programme to boost teacher recruitment. Press release, 2000/0140.

DfES (2001a) *Minutes of Evidence to the Select Committee on Education*. London: HMSO.

DfES (2001b) *Best Practice Scholarships Scheme* (www.teachernet.gov.uk/professional development/opportunities). Accessed 2 May 2003.

DfES (2002a) *Raising Boys' Achievement* (www.standards.dfes.gov.uk/ genderandachievement). Accessed 7 June 2003.

DfES (2002b) Press release, 22 April. Press notice 2002/0082.

DfES (2003a) *The Standards Site: Gender and Achievement* (www.standards.dfes.gov. uk/genderandachievement). Accessed July 2003.

DfES (2003b) *Using the National Healthy School Standard to Raise Boys' Achievement* (www.standards.dfes.gov.uk/genderandachievement). Accessed 12 July 2003.

DfES (2003c) *Statistics of Education: School Workforce in England (Including Teachers' Pay for England and Wales)*. London: DfES.

DfES (2003d) *Sure Start* (www.surestart.gov.uk/home.cfm). Accessed 8 April 2003.

Donovan, P. (1998) Men's brains, women's brains: study overturns century-old assumptions about cognitive functions, *University of Buffalo Reporter*, 30(7), 8 October.

Dowling, M. (2000) *Young Children's Personal, Social and Emotional Development*. London: Paul Chapman.

Duffy, M. (2002) Achievement gap, *Times Educational Supplement*, 15 November: 15–18.

Duveen, G. (1993) The development of social representations of gender, *Papers on Social Representations*, 2(3): 171–8.

Edmonds, S., Sharp, C. and Benefield, P. (2002) *Recruitment to and Retention on Initial Teacher Training: A Systematic Review*. London: TTA.

Education and Training Committee (2002) *Boys: Getting It Right*. Canberra: House of Representatives Education Committee, Parliament of Australia (www.aph.gov.au/house/committee/edt/eofb/report.htm). Accessed 15 March 2003.

Edwards, C. (1998) Partner, nurturer and guide: the role of the teacher. In C. Edwards, L. Gandini and G. Forman (eds) *The Hundred Languages of Children: The Reggio Emilia Approach – Advanced Reflections*. London: JAI Press.

Edwards, C., Gandini, L. and Forman, G. (eds) (1998) *The Hundred Languages of Children: The Reggio Emilia Approach – Advanced Reflections*. London: JAI Press.

Eisenberg, N., Martin, C. L. and Fabes, R. A. (1996) Gender development and gender effects. In D. C. Berliner and R. C. Calfee (eds) *The Handbook of Educational Psychology, Volume 1*. New York: Macmillan.

Epstein, D. (ed.) (1998) *Failing Boys? Issues in Gender and Achievement*. Buckingham: Open University Press.

Equal Opportunities Commission (2001a) News release: Billy Elliot and Bobby Moore join forces to challenge stereotypes. Manchester: Equal Opportunities Commission, October.

Equal Opportunities Commission (2001b) *What's Stopping You? Support from Other Organisations*. Manchester: Equal Opportunities Commission.

Fagot, B. I. (1978) The influence of sex of child on parental reactions to toddler children, *Child Development*, 49: 459–65.

Falk, D. (1997) Brain evolution in females. In L. D. Hager (ed.) *Women in Human Evolution*. London: Routledge.

Farver, J. A. and Shin, Y. L. (1997) Social pretend play in Korean- and Anglo-American pre-schoolers, *Child Development*, 68(3): 544–57.

Fausto-Sterling, A. (1992) *Myths of Gender: Biological Theories about Women and Men*. New York: Basic Books.

Ferri, K. and Smith, K. (1996) *Parenting in the 1990s*. London: Joseph Rowntree Foundation/Family Policy Studies Centre.

Finger, S. (2000) *Minds Behind the Brains: A History of the Pioneers and Their Discoveries*. London: Oxford University Press.

Foster, V., Kimmel, M. and Skelton, C. (2001) What about the boys? An overview of the debates. In W. Martino and B. Meyenn (eds) *What about the Boys? Issues of Masculinity in Schools*. Buckingham: Open University Press.

Foucault, M. (1980) *Power/Knowledge: Selected Interviews and Other Writings, 1972–1977*. London: Harvester Wheatsheaf.

Gambetti, A. (2001) Conversation with a group of teachers. In C. Giudici, C. Rinaldi and M. Krechevsky (eds) *Making Learning Visible: Children as Individual and Group Learners*. Reggio Emilia: Project Zero and Reggio Children.

Gardner, D. E. M. (1949) *Education under Eight*. London: Longmans, Green and Co.

Gardner, H. (2001) Introduction. In C. Giudici, C. Rinaldi and M. Krechevsky (eds) *Making Learning Visible: Children as Individual and Group Learners*. Reggio Emilia: Project Zero and Reggio Children.

Gender Equality Unit (1999) *Committee on Fatherhood: In Search of a New Kind of Fatherhood*. Helsinki: Ministry of Social Affairs and Health, Finland (www.vn.fi/ stm/english/equality_fset.htm). Accessed 13 June 2003.

General Teaching Council for Wales (2002) Big gender gap in Welsh classrooms. Press release, 15 March.

Giedd, J. N., Rumsey, J. M., Castellanos, F. X. *et al.* (1996) A quantitative MRI study of the corpus Callosum in children and adolescents, *Developmental Brain Research*, 91: 274–80.

Gingerbread (2001) *Becoming Visible: Focus on Lone Fathers*. London: Gingerbread.

Giudici, C., Rinaldi, C. and Krechevsky, M. (eds) (2001) *Making Learning Visible: Children as Individual and Group Learners*. Reggio Emilia: Project Zero and Reggio Children.

Gorard, S., Salisbury, J. and Rees, G. (1999) Revisiting the apparent underachievement of boys: reflections on the implications for educational research. Paper presented at the British Educational Research Association Annual Conference, University of Sussex, Brighton, 2–5 September.

Gould, S. J. (1981) *The Mismeasure of Man*. New York: W. W. Norton & Company.

Grosz, E. (1990) Inscriptions and body-maps: representation and the corporeal. In T. Threadgold and A. Cranny-Francis (eds) *Feminine/Masculine Representation*. Sydney: Allen and Unwin.

Gur, R. C., Turetsy, B. I., Matsui, M. *et al.* (1999) Sex differences in brain gray and white matter in healthy young adults: correlations with cognitive performance, *Journal of Neuroscience*, 19(10): 4065–72.

Gurian, M. (2001) *Boys and Girls Learn Differently: A Guide for Teachers and Parents*. San Francisco: Jossey-Bass.

Gurian, M. (2002) *The Wonder of Girls: Understanding the Hidden Nature of Our Daughters*. New York: Simon and Schuster.

Hager, L. D. (ed.) (1997) *Women in Human Evolution*. London: Routledge.

Haskey, J. (1998) One parent families and their dependent children in Great Britain. In R. Ford and J. Millar (eds) *Private Lives and Public Responses: Lone Parenthood and Future Policy in the UK*. London: PSI.

Haywood, C. and Mac an Ghaill, M. (2001) The significance of teaching English boys: exploring social change, modern school and the making of masculinities. In W. Martino and B. Meyen (eds) *What about the Boys? Issues of Masculinity in School*. Buckingham: Open University Press.

Hekman, S. (1991) Reconstituting the subject: feminism, modernism and postmodernism, *Hypatia*, 6(2): 44–63.

Hines, M., Golombok, S., Rust, J., Johnston, K. and Golding, J. (2002) Testosterone during pregnancy and gender role behaviour of pre-school children: a longitudinal, population study, *Child Development*, 73(6): 1678–87.

Hinsliff, G. (2003) It's who cares wins for the male nanny, *The Observer*, 9 March.

Holland, J. and Blair, M. (1995) *Debates and Issues in Feminist Research and Pedagogy*. Clevedon: Multilingual Matters/Open University.

Holland, P. (2000) Take the toys from the boys: an examination of the genesis of policy and the appropriateness of adult perspectives in the area of war, weapon and superhero play, *Children's Social and Economic Education*, 4(2): 92–108.

Holland, P. (2003) *We Don't Play with Guns Here: War Weapon and Superhero Play in the Early Years*. Maidenhead: Open University Press.

hooks, b. (1994) *Teaching to Transgress: Education as the Practice of Freedom*. London: Routledge.

Hyde, J. S., Fenema, E. and Lamon, S. J. (1990) Gender differences in mathematics performance: a meta-analysis, *Psychology Bulletin*, 107(2): 139–55.

Hyde, J. S. and Linn, M. C. (eds) (1986) *The Pyschology of Gender: Advances through Meta-analysis*. Baltimore: Johns Hopkins University Press.

Jaeger, J. J., Lockwood, A. H., van Valin, R. D. *et al.* (1998) Sex differences in brain regions activated by grammatical and reading tasks, *NeuroReport*, 9(12): 2903–7.

James, A., Jenks, C. and Prout, A. (1998) *Theorizing Childhood*. Cambridge: Polity Press.

Jancke, H. and Steinmetz, H. (1998) Brain size: a possible source of interindividual variability in corpus callosum morphology. In E. Zaidel, M. Iacoboni and A. P. Pacuel-Leone (eds) *The Role of the Human Corpus Callosum in Sensory–Motor Integration: Anatomy, Physiology and Behaviour and Individual Differences and Clinical Applications*. New York: Plenum Press.

Johnson, R. (1999) Colonialism and cargo cults in early childhood education: does Reggio Emilia really exist?, *Contemporary Issues in Early Childhood*, 1(1): 61–77.

Jones, G. (2002) *Killing Monsters. Why Children Need Fantasy, Super Heroes, and Make-believe Violence*. New York: Basic Books.

Jones, H. (2002) Big gender gap in Welsh classrooms. Press release, General Teaching Council for Wales, 15 March.

Jones, L. (2001) Trying to break bad habits in practice by engaging with poststructuralist theories, *Early Years: An International Journal of Research and Development*, 21(1): 25–33.

Jordan, E. and Cowan, A. (2001) Warrior narratives in the kindergarten classroom: renegotiating the social contract? In M. S. Kimmel and M. A. Messner (eds) *Men's Lives*. Needham Heights, MA: Allyn and Bacon.

Kamm, J. (1965) *Hope Deferred: Girls' Education in English History*. London: Methuen.

Katz, L. and Cesarone, B. (1994) *Reflections on the Reggio Emilia Approach*. Champaign-Urbana: University of Illinois, ERIC/EECE.

Killgore, W., Oki, M. and Yerelun-Todd, D. (2001) Sex specific developmental changes in the amygdala responses to affective faces, *Neuroreport*, 12: 427–33.

Kimmel, M. S. and Messner, M. A. (eds) (2001) *Men's Lives*. Needham Heights, MA: Allyn and Bacon.

Kimura, D. (1969) Spatial localization in left and right visual fields, *Canadian Journal of Psychology*, 23(6): 445–58.

Kimura, D. (1992) Sex differences in the brain, *Scientific American*, September: 118–25.

Knecht, S., Deppe, M., Drager, B. *et al.* (2000) Language lateralization in right-handers, *Brain*, 123(1): 74–81.

Kochanska, G. (1996) Inhibitory control in young children and its role in emerging internalisation, *Child Development*, 67: 490–507.

Kohlberg, L. (1966) A cognitive developmental analysis of children's sex-role concepts and attitudes. In E. E. Macoby (ed.) *The Development of Sex Differences*. Stanford, CA: Stanford University Press.

Krechevsky, M. (2001) Form, function, and understanding in learning groups: propositions from the Reggio classrooms. In C. Giudici, C. Rinaldi and M. Krechevsky (eds) *Making Learning Visible: Children as Individual and Group Learners*. Reggio Emilia: Project Zero and Reggio Children.

Langlois, J. H. and Downs, A. C. (1980) Mothers, fathers and peers as socialisation agents of sex-typed play behaviours in young children, *Child Development*, 51: 1237–47.

Leaper, C. and Gleason, J. B. (1996) The relationship of play activity and gender to parent and child sex-typed communication, *International Journal of Behavioural Development*, 19: 689–703.

Lehne, G. K. (1992) Homophobia among men: supporting and defining the male role. In M. S. Kimmel and M. Messner (eds) *Men's Lives*. New York: Macmillan.

Letts, W. (2001) Boys will be boys (if they pay attention in science class). In W. Martino and B. Meyenn (eds) *What about the Boys? Issues of Masculinity in School*. Buckingham: Open University Press.

Lingard, B. (1988) Contextualising and utilising the 'what about the boys?' backlash for gender equity goals, *Change: Transformations in Education*, 1(2): 16–30.

Lingard, B. and Douglas, P. (1999) *Men Engaging Feminisms*. Buckingham: Open University Press.

Lloyd, B. and Duveen, G. (1992) *Gender Identities and Education: The Impact of Starting School*. New York: St Martin's Press.

Lloyd, T. (1999) *Young Men, the Job Market and Gendered Work*. York: Rowntree Foundation/YPS.

Longino, H. E. and Hammond, E. (1995) Conflicts and tensions in the feminist study of gender and science. In J. Holland, M. Blair and S. Sheldon (eds) *Debates and Issues in Feminist Research and Pedagogy*. Clevedon: Multilingual Matters/Open University.

McGlone, J. (1980) Sex differences in human brain asymmetry: a critical survey, *Behavioural and Brain Sciences*, 3(2): 215–63.

McGuffey, C. S. and Rich, B. L. (2001) Playing in the gender transgression zone: race, class and hegemonic masculinity in middle childhood. In M. S. Kimmel and M. A. Messner (eds) *Men's Lives*. Needham Heights, MA: Allyn and Bacon.

McKie, R. and Gold, K. (2002) Testosterone levels may cause autism: research links social skills to hormones in the womb, *The Observer*, 19 May.

McMillan, M. (1919) *The Nursery School*. London: Dent.

McNaughton, G. (2000) *Rethinking Gender in Early Childhood Education.* London: Paul Chapman.

Macoby, E. E. (ed.) (1966) *The Development of Sex Differences.* Stanford, CA: Stanford University Press.

Macoby, E. E. (1998) *The Two Sexes: Growing up Apart, Coming Together.* London: Belknap Press.

Macoby, E. E. and Jacklin, C. N. (1974) *The Psychology of Sex Differences.* Stanford, CA: Stanford University Press.

Macoby, E. E. and Jacklin, C. N. (1983) The 'person' characteristics of children and the family as environment. In D. Magnussen and V. Allen (eds) *Human Development: An Interactional Perspective.* New York: Academic Press.

Macoby, E. E. and Jacklin, C. N. (1987) Gender segregation in childhood. In H. Reese (ed.) *Advances in Child Behavior and Development.* New York: Academic Press.

Mahoney, P. (2001) Girls will be girls and boys will be first. In M. S. Kimmel and M. A. Messner (eds) *Men's Lives.* Needham Heights, MA: Allyn and Bacon.

Mahoney, P. and Hextall, I. (2000) *Reconstructing Teaching.* London: Falmer/ Routledge.

Malaguzzi, L. (1998) History, ideas and basic philosophy: an interview with Lella Gandini. In C. Edwards, L. Gandini and G. Forman (eds) *The Hundred Languages of Children: The Reggio Emilia Approach – Advanced Reflections.* London: JAI Press.

Manchester Road School (n.d.) Archives (www.outerquest.co.uk/manchester/ archive/history.htm). Accessed 28 April 2003.

Marcus, D. E. and Overton, W. F. (1978) The development of cognitive gender constancy and sex role preferences, *Child Development,* 49: 434–44.

Martin, C. L. and Fabes, R. M. (2001) The stability and consequences of young children's same-sex peer interactions, *Developmental Psychology,* 37(3): 431–46.

Martin, J. (1999) *Women and the Politics of Schooling in Victorian and Edwardian England.* London: Leicester University Press.

Mazur, A. and Booth, A. (1998) Testosterone and dominance in men, *Behavioural and Brain Sciences,* 21(3): 353–97.

Mello, R. (2001) Cinderella meets Ulysses, *Language Arts,* 78(6): 548–55.

Men in Childcare (2002) When Men Become Carers. Conference, 1 November.

Messner, M. A. (2001) Boyhood, organized sports and constructions of masculinities. In M. S. Kimmel and M. A. Messner (eds) *Men's Lives.* Needham Heights, MA: Allyn and Bacon.

Messner, M. A., Hunt, D. and Dunbar, M. (1999) *Boys to Men, Sports Media: Messages about Masculinity.* Oakland, CA: Children Now.

Meyer, B. (1980) The development of girls' sex-role attitudes, *Child Development,* 51: 508–14.

Meyer-Bahlburg, H. F., Feldman, J. F., Cohen, P. and Ehrhardt, A. A. (1998) Perinatal factors in the development of gender-related play behaviour: sex hormones versus pregnancy complications, *Psychiatry*, 51: 260–71.

Meyers-Levy, J. (1994) Gender differences in cortical organization: social and biochemical antecedents and advertising consequences. In E. Clark, T. Brock and D. Stewart (eds) *Attention, Attitude and Affect in Response to Advertising*. Hillsdale, NJ: Lawrence Erlbaum Associates.

Miller, E. M. (1994) Prenatal sex hormone transfer: a reason to study opposite-sex twins, *Personality and Individual Differences*, 4: 511–29.

Milln, J. (2003) Cowed boys and Amazons, *Times Educational Supplement*, 14 February.

Ministry of Education (2000) *Review of Early Childhood Care and Education: Early Childhood Care Policy in Portugal, Background Report, Part 5*. Lisbon: Ministry of Education.

Moir, A. and Jessel, D. (1991) *Brain Sex: The Real Difference between Men and Women*. London: Mandarin.

Money, J. and Ehrhardt, A. A. (1972) *Man and Woman, Boy and Girl: The Differentiation and Dimorphism of Gender Identity from Conception to Maturity*. Baltimore: Johns Hopkins University Press.

Municipality of Reggio Emilia (2000) *The Municipal Infant Toddler Centres and Pre-schools of Reggio Emilia: Historical Notes and General Information*. Reggio Emilia: Reggio Children.

Munton, T., Mooney, A., Moss, P. *et al.* (2002) *Research on Ratios, Group Sizes and Staff Qualifications and Training in Early Years and Childcare Settings*. London: HMSO.

Murray, S. (1996) 'We all love Charles': men in childcare and the construction of gender, *Gender and Society*, 10(4): 368–85.

Myers, R. E. and Sperry, R. W. (1953) Interocular transfer of visual form discrimination habit in cats after section of the optic chiasma and corpus callosum, *Anatomical Record*, 115: 351–2.

Nimmo, J. (1994) The child in community: constraints from the early childhood lore. In C. Edwards, L. Gandini and G. Forman (eds) *The Hundred Languages of Children: The Reggio Emilia Approach – Advanced Reflections*. London: JAI Press.

Office for National Statistics (2000) *Living in Britain: Results from the General Household Survey 1998*. London: HMSO.

Office for National Statistics (2001) *Census: Children* (www.statistics.gov.uk/cc). Accessed 24 July 2003.

Ofsted (2003) *Yes He Can: Schools where Boys Write Well*. London: Ofsted Publications Centre.

Paley, V. G. (1984) *Boys and Girls: Superheroes in the Doll Corner*. Chicago: University of Chicago Press.

Penn, H. (1997) *Comparing Nurseries: Staff and Children in Italy, Spain and the UK*. London: Paul Chapman.

Penn, H. and McQuail, S. (1997) *Childcare as a Gendered Occupation*. Research Report No. 23. London: DfEE.

Perry, D. G. and Bussey, K. (1979) The social learning theory of sex difference: imitation is alive and well, *Journal of Personality and Social Psychology*, 37: 1699–712.

Piazza, G. and Barozzi, A. (2001) The city of Reggio Emilia. In C. Giudici, C. Rinaldi and M. Krechevsky (eds) *Making Learning Visible: Children as Individual and Group Learners*. Reggio Emilia: Project Zero and Reggio Children.

Piccinini, S. (2003) A city in evolution. Paper presented to the International Study Group, Dialogues on Education, Reggio Emilia, 19–24 January.

Press, F. and Hayes, A. (2000) *Thematic Review of Early Childhood Education and Care Policy*. Paris: OECD.

Putnam, R. D. (1993) *Making Democracy Work. Civic Traditions in Modern Italy*. Princeton, NJ: Princeton University Press.

Qualifications and Curriculum Authority (2001) *Curriculum Guidance for the Foundation Stage*. London: Department for Education and Skills.

Qualifications and Curriculum Authority (2003) Putting the fun in the foundation stage, *On Q*, 13 January.

Quigley, C. A. (2002) The postnatal gonadotrophin and sex steroid surge: insights from the androgen insensitivity syndrome, *Journal of Clinical Endocrinology and Metabolism*, 87(1): 24–8.

Rankin, B. (1998) Curriculum development in Reggio Emilia: a long-term curriculum project about dinosaurs. In C. Edwards, L. Gandini and G. Forman (eds) *The Hundred Languages of Children: The Reggio Emilia Approach – Advanced Reflections*. London: JAI Press.

Rich, D. (2003) Bang! Bang! Gun play and why children need it, *Early Education*, 40 (Summer): 7–10.

Rinaldi, C. (1998) Projected curriculum constructed through documentation. *Progettazion*: an interview with Lella Gandini. In C. Edwards, L. Gandini and G. Forman (eds) *The Hundred Languages of Children: The Reggio Emilia Approach – Advanced Reflections*. London: JAI Press.

Rinaldi, C. (2001a) Documentation and assessment: what is the relationship? In C. Giudici, C. Rinaldi and M. Krechevsky (eds) *Making Learning Visible: Children as Individual and Group Learners*. Reggio Emilia: Project Zero and Reggio Children.

Rinaldi, C. (2001b) Infant–toddler centers and pre-schools as places of culture. In C. Giudici, C. Rinaldi and M. Krechevsky (eds) *Making Learning Visible: Children as Individual and Group Learners*. Reggio Emilia: Project Zero and Reggio Children.

Rinaldi, C. (2003) Dialogue with the Reggio Emilia municipal infant–toddler center and pre-school experience. Paper presented to the International Study Group, Dialogues on Education, Reggio Emilia, 19–24 January.

Rodgers, C. S., Fagor, B. I. and Winebarger, A. (1998) Gender-typed toy play in dizygotic twin pairs: a test of hormone transfer theory, *Sex Roles*, 39(3): 173–84.

Ross, T. (2003) *Dearth of Male Primary School Teachers* (www.stuff.co.nz/stuff/ 0,2106,2539300a7694,00.html). Accessed 23 July 2003.

Rothbart, M. K., Posner, M. L. and Rosicky, J. (1994) Orienting in normal and pathological development, *Development and Psychopathology*, 6: 635–52.

Rowan, L., Knobel, M., Bigum, C. and Lankshear, C. (2002) *Boys, Literacies and Schooling: The Dangerous Territories of Gender-based Literacy Reform*. Buckingham: Open University Press.

Rubizzi, L. (2001) Documenting the documenter. In C. Giudici, C. Rinaldi and M. Krechevsky (eds) *Making Learning Visible: Children as Individual and Group Learners*. Reggio Emilia: Project Zero and Reggio Children.

Rutter, M. (1981) *Maternal Deprivation Reassessed*. Harmondsworth: Penguin.

Sanchez-Martin, J. R., Fano, E., Ahedo, L. *et al.* (2000) Relating testosterone levels and free play social behaviour in male and female pre-school children, *Psychoneuroendocrinology*, 25(8): 773–83.

Schneider, F., Habel U., Kessler, C., Salloum, J. B. and Posse, S. (2000) Gender differences in regional cerebral activity during sadness, *Human Brain Mapping*, 9: 226–38.

Scottish Executive (2001) *Statistical Bulletin Edn/G5/2000/1*. Edinburgh: Scottish Executive.

Scottish Office Central Research Unit (1998) *Women and Men in the Professions in Scotland*. Edinburgh: Scottish Executive.

Scottish Office Central Research Unit (1999) *Primary Education Teaching Staff*. Edinburgh: Scottish Executive.

Shaw, M. (2002) Assembly line for primary men, *Times Educational Supplement*, 18 October.

Shaywitz, B. A., Shawitz, S. E., Pugh, K. R. *et al.* (1995) Sex differences in the functional organisation of the brain for language, *Nature*, 373(6515): 561–2.

Shucard, D. W., Shucard, J. L. and Thomas, D. G. (1987) Sex differences in the patterns of scalp-recorded electrophysiological activity in infancy. In S. U. Phillips, S. Steele and C. Tanz (eds) *Language, Gender and Sex in Comparative Perspective*. New York: Cambridge University Press.

Singer, E. (1993) Shared care for children, *Theory and Psychology*, 3(4): 429–49.

Skelton, C. (1991) A study of career perspectives of male teachers of young children, *Gender and Education*, 3(3): 279–88.

Skelton, C. (2002) The 'feminisation of schooling' or 'remasculinising' of primary education?, *International Studies in Sociology of Education*, 12(1): 77–96.

Skelton, C. and Hall, E. (2001) *The Development of Gender Roles in Young Children*. Manchester: Equal Opportunities Commission.

Spence, K. and Chisholm (2001) *Male Students on Childcare Courses at Scottish Colleges*. Men in Childcare (www.meninchildcare.co.uk/Scotland.htm). Accessed 21 February 2003.

Sperry, R. W., Gazzaniga, M. S. and Bogen, J. E. (1969) Interhemispheric relationships: the neocortical commissures: syndromes of hemisphere disconnection.

In P. J. Vinken and G. W. Bruyn (eds) *Handbook of Clinical Neuropsychology*. Amsterdam: North Holland Publishers.

Steedman, C. (1985) 'Mothers made conscious': the historical development of primary school pedagogy, *History Workshop Journal*, 20: 135–49.

Steedman, C. (1990) *Childhood, Culture and Class in Britain: Margaret McMillan, 1860–1931*. London: Virago.

Steedman, C. (1998) The mother made conscious: the historical development of a primary school pedagogy. In M. Woodhead and A. McGrath (eds) *Family, School and Society*. London: Hodder and Stoughton/Open University.

Storey, A. E., Walsh, C. J., Quinton, R. L. and Wynne-Edwards, K. E. (2000) Hormonal correlations of parental responsiveness in new and expectant fathers, *Evolution and Human Behaviour*, 21: 79–95.

Strozzi, P. (2003) Advisories. Paper presented to the International Study Group, Dialogues on Education, Reggio Emilia, 19–24 January.

Strozzi, P. (2001) Daily life at school: seeing the extraordinary in the ordinary. In C. Giudici, C. Rinaldi and M. Krechevsky (eds) *Making Learning Visible: Children as Individual and Group Learners*. Reggio Emilia: Project Zero and Reggio Children.

Strozzi, P. and Vecchi, V. (eds) (2002) *Advisories*. Reggio Emilia: Reggio Children.

Sumsion, J. (2000) Negotiating *Otherness:* a male early childhood educator's gender positioning, *International Journal of Early Years Education*, 8 (2): 129–40.

Teacher Training Agency (2002) TTA welcomes increased male primary training. Press release, 5 February.

Terasawa, E. L. and Fernandez, D. L. (2001) Neurobiological mechanisms of the onset of puberty in primates, *Endocrine Reviews*, 22(1): 111–51.

Thorne, B. (1986) Girls and boys together, but mostly apart. In W. W. Hartup and Z. Rubin (eds) *Relationship and Development*. Hillsdale, NJ: Erlbaum.

Thorne, B. (1993) *Gender Play: Girls and Boys in School*. New Brunswick, NJ: Rutgers University Press.

Thornton, M. and Bricheno, P. (2000) Primary school teachers' careers in England and Wales: the relationship between gender, role position and promotion aspirations, *Pedagogy, Culture and Society*, 8(2): 187–206.

Times Educational Supplement (2001a) Early years drive to recruit male role models, *Times Educational Supplement*, 30 March.

Times Educational Supplement (2001b) Male models importance may have been overstated research suggests, *Times Educational Supplement*, 28 September.

Times Educational Supplement (2002) Study defies the 'boys need male teachers' belief, *Times Educational Supplement*, 8 March.

Tobin, J. J., Wu, D. Y. H. and Davidson, D. H. (1989) *Preschool in Three Cultures: Japan, China and the United States*. New Haven, CT: Yale University Press.

Turner, J. (2003a) Planet boy, where mum fades from the picture, *The Times*, 21 April.

Turner, J. (2003b) Look for WMD in my sons' playroom, *The Times*, 12 July.

Valentine, M. (1999) *The Reggio Emilia Approach to Early Years Education*. Dundee: Scottish Consultative Council on the Curriculum.

Van der Eyken, W. (1977) *The Pre-school Years*. Harmondsworth: Penguin.

Vecchi, V. (2001) The curiosity to understand. In C. Giudici, C. Rinaldi and M. Krechevsky (eds) *Making Learning Visible: Children as Individual and Group Learners*. Reggio Emilia: Project Zero and Reggio Children.

Von Marenholtz-Bulow, B. M. (1876) *Reminiscences of Froebel*. London: Cassell.

Vygotsky, L. (1978) *Mind in Society*. Cambridge, MA: Harvard University Press.

Walkerdine, V. and Lucey, H. (1989) *Democracy in the Kitchen*. London: Virago Press.

Walkerdine, V. and The Girls and Mathematics Unit (1989) *Counting Girls Out*. London: Virago Press.

Warden, K. (2003) Untitled article, *DfES Teachers' Magazine*, January (www.teachernet.gov.uk/teachers/November2002/Bridgingthegap Secondary/index). Accessed 21 June 2003.

Wearing, B. (1996) *Gender: The Pain and Pleasure of Difference*. Melbourne: Longman.

Weedon, C. (1987) *Feminist Practice and Post-structuralist Theory*. Oxford: Basil Blackwell.

Williams, C. (1992) The glass escalator: hidden advantages for men in 'female' professions, *Social Problems*, 39: 253–67.

Williams, C. (1995) *Still a Man's World: Men who Do 'Women's Work'*. Berkeley, CA: University of California Press.

Winter, J. S., Faiman, C., Hobson, W. C., Prass, A. V. and Reyes, F. I. (1975) Pituitary–gonadal relations in infancy. Patterns of serum gonadotrophin concentrations from birth to four years of age in man and chimpanzee, *Journal of Clinical Endocrinology and Metabolism*, 40: 545–51.

Wright, S. (2000) Why Reggio Emilia doesn't exist: a response to Richard Johnson, *Contemporary Issues in Early Childhood*, 1(2): 223–6.

Young Minds (1998) *Comments on the Consultation Paper: The National Childcare Strategy* (www.youngminds.org.uk/professionals/responses). Accessed 5 May 2003.

Zaidel, E., Iacoboni, M. and Pacuel-Leone, A. P. (eds) (1998) *The Role of the Human Corpus Callosum in Sensory–Motor Integration: Anatomy, Physiology and Behaviour and Individual Differences and Clinical Applications*. New York: Plenum Press.

Zinn, M. B. and Dell, B. T. (1996) Theorizing difference from multi-racial feminism, *Feminist Studies*, 22(2): 321–31.

Zipes, J. (1986) A second gaze at Little Red Riding Hood's trials and tribulations. In J. Zipes (ed.) *Don't Bet on the Prince: Contemporary Fairy Tales in North America and England*. New York: Routledge.

Index

aggression, 35–37, 78, 90, 92, 99, 106, 113, 124, 128, 129
attachment pedagogy, 10
attentiveness, 100
Australia, 141, 143
autism, 32–3

Batman, 30, 67, 81, 82, 86, 87, 88, 103
Bettelheim, B., 80, 83
binary construct of gender, 8–9, 62, 63, 64, 68–70, 72, 89, 95, 98, 106, 109, 125, 158
biological determinism, 6, 13, 23–7, 31–7, 56–7, 68–9, 71, 78, 101, 103–5, 113–14, 122
bodily inscription, 89–90, 129
Bowlby, J., 9
boys' 'underachievement', 94, 95, 112, 129, 141, 148, 154, 158
'boys will be boys' discourse, 112–14, 142
brain, 101, 103–4, 129
    corpus callosum, 25–26, 33
    emotional development, 24–5, 30
    hormones, 30–7
    language development, 24–5, 26, 27, 28–30, 33
    left-right laterality, 24–7
    maturation, 27–8
    physical structure, 22–7, 78
    processing emotions, 30
    self-regulation, 29–30
    size, 23–4
Bruner, J., 14, 17, 47

CAH (congenital adrenal hyperplasia), 32
category maintenance, 73–4, 76
child
    child and science, 12–13
    image of, 45, 59
    naturally developing child, 14–16, 110, 156, 158

childcare workers' status and pay, 134–5, 148–50
childhood, as a stage, 13, 15
    see also child
cognitive developmental theory, 71–72, 109
concept of self, 60, 61, 76
creationist theory, 102
critical thinking, 6, 8, 13, 19–20, 48, 157
culture, 9, 10, 12, 13, 16–18, 41, 49, 50, 57, 60, 61, 83, 89, 98, 103, 104, 107, 115, 124
    Anglo-American culture, 16
    Korean culture, 16
    school, 58

Darwin, C., 23
developmental psychology, 13–21, 55
developmental stages, 13–16
developmentally appropriate practice (DAP), 13, 17–19, 111
DfES (Department for Education and Skills), 94, 112, 132, 149, 151
Discourse, 48, 61–2, 64–5, 70, 72, 75–6, 83–84, 89,105, 110, 113–14, 116, 122, 156, 158
    discourse theory, 6–8
    dominant discourses, 6–13, 19–21, 72
    gender, 8, 65, 72, 95, 98, 106
    scientific, 12–13, 39–40
    'traditional', 52–55
    Unmasking discourses, 8–9
documentation, 44–45

educators' views about
    children's friendship patterns, 106–11
    see also friendship patterns
    girls and boys, 98–100, 106
    origin of gender differences, 101–4
emphasized femininity, 69, 71
English as an Additional Language, 79, 127

equal opportunities, 5, 20, 69, 94–98, 104, 109, 158
evolutionary biologists, 37–40

fairy tales, 80, 81, 82, 83
fathers, 35, 38–9, 101, 109, 115, 136, 137–9, 145
femininity, 65, 69, 73–77, 93, 105, 110, 114–16, 119, 125, 127–9, 154, 156
feminist, 6, 103, 113, 124, 137
feminization of schooling, 58, 112, 124–6
fighting, 6, 35–37, 67, 71, 81
Finland, 140–1
football, 118–20
Foucault, M., 6–8, 20
foundation stage, 7–8, 14,
   curriculum guidance, 5, 7–8, 14–15, 20
   profile, 5, 7–8, 125
friendship patterns, 66–9, 109–11
   see also educators' views
Froebel, F., 133

Gardner, D., 134
Gardner, H., 48
gender deviance, 69–77
gender equity strategies, 105
gender identity, 16, 18, 60–2, 110, 124, 129, 146–7
gender transgression zone, 73
'girly girls', 75
glass escalator effect, 152
good versus evil, 80–1, 84, 119, 123
group interactions, 51–5, 56–8
groups, 66, 91–92, 106–7, 110, 120
gun play, 19, 74, 81, 82, 90, 91, 92, 114, 121, 123, 127
   see also weapon play

hegemonic masculinity, 69, 71, 76, 73–4, 75–6, 84, 85, 92
   see also masculinity
heroes, 83, 85, 86, 87, 128
heroines, 86, 91, 128
home corner girls, 73, 75
homophobia, 74, 116
hormones
   activational influence, 30–1, 101
   adrenaline, 103
   cortisol, 38–9
   diethylstilbestrol, 33

early brain development, 31–35
   oestrogen, 31–32, 38
   organisational influence, 30–1
   prolactin, 38–9
   sex, 31
   testosterone, 31–8,

identity, 60, 62, 71
   identity formation, 18, 49, 53, 61, 124, 146–7
   multiple identities, 60–61, 65, 68
   'social duping', 147
imaginative role play, 16, 78, 82, 83, 84, 100, 157
immigration, 49
individual, focus on, 10–11, 13, 16, 17–19, 21, 96, 97

knowledge, 43–44
Kohlberg, L, 16, 71, 109

'laddishness', 142
language and gender, 9, 69, 88, 98, 105,106, 108, 143

McMillan, M., 133–5
magic wands, 91–2
Malaguzzi, L., 42, 43, 48–50
male educators proportion, 98, 132, 136–7
masculinity, 60, 64–5, 72–4, 76, 88, 89, 92–3, 105, 113, 114, 115, 116, 119, 121, 124, 127, 128, 129, 145, 154
   see also hegemonic masculinity
masculinization of schooling, 125–6
models, 76, 109, 130
   see also role models
moral panic, 94, 112
mother care, 9–12
mothers, 33–4, 37–9, 42, 88, 133–5, 136–7
multiple femininities, 124, 154
multiple masculinities, 113, 125, 154

'opposite' sex, 69, 108–9

patriarchy, 64–5
Pestalozzi, J., 133
Piaget, 13
planning for boys' interests, 96, 113–14

play choices, 32, 33–4, 66–9, 73, 99, 106,
115, 120
free choice, 16–17, 52–3, 156–7
playscripts, 79
'poor boys' discourse, 112, 141
Portugal, 133
positioning, 7, 54, 64, 70, 71, 72, 73, 74,
87–8, 93, 105, 110, 123–4, 129, 154
'positive masculinity', 154
Power Rangers, 67–8, 71, 81, 89, 92,
117–18
power relations, 20, 52–5, 59, 65, 69, 70, 75,
80, 84, 87, 88, 92–3, 106, 110, 116–17,
119, 121–2, 124, 126, 128, 153
Progettazione, 43–4
promotion, 150–3
psychoanalytical theory, 79

'race', 7, 9, 20, 23, 49, 50, 74, 75, 97
Raising Boys Achievement Project, 5, 94
'recuperative masculinity' strategies, 112–19,
124, 126, 128
'Reggio approach'
appeal of , 45–8
fundamentals, 42–5
image of child, 42
interface of theory and practice, 50
problems with, 48–9
Reggio Children, 46
Reggio Emilia, 41–2, 49
municipal infant and toddler centres and
preschools, 41–6, 48, 50–2
teachers, 41–5, 51–6
risk-taking
by children, 157
by educators, 157–8
gendered patterns, 29, 37
role models
men as, 76, 105, 124–5, 139–46
problems with, 146–8

schemas, 100
Scotland, 132, 142
Select Committee on Education and
Employment (Early Years), 47, 149
Sex roles, 38
sexuality, 54–5, 65
social capital, 49
social class, 7, 14, 15, 16, 20, 49, 69, 74, 75,
97, 142
social representations, 62
socialization, 28, 32, 34, 36, 65, 101, 104–5,
110, 124, 129, 143, 146
space – physical domination, 119
spatial development, 32, 33, 37
sport, 118–21
stereotypes, 6, 107, 109, 113, 116, 120, 122,
126, 136, 142–4
subjectivity, 51–5, 61, 99
superhero play, 71, 78–81, 88, 95, 100, 107,
114–16, 118, 120–4, 126–7, 129
adult intervention in, 22–4, 126–7, 130
Superman, 67, 82, 85, 87
Sure Start, 5

transformative practice, 20, 55
TTA (Teacher Training Agency), 149, 152–3
twins, 33

values, 50–8, 89
visio-spatial skills, 25, 37
Vygotsky, L., 14, 17–18

Wales, 132, 137
warrior narratives, 92–3, 118–19, 122
'ways of being', 76, 106, 110, 124
weapon play, 78–9, 81, 83, 88, 91, 114–15,
118, 121, 123, 127
see also gun play

Zipes, J., 83

WE DON'T PLAY WITH GUNS HERE

Penny Holland

War, weapon and superhero play has been banned in many early childhood settings for over 30 years. This book explores the development and application of a zero tolerance approach through the eyes of children and practitioners.

The author challenges the key rationale for linking aggressive play themes to violent behaviour. She examines play where children are allowed to construct weapons and enact goodies/baddies and superhero scenarios with sensitive adult guidance, and explores the generally positive experiences of children and practitioners. Rather than reading this form of play as the beginning of the slippery slope towards anti-social behaviour, readers are invited to view it as an entry point to imaginative play and social development.

We don't play with guns here is a fascinating and insightful contribution to this area of much debate in the early childhood community. The book is key reading for early childhood practitioners, teachers, students, parents and policy makers.

Contents

Series editor's preface – Introduction – Zero tolerance of war, weapon and superhero play: where does it come from and why do we do it? – Boys will be boys and girls will sit nicely – The power of imagination – Relaxing zero tolerance: the experience of one setting – The bigger picture: a summary of findings from 13 settings where zero tolerance has been relaxed – War, weapon and superhero play: what does it look like? – Conclusion – Bibliography – Index.

128pp   0 335 21089 9 (Paperback)   0 335 21090 2 (Hardback)

BOYS AND GIRLS IN THE PRIMARY CLASSROOM

Christine Skelton and Becky Francis (eds)

This book sets out to illustrate how gender equity (and inequity) transpires in primary classrooms. It uses the findings of current research to provide teachers with recommendations for promoting equity amongst boys and girls.

Renowned educational researchers have taken their area of specialism and summarized recent research in the area before looking specifically at issues relevant to primary teaching and learning. The areas of the primary school covered in the book include the National Curriculum subjects of literacy, numeracy and science, and broader topics such as working with boys, children with special educational needs, primary/secondary transition, playground cultures and children's construction of gender identities.

Boys and Girls in the Primary Classroom uses 'evidence based' research to provide accessible accounts of investigations into gender and primary schooling. At the same time, it offers a critique of the whole drive towards 'evidence based' research. The book is aimed particularly at primary teachers and student teachers although the research will be of interest to academics and undergraduate students.

Contents
Introduction – Evidence-based practice and educational research: when 'what works' doesn't work – Working with children to deconstruct gender – Gender in the playground – 'Troubling, troubled and troublesome?': working with boys in the primary classroom – Some neglected aspects of transfer: issues of identity, status and gender looked at from the pupils' perspective – Gender and special educational needs – Superhero stories: literacy, gender and popular culture – Gender equity in science – Girls and boys in the primary maths classroom – Index.

192pp   0 335 21154 2 (Paperback)   0 335 21155 0 (Hardback)

SUPPORTING ICT IN THE EARLY YEARS

John Siraj-Blatchford and David Whitebread

Supporting ICT in the Early Years helps readers understand how very young children (from birth to six) develop an early awareness, and subsequently develop their knowledge, skills and understandings of information and communication technologies (ICTs).

The rapid growth of ICT has prompted concerns among parents, educators and policy-makers over the suitability of many educational applications, and electronic toys, for young children. However, evidence is presented to show that the use of ICT by young children is compatible with the principles of a developmentally appropriate curriculum (DAC). In fact the authors argue that used imaginatively, many applications of ICT can make a significant and unique contribution to children's social and cognitive development.

This is a significant book for parents, carers, teachers and other professionals who want to provide a rich learning environment in this area of experience.

Contents
An integrated approach to ICT education – ICT in the home, the local environment and early years education – Responding to the differing needs of children – Programmable toys, turtles and control technology – Painting, drawing and constructing images – Stories, narratives, simulated environments and adventure games – The internet, websites and communications – Conclusions: the way forward – Appendices – References – Index.

128pp   0 335 20942 4 (Paperback)   0 335 20943 2 (Hardback)